Managing
Communication
Processes

Managing Communication Processes

From Planning to Crisis Response

E. W. Brody

PRAEGER

New York
Westport, Connecticut
London

Library of Congress Cataloging-in-Publication Data

Brody, E. W.
    Managing communication processes : from planning to crisis
response / E. W. Brody.
      p.   cm.
    Includes bibliographical references and index.
    ISBN 0-275-93467-5 (alk. paper). — ISBN 0-275-93468-3 (pbk. :
alk. paper)
    1. Communication.   I. Title.
P90.B745   1991
302.2—dc20   90-23751

British Library Cataloguing in Publication Data is available.

Library of Congress Catalog Card Number: 90-23751
ISBN: 0-275-93467-5 (hb.)
      0-275-93468-3 (pb.)

First published in 1991

Praeger Publishers, One Madison Avenue, New York, NY 10010
An imprint of Greenwood Publishing Group, Inc.

Printed in the United States of America

The paper used in this book complies with the
Permanent Paper Standard issued by the National
Information Standards Organization (Z39.48-1984).

10 9 8 7 6 5 4 3 2 1

For Sandy

Contents

Contents

Preface

The content of the pages that follow departs from traditional discussions of communication case problems and campaigns—which were to have been the primary focus of this book—in several respects. While usually treated as separate and distinct, communication efforts are treated here as closely interrelated. More important, mass communication is viewed as one of several sources of organizational messages, all of which require careful management if objectives are to be achieved.

While usually viewed in isolation, the several varieties of communication efforts—plans, programs, campaigns, special events and crisis or disaster response mechanisms—are more logically viewed holistically. Strategic and operational communication plans should flow naturally out of organizational plans. Communication programs should be developed within planning guidelines. Campaigns and special events usually are, or should be, constructed as components of campaigns. Crisis and disaster response plans may vary to some extent from the basic pattern, but the differences result more from necessary variation in level of detail than any other factor.

A similarly holistic approach is preferable in examining the several ways in which organizations communicate. Success and failure in mass communication too often are assumed to be governed by three primary variables: message, medium and audience. That assumption might be valid were the process completed as messages are received, but more is required. Clients and employers measure communicator success in audience responses, and those of audiences whose behaviors are shaped only in part by communicators' messages. Those responses may or may not be influenced positively or negatively by communicators' messages.

Near limitless numbers of messages are transmitted from minute to minute by and about organizations, their products or services, their environments, and their behaviors. Only a small part of the messages originates in formal communication systems. The larger and more credible portion is generated elsewhere. Messages are transmitted continuously by the quality of organizations' products or services; by the environments they create for consumers and workers; and by their behaviors and their workers' behaviors. Integrity and consistency in these messages arguably are the most important elements in mass communication.

Credibility is prerequisite to positive response for most messages. Integrity and consistency across messages, in turn, are prerequisite to credibility. This especially is the case where messages originate in mass communication, a process whose messages are accurately perceived as more prone to distortion than is the case elsewhere. Quality in products and services speaks for itself. So do organizational environments and organizational and individual behaviors. Their messages are experienced rather than merely being seen, heard, or read.

Viewed from another perspective, communicators shape expectations while quality, environments and behaviors create experiences in a world in which satisfaction equals expectation divided by experience. Where the calculation produces values greater than 1.0, credibility is enhanced and organizations benefit. Where values are less than 1.0, credibility is lost and organizations suffer.

All of the foregoing can be summarized as follows. Messages transmitted by communicators through mass media are inherently weak and prone to failure unless supported by those emanating from products or services, environments, and behaviors. Any tendencies on the part of communicators to plunge ahead with message development and transmission therefore create unnecessary risks to sponsoring organizations. No message can be rationally created or disseminated through mass media until those originating from other sources have been carefully examined. Only where this has been done, and where conflicts first are eliminated, should mass communication proceed.

While not new, these concepts are rarely embraced in their totality in contemporary organizations. Some 60 percent of the billings of the nation's 100 leading public relations firms, for example, is said to arise from publicity work. Continuing decline in mass media audiences coupled with growing public skepticism of large organizations nevertheless suggests that the efficiency and effectiveness of publicity must continue to decline, and that more sophisticated techniques will become predominant.

This book was written to provide tomorrow's communicators with a broader view of their discipline and with greater insight into the diverse factors that influence the results of communication. Like most such efforts, it is not mine alone. I am especially indebted to Dan Lattimore, chairman of Memphis State University's Department of Journalism, whose comments and suggestions helped shape the final product; to Richard R. Ranta, dean of the university's College of Communication and Fine Arts, for his continued support; and to the many students who demand to know the why's as well as the how's of communication, for their continued inspiration.

I would be derelict were I to fail to mention the support and assistance of the Praeger editorial team, especially Alison Bricken, who shepherded this project almost to conclusion while in transition from editor to mother, Anne Davidson, who succeeded Alison, and John Roberts, for his help in dealing with hyphen-happy copy editors.

1

Mass Communication Revisited

Traditional concepts of mass communication often undermine efforts to develop productive plans, programs, campaigns, special events, and crisis response strategies. Those preoccupied with the classic information processing model of communication and with a perceived need to persuade message recipients to behave as employers or clients desire often fall short of achieving objectives.

Their problems arise out of several perceptual problems. They tend to define "communication" in overly narrow terms and perceive persuasion to be as a less-than-ethical process. They fail to recognize the potential destructiveness inherent in conflicting messages and the essentially transactional nature of communication. These failings often produce a distorted view of the basic steps in mass communication.

Those who apply too-narrow definitions to "communication" fail to recognize that individuals assimilate information from many sources that vary in strength and credibility. The mass media, unfortunately, are among the weakest and least credible.

Popular misconceptions of persuasion usually are based on unsupported assumptions as to the ethical legitimacy of the process. Persuasion is value-neutral. Persuasion can be applied to achieve unethical objectives, but the process remains no less ethical than the crowbar used in a burglary.

Persuasion and communication are better understood as human transactions or social exchanges. The transactional approach better arms communicators to more efficiently and effectively manage the broad range of communication efforts in which most organizations engage. Plans, programs, campaigns, special events, and crisis response systems are interrelated. Each contributes to organizational success or failure. And each benefits or suffers from the others' strengths or weaknesses.

Mutual supportiveness is virtually essential in an era in which the national population is "tuning out" the mass media at an accelerating rate. Only 30 percent of 21- to 34-year-olds were regularly reading newspapers in 1990 as compared to 67 percent in 1965, according to a report by the Times Mirror Center for the People & the Press. Regular use of television newscasts declined by 11 percent among the same age group over the same time span. In fact, newspaper readership was down in every age group and television news usage declined in all but the 50-and-older group.

CONCEPTUAL INADEQUACIES

Mass communication's most prevalent problem has been created by tunnel vision, the inability to comprehend that communicators control only the smallest and least effective portion of the messages to which stakeholders are exposed. The bulk of the messages that organizations transmit first appear to originate in mass and interpersonal communication. Closer examination reveals different conditions.

Information is more easily transmitted and assimilated through experience than other forms of information transfer. Exposure to reality transmits concepts and ideas more quickly and effectively than words delivered orally, on paper, or by videotape. These conditions create the basis for a broader concept of communication.

Types of Communication

Many contemporary textbooks divide communication into mass and interpersonal categories. The interpersonal category usually is subdivided into one-on-one, small-group, and large-group varieties. Other authors consider communication as consisting of interpersonal, small-group, large-group, and mass categories.

Mass communication, in either case, has been subdivided into print and electronic varieties but technological change has been blurring the boundary between the two groups. Devices such as billboards, direct mail and transit signs have been considered print media because they are printed. Billboards today often contain electronic devices. Direct mail materials may include audio and video recordings. And video monitors are being installed to deliver advertising messages in retail stores.   There also are emerging what Everett Rogers (1986) has described as the interactive media (p. 32). These include computer and satellite-based systems that enable individuals to transmit and receive information using computers, teleconferencing, teletext and videotext systems, interactive cable-television systems, and communication satellites.

Where communication is defined as the transfer of information, however, the traditional and emerging forms together encompass only a small part of the communication universe. Humans receive and assimilate information from multiple sources that vary in impact and credibility. Information originating with individuals—interpersonal information—varies in credibility with senders' credentials and their positions. Information received from mass media—mediated information—varies in credibility in similar fashion. Even greater variation is found in information delivered in other ways.

Information transmitted by organizational behaviors, for example, usually is more convincing than that contained in interpersonal or mediated messages. What an organization does—the sum of the behavioral messages it sends—readily overpowers its advertising or the statements of its personnel.

Environments transmit messages in similar fashion and with nearly equal strength. The extent of organizations' concern for stakeholders is demonstrated most convincingly by the environments they create. Patrons and workers take cleanliness and comfort as incontestable evidence of caring.

Finally, and often most importantly, quality communicates. The quality of organizations' products and services overcomes any conflicting information delivered through mass media or sales persons.

Variation in Effectiveness

Product and service quality ultimately become known to consumers with or without formal communication efforts. Honesty and dishonesty become evident with sufficient frequency to discourage any tendency to mislead. The nature of environments that organizations create for stakeholders is apparent to those involved. Each of these factors contributes, positively or negatively, to the success of organizations' communication efforts.

The communication spectrum, as a result, logically can be defined to include five message sources:

1. Mass communication, consisting of messages that originate in the mass media—print, electronic and interactive.
2. Interpersonal communication, including the one-on-one, small group and large-group varieties.
3. Behavioral communication, encompassing organizations' behaviors and those of their personnel, which usually are perceived as authorized or condoned by the organization.

4. Environmental communication, as expressed through the environments organizations create for consumers, employees, and others.
5. Qualitative communication, consisting of messages conveyed by the
   quality of organizations' products and/or services.

The latter three forms of communication are highly effective and
efficient. Where messages delivered qualitatively, environmentally, or
behaviorally conflict with those conveyed in interpersonal or mediated
form, qualitative, behavioral, and environmental messages usually are
believed. These conditions can be a curse or a blessing as communicators try to persuade organizational stakeholders to behave as organizations prefer.

THE NATURE OF PERSUASION

Efforts to induce predetermined behaviors among specific groups
often are viewed as manipulative, as something less than ethical.
Advertising, marketing, public relations, and sales promotion are
popularly perceived as persuasive disciplines, often misleading in their
strategies and tactics. These perceptions at worst are only partly based
in reality. All interpersonal and mediated communication is purposeful.
Strategies and tactics may or may not be misleading. And persuasion
is not a manipulative exercise.

As defined by Petty and Cacioppo in *Communication and Persuasion: Central and Peripheral Routes to Attitude Change* (1987, p. 25),
persuasion includes "any effort to modify an individual's evaluations
of people, objects or issues by the presentation of a message." As such,
persuasion is value-neutral. Ethical problems that may attach to
specific efforts to persuade are a function of purpose rather than
process. Ethical propriety is a product of communicator intent.
Persuasion can be considered unethical only where persuaders
intentionally misinform or induce individuals to behave contrary to
their best interests or to prevailing moral standards.

Persuasion, in other words, is no more unethical than a gun is
criminal. Persuading friends to use firearms for target practice is an
ethical pursuit. Persuading them to use guns criminally is unethical.

Ethical factors in persuasion are important for several reasons.
First, the bulk of interpersonal and mass communication is persuasive
under the Petty-Cacioppo definition. To the extent that their messages
are intentional rather than inadvertent, qualitative, environmental,
and behavioral forms of communication also are persuasive. Second,
inconsistencies in messages created inadvertently or through unethical
behavior destroy efficiency and effectiveness in communication and
credibility in sponsoring organizations.

The need for consistency creates a thicket of problems and opportunities. Productivity in communication compounds where message content is consistent, but inducing consistency may require redrawing the boundaries of communication. Communicators usually deal only in mediated communication. Some become involved in interpersonal communication through speech writing, but these circumstances are rare. Other forms of communication are managed by noncommunicators or left to chance.

Behavioral communication is controlled primarily by senior managers and to a lesser extent by those who write policy and procedure manuals. Environmental communication usually is the responsibility of maintenance personnel, although designers or decorators may be involved in some settings. Qualitative communication presumably is everyone's job but usually is no one's responsibility. Where communicators are involved, quality usually is considered a given rather than a variable, an established fact around which mediated messages must be fashioned. Coordination is rare across these forms of communication and seldom occurs between them and the interpersonal and mediated varieties.

CONFLICTS AND INCONSISTENCIES

Conformity in messages is vital to avoid destructive conflicts and inconsistencies. Much of the intended benefit of communication can be lost through conflicts in messages and sources. Organizational priorities, management experts claim, are more clearly expressed in budgets than in chief executives' speeches. Organizational commitment to stakeholders similarly is better seen in behaviors, environments, and quality of products or services than in mediated or interpersonal messages.

What organizations do speaks more loudly than what they say. The content of behavioral, environmental, and qualitative messages is overpowering. No mediated or interpersonal messages can long stand against them. Where behavioral, environmental, and qualitative messages go counter to mediated and interpersonal, the former prevail. Interim confusion, moreover, negates short term benefits usually expected of interpersonal or mediated messages.

The persuasive ability of arguments demonstrably is enhanced by consistency and repetition. Limited communicator ability to manipulate other variables makes these factors especially important. Communicators' tasks become more complex, unfortunately, as they address the implications of the consistency problem.

Consistency in messages from different sources can be gained in one of two ways: by changing messages or by changing realities. Potential for success compounds where behavioral, environmental, and qualitative messages are consistent with mediated and interpersonal. Failure becomes almost inevitable where the reverse is true.

While often undetected, all delivered messages produce responses of one sort or another, for better or worse. To the extent that communication can be said to occur only where messages are delivered, the process is controlled by recipients rather than senders. Those exposed to messages may elect to respond in any of several ways. The potential range of responses is greater than many acknowledge. The extremes, in any given situation, are not the desired response and no response. No response, instead, is a midpoint on a response continuum ranging from wholly positive to totally negative. Consider, for example, this bit of prose of anonymous origin quoted by Michael LeBoeuf (1987):

> I'm a nice customer. You all know me. I'm the one who never complains, no matter what kind of service I get.
>
> I'll go into a restaurant and sit quietly while waiters and waitresses gossip and never bother to ask if anyone has taken my order. Sometimes a party that came in after I did gets my order, but I don't complain. I just wait.
>
> And when I go to a store to buy something, I don't throw my weight around. I try to be thoughtful of the other person. If a snooty salesperson gets upset because I want to look at several things before making up my mind, I'm just as polite as can be. I don't believe rudeness in return is the answer.
>
> The other day I stopped at a full service gas station and waited for almost five minutes before the attendant took care of me. And when he did, he spilled gas and wiped the windshield with an oily rag. But did I complain about the service? Of course not.
>
> I never kick. I never nag. I never criticize. And I wouldn't dream of making a scene, as I've seen some people do in public places. I think that's uncalled for. No, I'm the nice customer. And I'll tell you who else I am.
>
> *I'm the customer who never comes back!*

Professor LeBoeuf's anecdote (p. 11) underscores several points. First, as indicated earlier, behavioral, environmental, and qualitative communication are highly effective. Second, delivered messages produce responses. This cause-and-effect relationship exists regardless of message origins and whether or not responses can be immediately observed or measured. Departures of unhappy customers rarely are recorded. Unexpressed complaints are never heard. Loss of patronage is not easily detected.

The events and their results nevertheless are real. Messages may be rejected out of hand, as doubtless would be the case among those subjected to the sort of indignities described above. Message content may be noted and forgotten, or noted and mentally filed for future reference. Measurable behavioral response may occur only after several messages from diverse sources have been received and cumulatively weighed. Each message received nevertheless produces a reaction. The circumstances are not unlike those that prevail in decision making where, as others have observed, "no decision is a decision." In communication, no reaction to received messages is equally significant, signaling uncertainty or rejection.

There exists no comprehensive model of communication that embraces the origins and outcomes of all messages. The best of those available offer valuable insights, however, into what communication is and should be. The importance of response or feedback in communication is emphasized, for example, in a two-way symmetrical model of mass communication offered by James E. Grunig and Todd Hunt (1984). They envision the process as an exchange of ideas and underscore the weaknesses inherent in one-way communication.

The Grunig-Hunt view of mass communication as exchange leads logically to considering other forms of communication in like manner. If communication can be considered an exchange, can relationships between individuals, and between organizations and individuals, also be viewed as series of exchanges or transactions? Finally, if relationships are transactional, should not exchange be considered a primary function of communication?

SOCIAL EXCHANGE THEORY

Human and organizational behavior give every appearance of being transactional in nature. Emotions, ideas, products, and services all are exchanged by individuals and organizations. Exchanges produce benefits or profits in several forms, including psychic and emotional as well as economic, but the transactions involved nevertheless constitute exchanges.

The most appropriate model of a transactional world arguably is found in sociology in what is called social exchange theory. Social exchange theory embraces transactions of all kinds. The concept extends from products and services at one extreme to emotions at the other. Thoughts and ideas, the content of communication, are closer to the emotional end of the continuum.

Mass communication, by extension, becomes a process of exchange applied by organizations to establish, enhance, or maintain relationships with stakeholder groups. As defined here to include behavioral, environmental, and qualitative communication, the process necessarily is transactional. Some information is transmitted intentionally in hope of gaining understanding, patronage, and loyalty. Intentionally transmitted information is delivered interpersonally or through mass media. Behavioral, environmental, and qualitative information should be transmitted by design but is transmitted in any event, with necessarily varying results.

Stakeholder Reactions

Organizational stakeholders exposed to a mix of intentional and unintended messages may or may not react as organizations anticipate. Messages may be rejected out of hand rather than weighed on their merits. Where received and examined, messages may produce disbelief, especially where conflict occurs.

Communication succeeds where exchanges produce mutual understanding, where transactions are acceptable to both parties. Mutual satisfaction requires exchanges on value-for-value-received bases. Durable relationships develop where transactions occur in this manner. Individual needs are satisfied and organizations prosper. Successful communication, in other words, produces public relationships built on serial transactions that engender mutual trust, confidence, and gain.

These conditions produced a surge in attention to "relationships" during the late 1980s and early 1990s. Beset on all sides by social pressures, individuals increasingly are concerned with durable, problem-free relationships. They seek organizations as well as friends with whom they can be comfortable. They look for businesses that will reliably and pleasantly meet their needs on continuing bases. They want to deal with firms to which they can send their spouses and children for products or services without fear of poor service or exorbitant prices. Cost increasingly is a secondary consideration.

Implications of Communication

The implications of these conditions for communication are extensive. The relative strength of nonmediated messages and the nature of social exchange should be both enlightening and humbling to communicators. These factors demand a different approach to communication. If exchange is communication, and communication is exchange; if communication encompasses behavioral, environmental, and qualitative exchanges; then those who manage communication must:

1. Control the origins and content of all messages.
2. Ensure that exchanges are fair and equitable in order to validate messages.
3. Measure results in strength of constituent relationships.

Only when these prerequisites have been satisfied can communicators proceed without risk to implement plans, programs, campaigns, special events, and crisis response strategies. Planning is necessary to meet the prerequisites, but that planning is as readily accomplished at the organizational level as at the communication level.

COMMUNICATION PROCESSES

Meeting the three specified criteria requires two departures from traditional communication planning. First, the primary process emphasis shifts from channel selection and message delivery to research and planning. Second, the process requires greater integration in planning, programming, campaign and special event design, and crisis response.

Dealing with communication as a transactional process requires early decisions concerning the proposed content of social exchanges. Details of transactions attractive to stakeholders and advantageous to the organization must be completed early. The process involved is more complex than selecting communication channels and fashioning messages and produces two secondary consequences. First, communicators become parties to organizational strategic and operational planning. Second, communicators assume primary responsibility for nonmediated as well as mediated communication.

Communication planning concurrently becomes comprehensive, embracing activities collectively rather than individually. Plans, programs, campaigns, special events, and crisis response mechanisms are integrated in content although necessarily separated to varying degrees in operational terms.

Process Beginnings

Communication is rooted in organizational planning processes —usually more in operational (one-year) rather than strategic (typically five-year) plans. Operational plans specify organizations' goals and objectives, usually numerically and in terms of market share, revenue, memberships, or profit. Achieving organizational goals and objectives invariably requires inducing stakeholders to behave in predetermined ways.

Organizational plans are critical to communication because those plans define, although often indirectly, the nature of the exchanges that organizations offer their stakeholders. Proposed exchanges must be known before they can be incorporated into messages preparatory to communication.

Significant effort often is necessary to define proposed exchanges. Expenditures prescribed in organizational plans limit the quality of goods and services and the comfort of environments. Policies and procedures that influence organizational and individual behaviors are molded to conform to available resources. Organizational planning thus defines proposed transactions and limits the content of messages that may be used to encourage stakeholder acceptance. Plans, programs and other components of communication—campaigns, special events, and crisis responses—all are shaped by organizational plans.

Organizations' philosophies, mission statements, and stated goals and objectives may or may not accurately reflect the realities that communicators encounter in planning, programming, designing campaigns, staging special events, managing issues, and responding to crises. Organizations' qualitative, behavioral, and environmental messages determine, over time, the nature and strength of relationships between organizations and stakeholders. Consistent and salutary messages produce trust and loyalty. Inconsistent messages, or messages of questionable validity, destroy credibility and breed cynicism and distrust. Levels of stakeholder trust, loyalty, and credibility govern potential for success in communication, especially under crisis conditions.

The influence of organizational plans on communication is so strong that some in management have been persuaded that communicators must be involved in *organizational* planning. Columbia University Professor Melvin Anshen, for example, argues that contemporary social conditions require that senior communicators participate in the process as planners and ombudsmen.

Planning

With or without such involvement, communicators must prepare plans to guide their own activities. Communication planning is a straightforward process through which communication goals and objectives are established in support of organizational goals and objectives. Communication plans specify general guidelines and points of emphasis for communication programs. In the absence of detailed organizational plans, communication plans specify the nature of proposed transactions. Communication plans provide direction for those responsible for developing stakeholder-specific communication programs.

Communication plans are general in nature and parallel the plans of parent organizations. While cast in general terms, however, communication plans provide guidance to those who design the components of the organization's communication system. Guidance is especially necessary as to the nature of transactions offered to stakeholders.

If an auto manufacturer's objectives include a greater market share, for example, the communication plan should specify the reasons the organization will give each group to behave in ways that will permit the objective to be reached. Proposed transactions might include bonuses for workers who reduce defect rates, improved products and better delivery schedules for dealers, and more reliable transportation for consumers.

The communication planning process should ensure that proposed benefits will accrue to each group. Unfulfilled promises—implied or implicit—create conflicting messages of the sort discussed earlier. No communication plan can be considered final until planners have assured themselves that proposed mass-media message content will be accurate and consistent with messages originating from other sources.

Communication plans, to summarize, should specify proposed transactions with stakeholder groups and the reasons why those transactions will be mutually advantageous. Proposed transactions should be incorporated into general statements as to what communication is expected to accomplish and why stakeholders should respond to proposed messages in keeping with organizational desires. Such statements tend to be cumbersome, but communication plans need not be cast in the language of advertising. Their purpose is to provide guidance for communicators.

Programming

Where plans deal directly with transactions and indirectly with the nature of information to be transmitted to stakeholders, communication programs define the ways that information is to be transmitted to stakeholder groups. Where plans are general and fashioned at the organizational level, programs are stakeholder-specific. Stakeholder groups vary little from one organization to another. All deal with consumers, employees, vendors, owners, and media. Donors, voters, and volunteers are among other groups that can be important to specific organizations. Programs must be designed for each stakeholder group in keeping with group and organizational interests.

Program and programming traditionally have been used to refer to planning as well as programming. Communication efforts in their totality have been called programs rather than plans, and the word also has been applied to narrower efforts to communicate with employees, consumers, and other groups. The differences are more important for practical than semantic reasons. Need for planning and, especially, for a clearly defined set of proposed transactions, is too easily overlooked. Absence of a communication plan can tempt communicators to proceed to message design and channel selection without adequate attention to the transactions that messages should be designed to encourage. Where transactions are not defined in the course of organizational or communication planning, they must be addressed in the first phase of what then becomes a more complex programming process.

Where adequate plans exist, programming is more readily accomplished. Programs are the operational components of mass communication systems. Programs are continuing efforts to encourage exchanges with organizational stakeholders. Programs usually are designed on annual bases, conforming to communication plans and the philosophies, mission statements, goals, and objectives of organizations. Programs are intended to develop and maintain mutually beneficial relationships between organizations and stakeholders through serial exchanges.

Within these general parameters, programs are designed to convey the terms of proposed transactions to stakeholders and elicit responses that will enable organizations to make any adjustments necessary to ensure success. Program goals and objectives are expressed in communication rather than management terms. Where organizational goals for a year might include a 5 percent increase in sales of a specific product, communication goals might require similar improvement in consumer perception or knowledge of the product. An organizational decision to reduce turnover rates, in similar fashion, might suggest parallel improvement in perceptions of the company among employees or prospective employees.

Programs are based on stakeholder-specific sets of goals and objectives, with each objective expressed in measurable terms. One or more strategies, each involving one or more tactics or activities, is specified to accomplish each objective. Objectives in each case are expressed in terms of measurable behavioral responses among stakeholders. Ability to measure results, and mutually understood definitions of "success," are essential if those involved are subsequently to determine whether success was achieved.

Activities or tactics used in communication programs are designed to transmit information to stakeholders. The word activity is broadly defined. An activity can be as readily managed as an after-dinner speech and as demanding as a national or international speakers' bureau. Activities range from writing letters to publishing magazines, from sending a team to a charity bowling competition to organizing a membership or fund-raising campaign.

Campaigns and special events can be among the activities of which programs are structured but often are conducted as free-standing units, independent of plans and programs. Fund raising and membership campaigns often are conducted in this manner, and may be less productive as a result.

The strength of relationships established and nurtured through communication programs governs the magnitude of campaigns and the difficulties communicators experience in dealing with these specialized communication situations. Communication programming therefore tends to be developmental and preventive while campaign and special-event design and execution as well as crisis management are equally apt to be remedial. Where communication programs are oriented to avoiding disputes and conflicts, campaigns and crisis-related efforts often are confrontational. Programs may include campaigns and special events and frequently are extended to encompass crisis communication efforts.

Campaigns and Special Events

From an organizational standpoint, campaigns and special events are programs in miniature. Campaigns and special events tend to be more obviously transactional in nature than plans or programs. Both are typically built around clearly defined exchanges. Memberships, dollars, and votes are the coinage of campaigns and, to a lesser extent, of special events as well.

Most campaigns and special events are components of continuing communication programs, as in the periodic fund raising efforts of nonprofit organizations or the re-election campaigns of public office holders. Others may revolve around special interest groups' episodic efforts to influence organizational or governmental policy. Potential for success or failure and level of communicator difficulty, in any case, will be influenced by parent programs. Response to messages is cumulative. Stakeholders whose trust and confidence have been earned over time through performance and communication tend to respond favorably to campaign and special event messages. Where skepticism or distrust prevail, the reverse is true.

Campaigns and special events are designed to accomplish more narrowly drawn objectives than is the case with programs. They also tend to be confined to more limited time spans. Campaigns and special events usually are cyclical or episodic rather than continuing, as is the case with programs. They often are adversarial and usually are to some extent competitive.

Campaigns typically are launched to achieve narrowly defined political, economic, or social objectives and in general are of less than one year in duration. While campaigns for public office may extend beyond 12 months, most political campaigns are shorter lived and deal with pending or anticipated legislation. Fund-raising campaigns, whether their objectives are expressed as contributions or member- ships, usually are measured in weeks or months.

Crises

Frequency and intensity of organizational crises, like need for campaigns and special events, are governed in part by the efficiency and effectiveness of communication plans and programs. Crises differ from campaigns and special events primarily in that campaign and special-event time factors are known where crises are unpredictable. Demands on communicators vary accordingly.

The nature of communication systems is such, however, that crisis communication is no more readily examined in a vacuum than are campaigns or special events. Numbers of crises in which communica- tors become involved, and the severity of those difficulties, are functions of the effectiveness of communication plans, programs, campaigns, and special events. Strong plans and programs, and effective campaigns and special events, prevent many crises from developing. Organizations that have earned the stakeholders' respect are relatively invulnerable to deliberate attack although quite subject to disaster.

Most crises are predictable and can be sorted into two categories: neglected issues that have grown to critical proportions, and human errors that create life threatening or environment threatening problems. The conclusion of a very old joke suggests that those waist- deep in alligators rarely remember that their primary responsibility is to drain the swamp. Alligators, like issues, are born vulnerable and helpless. Both become man-eaters through neglect.

Crises require attention, however, regardless of origin. Crisis communication efforts, like campaigns, are simplified or complicated by the presence or absence of comprehensive communication systems. Effective systems are based on comprehensive plans. Appropriate plans provide for issues tracking to facilitate early identification of potential crises. Most plans also incorporate crisis response mechanisms that enable communicators to better meet the problems involved.

The difference between crises and disasters is small but significant. The former can be anticipated. The latter, spawned by human error or natural forces, cannot be predicted. Most organizations use the same sort of contingency planning and apply the same management systems to deal with disasters and crises. Plans are more mechanical than creative. They do little more than define responsibilities and provide for temporary organizational structures.

THE BASICS PREVAIL

None of the factors explored above should be interpreted as departing from the basic communication process: research, planning, implementation, and evaluation. The greater complexities that arise where communicators attempt to deal with a broader definition of communication and with the transactional nature of the process makes the four-step approach more important than before.

Research is vital, for example, in fashioning exchanges that will be welcomed by stakeholder groups. Communicators must be aware that consumers value quality as much as appearance, and that workers value participation as much as wages.

The complexities of planning compound apace where organizations' needs for consistency in messages is addressed. Mass-mediated and interpersonal messages must be consistent with those transmitted environmentally, behaviorally, and qualitatively. Each of the latter sectors therefore must be addressed in communication plans and programs.

Assessment becomes at least proportionately more complex in that valuative processes must be made sensitive to more messages delivered through more channels. Communicators must develop capabilities to separately analyze the impact of messages by source, and to make adjustments accordingly.

Perhaps most important, need for coordination within the mediated and interpersonal communication categories becomes significantly more pressing. Greater complexity in communication systems inevitably is expressed in higher cost as well as greater potential for productivity. Added costs can be best absorbed by ensuring a level of coordination that compounds results.

Step One: Research

Research encompasses a broad range of functions that vary in formality in communication. Formality in research or information gathering systems is governed more by academic definition than by complexity or sophistication. Formal research is designed to add to knowledge and conducted in keeping with rigorous procedural standards. Most communication-related research is less rigorous although no less important to the process. Communicators depend primarily on informational mosaics fashioned of data gathered from multiple organizational and external sources.

Organizational information includes all data—quantitative and qualitative—that may directly or indirectly produce insights into the strength of relationships between organizations and stakeholders. This information category also may include reports and other data that may indicate environmental change. Data about potential change in cost and availability of production resources is especially important.

More precise estimates of resource availability and stakeholder concerns often originate externally. Data from the Bureau of the Census and other U.S. Department of Commerce components can be valuable in assessing trends and their potential impacts. Information published in business and trade magazines and leading newspapers also can be helpful, especially in a process called environmental assessment.

Environmental assessment is a two-phase early warning system. The phases are scanning and monitoring—scanning to identify incidents that may trigger trends and monitoring to track developing trends important to the organization.

Efforts to develop mass communication programs, campaigns, special events, and crisis control strategies without adequate information are akin to building office towers on quicksand. Resulting structures will not endure, no matter how well designed or constructed. Information-gathering techniques vary with types of communication efforts, but basic processes, with few exceptions, remain operative.

Step Two: Planning

With research completed, communicators traditionally have designed programs, campaigns, and crisis responses in keeping with responses to a series of critical questions. The questions, subject to logical and rational consideration only where communicators maintain adequate knowledge of organizations and their environments, are:

1. What are the organization's goals and objectives?
2. What communication goals and objectives are implicit in or implied by organizational goals and objectives?
3. What stakeholder groups are involved in each goal and objective from organizational and communicator standpoints?

4. What behaviors should the organization seek to encourage among stakeholder groups?
5. What messages must be conveyed to group members to induce them to behave as the organization would have them behave?
6. What interpersonal, mediated, behavioral, and environmental techniques or communication channels can best be used to deliver messages to each group?
7. How can stakeholder responses be measured as communication efforts proceed?

Responses to these questions enable professionals to establish the communication programs for which they historically have been primarily responsible. Communication goals are developed as a function of organizational goals. Objectives and strategies then are based on communication goals and sets of activities are planned to convey information.

Step Three: Communication

Communication deals with two major variables: messages and media. Messages, ranging from behavioral to mediated, contain information to be delivered to stakeholders. Media are channels of communication through which messages may be delivered. They range from traditional mass media to organizational behaviors and environments. Message content varies with the nature of campaigns or events, and stakeholders involved. Fund-raising efforts, for example, usually bear little resemblance to political campaigns.

Communication during the course of crises presents different problems, most of them influenced by the extent of organizational preparedness. While volume of headlines and public hand-wringing often suggest otherwise, most organizational and communication crises are at least in part predictable. Early experiences with nuclear energy in the United States and the Soviet Union, for example, should have served as precursors of the similar incident Chernobyl. Exxon's Gulf of Alaska oil spill of 1989 should have been expected in the wake of a similar but less traumatic incident off the coast of France a few years earlier. The only real unknowns in the second incidents involved dates, places, magnitudes, and the identities of organizations and individuals involved.

The communication sequence usually follows a pattern based on answers to six questions:

1. What are the nature and origin of the problem at hand?
2. What stakeholder groups are involved?

3. What changes, if any, must be made in organizational policy or
   procedure to assure fair and equitable treatment of those groups?
4. What messages do we want to send them?
5. What media are best suited to convey those messages?
6. How can we measure results of the communication process?

Step Four: Assessment

Measuring the results of communication is a complex process
regardless of the apparent simplicity of the problem. Assessment
requires a precise answer to a complex question: To what extent did
messages sent in the course of the communication effort produce
desired results? Complexity develops because communicators are
interested in the extent to which results were produced by messages
delivered. Results may be inadequate to justify continuing massive
communication efforts. Large percentages of product sales, for example,
occur with or without attendant product publicity programs. Such
programs can be justified economically only where additional sales are
adequate to support expenditures involved.

Results of communication can be measured directly or indirectly.
Assessment can be accomplished by using existing or new measuring
devices. Decisions by organizations and communicators as to types of
measurements to be used usually are governed by levels of precision
required and costs involved. Costs are lowest where existing indicators
can be used but indirect measurement usually is relatively imprecise.

Assessment efforts must accomplish two objectives. First, they must
produce data that demonstrate results to the satisfaction of senior
managers or clients. Requirements vary among members of these
groups. Communicators therefore must come to agreements with
clients or superiors before programs begin in order to later provide the
information they require.

Assessment techniques designed to determine the relative efficiency
of media and messages are more important to communicators.
Communication efforts can be fine tuned as they proceed only to the
extent that communicators can obtain accurate information (a) as to
the ability of media to convey messages and (b) recipient responses to
those messages. Too often, however, employers and clients are
unwilling or unable to fund research necessary to provide such
information.

Pragmatically, clients and employers often are less than ideal
sources of information. Most are too close to their businesses or other
endeavors to accurately perceive their communication needs. Those
called upon to plan and implement communication efforts always are
best advised to perform their own inspections and reach independent

conclusions as to organizational needs. Client or employer perceptions deserve consideration but rarely should be accepted at face value.

Senior managers especially tend to be unaware of attitude and opinion among stakeholders. Employee and labor relations consultants called upon to deal with union organizing problems, for example, almost invariably find corporate managers surprised and disappointed over their subordinates' failings. A typical chief executive's comment on being confronted with union organizers is: "our working relationships always have been the best."

IN SUMMARY

Little that transpires in the development of communication strategies and tactics deals with communication in the sense that most use that word. Developing, packaging, and distributing messages is but a small part—and the least effective part—of contemporary communication. The developmental challenge that communicators face is most readily described in a series of four preliminary questions:

1. What stakeholder groups are parties to the program, campaign, special event, or crisis?
2. What behaviors are sought on the part of each group?
3. What messages must be sent to induce such behaviors?
4. What must the organization do to validate the messages?

In other words, what changes in organizational policies, behaviors, or environments may be necessary to ensure that (a) mediated messages are consistent with environmental, behavioral, and qualitative messages and (b) that the organization's position is logical, rational, equitable, and honestly portrayed? Here, again, the role of exchange theory should be evident. Simply put, the task involves designing an exchange or exchanges that will satisfy the needs of both parties. The cosmetic manufacturer that wants to successfully introduce a new fade cream need only ensure that the product removes skin blemishes without adverse side effects. Product attributes then will enable communicators to honestly send irresistible messages to prospective consumers. Employers who want greater productivity similarly need only announce themselves ready to compensate workers accordingly. Real estate developers who want to offer "the most luxurious offices in town" first must make certain that products conform to that description.

Where realities fail to support proposed messages, changes must be made in one area or both. Failure to make necessary changes, other than in rare instances, destroys potential for successful communication. Misleading or conflicting messages ultimately are destructive. Gross exaggeration rarely is tolerated other than among those promoting traveling entertainment events. Those involved will not soon return and promoters are not held accountable for the quality of the events they stage. Other organizations are held accountable by consumers for the quality of products and services. Failure to deliver on promises destroys prospective relationships. Long-term sales potential for products or services dies with those relationships.

Message content is—or should be—a product of organizational environments, behaviors, and product/service qualities. More specifically, messages should reflect relative advantages that the organization enjoys in those areas. They should focus on those attributes—environmental, behavioral, and qualitative—in which the sponsoring organization excels.

ADDITIONAL READING

Anshen, Melvin, ed. *Managing the Socially Responsible Corporation.* New York: Macmillan, 1974.

————. *Corporate Strategies for Social Performance.* New York: Columbia University Press, 1980.

Blau, Peter M. *Exchange and Power in Social Life*, 2nd ed. New Brunswick, NJ: Transaction Publishers, 1989.

Grunig, James E., and Todd Hunt. *Managing Public Relations*, New York: Holt, Rinehart and Winston, 1984.

Kellerman, Donald S., Andrew Kohut and Carol Bowman. *The Age of Indifference: A Study of Young Americans and How They View the News.* Washington, D.C.: Times Mirror Center for the People and the Press, 1990.

LeBoeuf, Michael L. *How to Win Customers and Keep Them for Life.* New York: Berkley, 1987.

Petty, Richard E., and John T. Cacioppo. *Communication and Persuasion: Central and Peripheral Routes to Attitude Change.* New York: Springer-Verlag, 1987.

Rogers, Everett M. *Communication Technology: The New Media in Society.* New York: Free Press, 1986.

2

The Communication Environment

Life on earth began, some scientists speculate, when basic chemical elements came together in a sort of nutrient broth. Heat levels probably were low and development progressed slowly. Contemporary society more closely resembles a pressure cooker in which individual and organizational survival depend on ability to adapt quickly to changing conditions.

Pressure and accompanying stress levels have increased steadily over the centuries. Several trends, some generally recognized and others only now gaining attention, have contributed to contemporary circumstances. Societies have become progressively larger and more complex, more specialized, and more interdependent. Nations once composed of thousands of independent towns and cities have become components of global economic systems.

Interdependence has prompted a continuing rethinking of social relationships. Organizations ranging from governments to for-profit corporations find it necessary to rethink their missions, goals, and objectives as well as their products or services in keeping with emerging social standards and conditions. Social conditions are especially demanding. The interdependency that characterizes industrial and postindustrial societies has become equally prevalent among organizations and their stakeholder groups. Among the many engines of change:

1. The industrial revolution, especially its social aspects
2. The capital requirements crisis
3. Growth and centralization in government
4. Growth and urbanization of populations
5. Concurrent change in social beliefs and customs
6. Equal opportunity
7. Consumerism
8. The energy crisis

9. Environmental problems
10. The information explosion
11. Increasing numbers of knowledge workers and their economic and
    political influence
12. Change in social emphasis from technology to quality of life

While environments are changing rapidly, neither humankind nor
humanity's creations have become more adaptable. Organizations have
proven most resistant to change and, as a result, are most threatened
in contemporary society. The term organizations is used here to include
corporations of all kinds as well as the governments that spawn them.
Organizations encompasss sole proprietorships and partnerships, for
profit and not-for-profit corporations, foundations and think tanks,
educational and health care institutions, membership organizations,
and governmental agencies of all kinds at all levels. All are subject to
progressively more critical and demanding scrutiny. Recent history
suggests that society's demands on corporations may be especially
onerous. The demands nevertheless exist and must be dealt with by
corporations attempting to survive in an emerging postindustrial
society.

ORGANIZATIONAL EVOLUTION

Organizations are creatures of society. Most of the largest were
established in law to serve specific purposes for the common good. First
among them were state and national governments, each soon followed
by a parallel bureaucracy. State governments spawned counties and
municipalities. Federal government created a host of zones, districts,
territories, and the like.

The governmental structure of the United States was built on the
premise that the best government was the least government; that
freedom of economic opportunity, individual initiative, and private
property would be sufficient to "the American dream." Distortions set
in as corporations, labor unions, and special interest groups each
sought advantages at others' expense.

Corporations deserve special attention. Society, acting primarily
through state governments, gave corporations life to solve a specific if
often forgotten economic problem. The problem was a shortage of
capital to fund economic growth. Successful businesses rarely generate
adequate profits to finance the growth of which they are capable.
The onset of the industrial age brought unprecedented demand for
resources to fuel expansion. The solution, in the form of corporations,
was intended to create benefits for society as well as businesses.
Corporations were conceived as vehicles to enable capital to be

accumulated and applied, stimulating growth and development. Society, acting through state legislatures, authorized corporations in hopes they would foster democracy by creating economic abundance. Entrepreneurs received special concessions or franchises in return for undefined benefits that were to accrue to the general welfare. That ambiguity is the source of contemporary debate over the social responsibility of corporations large and small.

The On-Going Battle

Governments and their corporate offspring now are locked in battle over social and economic legitimacy. As creatures or franchises of the states, corporations presumably are indebted to the states and dependent on public good will, as expressed through the states, for the continuance of their franchises. Conflict inherent in these conditions has developed at several levels and has come to preoccupy both Republican and Democrat parties.

Fundamental conflict is produced by the collision of democratic values on which government is based with the economic values that drive the free enterprise system. Democracy is based on freedom and equality while capitalism is founded on efficiency and productivity.

Changing public expectations of government and corporations produce more complex conflicts. Elective offices often are won through grandiose promises illogically combined with commitments to fiscal austerity. Having created these dilemmas, elected officials attempt to redeem their pledges by shifting social burdens from government to corporations. Rather than come to grips with escalating health care costs during the 1980s, for example, governmental agencies sought to shift the burden to employers.

A Persistent Dilemma

Organizational problems of this sort are compounding. The diversity and complexity of demands leveled at contemporary organizations is reminiscent of a whimsical admonition to workers: "Keep your eye on the ball, your shoulder to the wheel, and your nose to the grindstone. Now, just try to work in that position." The organizational challenge has been defined by contemporary management theorists Marcus, Kaufman, and Beam (1987):

> Corporations are simultaneously economic instruments that must succeed according to the criterion of efficiency and social systems that have to perform acceptably in light of society's values. They have to

do well—efficiently transform goods into products and services—and
do good—maintain legitimacy in the face of changing values. Efficiency is easier to define, quantify and measure but legitimacy is no less
important. (8)

The demands that society makes of organizations, however, are not
necessarily logical and rational. Accepted and implemented unques-
tioningly, these demands can be self-defeating, as management theorist
Peter F. Drucker pointed out in 1989. Appeals to social responsibility,
Drucker said, must be viewed in light of the designs and capacities of
organizations involved.

> We may well decide that the social good outweighs the cost of the
> sacrifice in performance. But it is dangerous, it is indeed irresponsible,
> not to ask the question or to pretend that it is irrelevant—which is
> what we did in the United States when we decided to make the school
> the agent of racial desegregation. Had we then asked the question, we
> would almost certainly still would have desegregated the schools. The
> great sin of segregation and racial discrimination had to be corrected,
> had to be expiated. But we might have found ways to avoid, or at least
> contain, the damage to the capacity of the school to teach. We might,
> for instance, have started with experimental programs in a few
> schools selected for their high standards and their strict discipline. By
> brushing aside as racist and irrelevant all questions regarding the
> school's primary task, we only assured that we got neither desegrega-
> tion nor scholastic achievement. (87)

Conflicts of this sort will plague corporations and governments for
decades. Neither group always will be correct in judging prevailing
conditions or the appropriateness of proposed strategies to deal with
social problems. Corporations and governments each can be expected
to attempt to meet society's expectations. Each also can be expected to
avoid the economic costs involved. The process is something of a
charade. Consumers ultimately pay, whether in taxes or higher prices.
The contestants nevertheless persist because winners in wars of ideas
are those who appear to have won, regardless of realities.

Continuing Conflict

Intergroup and intragroup conflict are fueled by struggles to meet
social expectations and maintain legitimacy, as expressed informally
in social norms or formally through statute or administrative regulation. The pursuit of efficiency continues apace, even where such efforts
conflict with an organization's need for legitimacy. Marcus, Kaufman,
and Beam (1987) described the dilemma in these words:

To be efficient, the corporation needs the cooperation of such relevant stakeholders as customers, suppliers and workers. If these constituencies withhold vital resources for a significant period of time because of a perceived lack of legitimacy, the corporation is hard-pressed to produce saleable goods and services. On the other hand, there are cases where legitimacy and efficiency conflict, such as where corporations meet the needs of their immediate constituencies but bring harm to society by damaging the environment or failing to employ minorities. In these cases, resources may have to be diverted from efficiency-enhancing activities to ones that are designed to maintain social legitimacy. . . . (8)

Legitimacy is a political resource that is granted on a contingent basis and is subject to alteration as social demands are modified. (9)

The legitimacy problem is difficult for managers to handle. Several factors are involved. First, managers have little influence over matters of legitimacy. Managerial and organizational destinies are as inextricably intertwined as those of organizations and their environments. Second, managers often are ill-equipped to handle the intangible and subjective rather than the tangible and objective. Most are more comfortable coping with products and their manufacture or distribution than with people and communication.

Most managerial difficulties are generated by this conflict between productivity and legitimacy; by what has and what usually has not been taught in business schools. The problem is doubly difficult because society is ill-prepared to deal with complex issues. Contemporary consumers are products of a convenience or fast-food society. They have neither time nor inclination to become involved with anything that cannot be cooked, packaged and delivered ready to eat in less than two minutes. Any remnants of the meal, moreover, must be amenable to being disposed of in 15 seconds.

Ideas rarely are compatible with the convenience mentality although packagers keep trying. The complexities of the legitimacy versus productivity issue, for example, have been dehydrated, compressed, packaged, and delivered under a deceptively simple label: social responsibility. The label is attractive but it makes the product no more readily digested by any of the parties.

Managerial Problems

Organizations' difficulties are compounded by conditions within their management ranks. Today's middle-aged managers were reared and educated under economic, political, and social conditions that no longer exist. Two sets of problems arise as a result.   First, most managers are underequipped or unwilling to address contemporary circumstances. Second, those circumstances continue to change.

Misperception. Managers in business and communication often fail to perceive and understand the changes that occur around them. They are unable to adequately comprehend the environments in which their organizations function, the limitations those environments impose, and the ways organizations must respond in order to survive.

Managers most often are concerned with organizations' economic functions to the exclusion of the social. They fail to grasp the interdependence created by continuing economic and social change. Progressive concentration of wealth and power in corporations has produced concomitant social responsibility. The extent of the responsibility, and the parallel vulnerability, have been demonstrated by the alacrity with which government and special interest groups are prepared to step forward in the absence of organizational response.

Changing circumstances. Special interest groups have been especially aggressive in bringing to corporate and governmental attention many trends that are transforming human and organizational life. Several trends have proven especially influential in convincing large segments of the population that economic performance is inadequate to justify the existence of corporations. They include:

1. Increasing recognition that natural resources are finite and that national resource independence is being supplanted by interdependence.
2. Developing energy problems that ultimately will contribute to radical change in society and in the costs of production.
3. Growing acceptance of the fact that unrestricted industrial activity can harm the environment and public health.
4. Increasing support for the thesis that the power society vests in organizations is accompanied by both social and economic responsibilities.

Drucker identifies the social imperatives of contemporary organizations in declaring:

> The single most important thing to remember about any enterprise is that results exist only on the outside. The result of a business is a satisfied customer. The result of a hospital is a healed patient. The result of a school is a student who has learned something and puts it to work ten years later. Inside an enterprise there are only costs. (230)

Outside the organization, managers are confronted with an environment in which concepts of freedom, capitalism, and society have been redefined. Freedom is becoming progressively more circumscribed by society for organizations as well as individuals. The capitalist system continues to evolve. Rather than accept and respond to changing realities, organizations too often attempt to substitute rhetoric for performance. The result is loss of credibility, which compounds communication problems.

SOCIAL RESPONSIBILITY

Social change is spurred on in part by the mass media. Relatively few of them, however, are equipped or disposed to deal with major social issues. Close inspection of most media reveals a fast-food or quick-fix mentality as prevalent as in the population the media serve. Editorial writers, like activists, early concluded that the demands of social responsibility will be met where organizations are fed strong and repeated doses of ethics. The prescription is no more practical than fast foods for those who need healthy diets.

Conflicts today are presumed soluble by socially responsible organizations even where difficulties involved are environmental rather than organizational in origin. Environmental problems rarely respond to internally developed codes of organizational conduct based on management values. Resolution instead requires attention to society's values as expressed in expectations of or demands on organizations. Responsive solutions must address values and demands in ways that are feasible economically and in terms of results. Equally important, as Drucker pointed out, responses must be compatible with the purposes of organizational systems. Only some 30 years after burdening its public schools with solving the nation's segregation problem, did domestic society recognize that the product of the system had deteriorated to a point at which the nation's status as a world economic power was imperiled.

Definition Established

Social responsibility already has been defined in some detail in the United States. Considerable controversy attached to the concept when it first was advanced in the 1950s and 1960s. By the 1990s, freedom, capitalism, and society had become relative rather than absolute terms, with their functional limits defined by society rather than special interest groups. The evolution of capitalism had entered a new phase and most accepted the fact that the process would continue. What might then have been termed a new definition was advanced in June of 1971 in New York City by the Committee for Economic Development in a paper entitled "Social Responsibilities of Business Corporations":

The corporate interest broadly defined by management can support
involvement in helping to solve virtually any social problem, because
people who have a good environment, education, and opportunity make
better employees, customers and neighbors for business than those who
are poor, ignorant, and oppressed.

The committee listed ten major categories of socially responsible
actions: economic growth and efficiency, education, employment and
training, civil rights and equal opportunity, urban renewal and
development, pollution abatement, conservation and recreation, culture
and the arts, medical care, and government.

Organizational activity in these areas has not been maintained at
uniform levels across the set of categories or over time. Some variation
is more a function of governmental action than organizational preference. As government became progressively more involved in civil rights
legislation, for example, organizational leaders turned their efforts to
ecological, urban, and other problems basic to their operations.

Remaining Issues

Organizations have made substantial progress in accommodating to
governmental activity, especially where that activity appears driven by
public opinion. Several social issues nevertheless remain to be resolved.
Some are primarily economic in nature; others are almost entirely
political.

The economic issues revolve around matters of cost as well as scope.
Succinctly stated, the questions are, "What shall be done?" "What will
it cost?" and "Who shall pay?" The political issues are matters of credit
and blame: "Who shall be acclaimed for successes?" and "Who shall be
condemned for failures?"

Economic issues. Payment is the focal point of most economic
matters. As budgets and trade balances became more troublesome to
Washington, the Federal government "backed away" from social
programs, new and existing. Some of the burdens involved were shifted
to the states. Others were placed, directly or indirectly, on taxpayers'
shoulders.

What amounts to "trickle down cost shifting" has continued,
moreover, within the several states. Legislatures have passed along
expenses as user fees, delegated responsibilities to counties or cities,
or otherwise managed to dodge the bullet for a time. Taxpayers, in
part as a response, have become resistant to new or increased taxes in
any form, creating political pitfalls of substantial size.

Political issues. The primary political issue is survival. Politicians
universally are more adept at counting votes than dollars. Those bent

on survival spend most of their time gaining credit for efforts that most voters approve and avoiding responsibility for developments that voters find distasteful. The result often consists of voting for new programs and against taxes necessary to fund them.

The newest twist in this game occurs when the political establishment drags business into the process. Much of the cost of toxic waste cleanups, for example, was levied against organizations that disposed of waste legally under then-existing laws. In like manner, legislators concerned over increasing costs of federal health care programs at this writing were considering requiring *all* employers to provide insurance for all of their personnel.

Tactics of the latter sort enable politicos to create benefits without increasing taxes or, at least, appear to be doing so. Costs incurred by organizations in meeting social responsibilities, to the extent that evidence is available, ultimately are paid by consumers. "General Motors Public Interest Report 1989," published in the Spring of that year, contained 64 elaborately printed pages detailing activities in areas ranging from clean air to solid waste management. Readers were left to decide for themselves whether associated costs were added to product prices or funded with profits that otherwise would have been allocated to primary stakeholders.

The largest long-term economic and political risks attendant to social responsibility may involve threats to productivity, potential for increased inflation, and resulting unemployment. The elemental question involved is simple: "What happens when organizations pass along social costs to the extent that their products or services are priced out of the market?" How high can General Motors' prices become before erosion in the company's share of the domestic auto market accelerates? How much social responsibility would the company be able to afford in the absence of governmental controls on numbers of vehicles imported from overseas?

Pressure groups. Both political and economic concerns are engaged where jobs are lost or job losses are threatened. Labor organizations and many other pressure groups are at work in the United States. They are effective because they focus on single issues, in the process becoming powerful despite their small size. Mass movements in modern politics, as Drucker points out, usually involve no more than 5 to 10 percent of the electorate. Minorities rarely provide margins of victory and succeed by blocking actions of which they disapprove. Drucker continues:

> Unlike the totalitarians, the single-cause group does not attempt to seize power. It does not even perceive itself as political, but moral. The totalitarians were predators; the new mass movements are parasites. The totalitarians killed. The single-cause pressure group paralyzes. (103)

Establishing Limits

The conditions Drucker describes are recognizable in many parts of contemporary society. They raise complex issues for organizations and managers, even where both endorse contemporary standards of social responsibility. How far can and should organizations and managers go in socially responsible action? At what point do socially responsible actions compromise the economic and, perhaps, the legal rights of shareholders and other stakeholders? How can the responsibility of individual organizations be accurately measured as to specific social issues?

How much, in other words, is enough socially responsible activity on the part of an organization? Stakeholders—those who have stakes in organizational conduct and economic success—already are challenging organizations on several fronts. In some cases, as with domestic auto manufacturers, challenges are revealed in sales figures. Customers have been "voting with their feet" ever since Volkswagen introduced the United States to what came to be called "the beetle" some 40 years ago. The ranks of organizations that have been abandoned in whole or part by their customers are legion.

Other expressed stakeholder concerns of late have included profit levels, illegal or unethical behavior, secrecy concealing corporate misconduct, disregard for potentially damaging results of corporate action, excessive political influence, and unsatisfactory executive behavior. Lists of companies involved in such pursuits change from day to day as newcomers "go to the head of the class." A review of the past few decades, however, would produce a list including most of *Fortune*'s list of the nation's 500 largest corporations.

Self-imposed problems aside, the electorate expects and, increasingly, demands organizational behaviors radically different from previously accepted and approved patterns. Pragmatically, society is forging a new social contract; rewriting franchise agreements represented by corporate charters. Public needs and expectations are the first expressions of those changes. Absent appropriate organizational response, the changes will be written into law by legislation, regulation, or adjudication.

ENVIRONMENTAL FACTORS

The influence of environmental factors on organizations can be analyzed, as management theorists have demonstrated, from an almost limitless number of perspectives. Perspectives vary in value to communicators with the extent to which they focus on organizations' relationships with stakeholder groups.

Two perspectives have proven valuable in analyzing the interplay of influence between organizations and stakeholder groups. One, mentioned earlier, involves organizational functions—inputs and outputs. Any change in any of these elements engages the interests of one or more stakeholder groups. The other perspective is somewhat broader, involving a stronger emphasis on organizational environments.

Organizational Functions

The functional view of organizations suggests that any disturbance in input, throughput, or output flows threatens stability, productivity and, by implication, the welfare of one or more stakeholder groups. Consider, for example, a product as simple as the common paper clip, a bit of plated wire bent into one of several common forms to temporarily hold two or more sheets of paper. The product appears simple but its manufacture requires more than is immediately evident.

Wire and plating material are essential, of course, as are manufacturing personnel, machinery, buildings, and all of the elements necessary—including capital—to maintain them. With these resources in hand, paper clip production can begin. Manufacturing processes thus are vulnerable to interruption through change in labor, material, and energy supplies. As paper clips are produced, they must be marketed, sold and distributed—processes also subject to disruption. Even then, the organization's work is incomplete. Accounts receivable must be collected, deposited and, in a sense, recycled.

Identifying groups. Groups involved in organizations as uncomplicated as paper clip manufacturers thus are more numerous than many perceive to be the case. Assuming, for illustrative purposes, that such a company is in process of being organized, the following groups would form:

1. Investors to provide capital to fund construction of the plant, install equipment, purchase raw materials, hire personnel, maintenance inventories, ship orders, maintain facilities, and collect payables.
2. Members of the financial community and regulatory agencies at state and, perhaps, federal levels if funding requires a public stock offering.
3. Senior managers who must be hired early to develop the organization; individuals often called upon to risk the relative economic safety of other positions who must be offered offsetting incentives during the recruiting process.

4. Municipal, county, and state governments that may be involved in zoning, construction permits or variances, operating licenses, and the like. As operations begin, state and federal agencies that regulate manufacturing processes, waste disposal, occupational safety and health, and other aspects of business also become involved.
5. Business and financial news media, as plans are announed.
6. Employees, prospective employees and, later, former employees who may be entitled to benefits of one sort or another.
7. Vendors ranging from contractors who will build the plant to those who will supply raw materials, packaging, energy to keep machinery running, trucks in which to transport products, and literally thousands of other durable and consumable products and services.
8. Creditors, including banks, finance and leasing companies and other sources of short- and long-term capital, as well as vendors.
9. Business and trade associations in the organization's industry and in industries to which the organization sells products or services.
10. Prospective customers, customers and, later, former customers.
11. News media serving the office supply industry; those in which the company may elect to advertise and those who might be interested in news releases.
12. Residents of neighborhoods near the plant, especially if processes involved are going to involve discharge of any hazardous, toxic, or noxious waste.
13. Members of community nonprofit groups ranging from schools and colleges to charitable and civic organizations who might come to the organization for support.
14. Members of special interest groups that might become interested in the organization's activities. These include labor unions, environmental groups, and any others whose interests may be engaged intermittently or on an on-going basis.

Organizational variation. Paper clip manufacturing is not a complex business, but managers must cope with all of the stakeholder groups identified above. Should the company elect a multifaceted marketing strategy, selling direct to some customers and through distributors to others, two customer groups would be involved. Were the company to create a designer paper clip identifiable by consumers, that group also would be added to the stakeholder list. If the company grows and moves into international markets, numbers of stakeholder groups compound with numbers of nations involved. The total becomes even greater, of course, should the company elect to manufacture overseas or subcontract manufacturing to overseas firms. Multinational firms that manufacture and sell overseas and deal in multiple product lines become involved with hundreds of stakeholder groups varying in size and complexity with plant and office locations.

These circumstances require that communication planners be familiar with all operations in which clients or employers may be engaged. Identifying stakeholders, especially in terms of specific issues, becomes difficult without such knowledge.

Stakeholder Linkages

Organizations' relationships with stakeholders can be complicated by environmental factors. Environments that influence stakeholders can produce strong, immediate, and significant problems for organizations. Resulting difficulties are best described as secondary or derived problems but are no less troublesome from a managerial standpoint.

Environmental factors of all kinds can change usually predictable stakeholder behavior in ways detrimental to organizations. Labor problems in suppliers' plants or in the transportation industry, for example, can prevent vendors from delivering material as the organization requires. Increases in fuel costs can create losses as organizations fill pending orders. Electricity shortages can limit production and destroy ability to meet customer delivery deadlines.

Tertiary problems are even more difficult to identify on a timely basis in the absence of complete information. Consider for example, the extent to which an increase in the price of silver can create difficulties for hospitals. Silver in pure form is rarely used in hospitals but the metal is a vital ingredient in film used in radiology and imaging departments.

Hospitals nevertheless are better able to respond to higher silver prices than are film manufacturers. At minimum, hospitals can adjust prices to avoid losses due to higher film costs. Volume short-term purchases could be arranged in anticipation of higher prices. Vendors also might be induced to enter into longer-term contracts affording greater price protection.

More important from a communication standpoint, ability to anticipate change enables organizations to inform stakeholders of prospective cost increases. Price increases somehow seem more palatable when consumers are informed far in advance of effective dates. Knowledge of environmental factors that influence organizational welfare for these reasons is as important to communicators as to managers. Communicator ability to assist organizations in meeting their objectives is governed by knowledge of (a) client or employer operations, (b) environments in which client or employer organizations function, (c) environments in which stakeholders function, and (d) environmental trends in all of those areas.

Environmental Functions

Identifying and tracking environmental factors is tedious but not difficult. Factors involved are readily identified where communicators are familiar with two sets of environments with which organizations are concerned: internal and external.

Internal environments or subsystems include the psychological, social, political, and technological. The first three have been more or less bound together by some contemporary theorists with the term "organizational culture." External or suprasystems include the socio-cultural, political-legal, economic, and technological. They are equally complex and usually are greater sources of tension and conflict.

Subsystems

Psychological. The psychological subsystem is the most complex of the four internal subsystems. It consists of the motivations, needs, values, attitudes, perceptions, beliefs, emotions, and personality structures of organizations' members, from executive suite to shipping department. Complexities in psychological subsystems, in which social subsystems originate, can create inconsistencies in organizational behavior.

Social. Organizational cultures are created by social subsystems. Cultures are shaped by the collective aspects of human behavior in groups. These behaviors involve more than the aggregate of individual behaviors and usually are viewed as a sort of collective consciousness or intelligence.

Political. Rooted in the informal power structures of social systems, organizations' political subsystems generate the power and influence wielded by natural rather than formal leaders. Individuals who are part of the this informal elite, and the roles they occupy in organizations, originate in political subsystems. Formal leadership structures may or may not be based in these subsystems.

Technological. The collective attributes of machines and the individuals and organizations that support them are created in organizations' technological subsystems. These elements encompass the roots of mechanization, computerization, automation, and robotization. Scientific advances that enhance the importance of technologies also increase the stature and power of the disciplines involved.

While necessarily described individually, organizational subsystems can not be viewed as independent units. Subsystems and suprasystems necessarily interact in near infinite ways.

Suprasystems

Interactions vary across and within systems. Conflict originating in any subsystem or suprasystem can dominate organizational concerns at any given moment. Potential for conflict among suprasystems also is compounded by their complexity.

Socio-cultural. Change tends to occur at a relatively slow—some would say generational—pace in the socio-cultural suprasystem. Socio-cultural suprasystems encompass life styles, career expectations, consumerism, family formation, population trends, and life expectancies. Social values, cultural characteristics, societal inequalities, educational characteristics, and demographics also fall within the socio-cultural group. All these factors changed perceptibly during the 1980s and change continues to occur.

Political-legal. Rates of change in political-legal suprasystems tend to parallel those prevailing in the socio-cultural. The political-legal suprasystem includes the executive, legislative, and judicial as well as bureaucratic "branches" of government at all levels. Political parties and pressure groups are involved as well. The political-legal suprasystem tends to be reactive rather than active; responding to socio-cultural trends with laws and regulations. Potential for sudden change nevertheless exists where political-legal suprasystems are defined globally or hemispherically, as increasingly is the case in contemporary society.

Economic. Potential for sudden change is greater in the economic suprasystem than in the socio-cultural. Trends in gross national products, interest rates, money supply, inflation rates, unemployment levels, and the availability and cost of energy and raw materials all are components of the economic suprasystem. Capital, natural resources, and labor also are included.

Technological. Change can come at least as suddenly in the technological suprasystem as in the economic. The two differ, however, in that technological changes usually are considered "progress" while economic changes vary in direction. The technological suprasystem also includes more than laboratory and product developments. Magnitude and focus of research and development efforts and trends in patent protection are important here. Emerging technologies, new product lines, management of computer information and other innovations also are involved.

Analyzing Systems

Organizational analyses are readily accomplished by examining suprasystems and subsystems. Several additional elements also require attention, however, if communicators are to maintain sensitivity to potential conflict. Analyses are most readily accomplished by examining organizations, their subsystems, and their suprasystems from five perspectives:

1. System objectives—where the organization is and where it wants to go.
2. Environmental constraints—current conditions in suprasystems and subsystems and limitations they impose.
3. System resources—the extent to which organizations can command, control or can gain access to *all* resources necessary to achieve objectives.
4. Systemic components—the several activities, goals and measures of performmance used by organizational sub-units.
5. System management—the knowledge, abilities and talents of those who direct systemic operations.

Managements and systemic components are givens from communicators' standpoints. For better or worse, communicators work within limitations imposed by the personalities, talents, and abilities of management teams and structures. Under these conditions, communicator effort must be oriented toward organizational objectives, environments, and systemic resources. Interplay among these elements produces shifting tensions that generate conflict.

The paper clip manufacturing concern discussed earlier can serve as a model in examining these factors. As a start-up organization, the firm begins at "ground zero" and seeks a share of the paper clip market. Company subsystems presumably are supportive and malleable. Few established internal patterns exist in new organizations. Major obstacles in socio-cultural or political-legal suprasystems presumably would have prevented the firm from being established and therefore can be assumed to have been overcome.

Economic and technological suprasystems are another matter. Resources must be assumed to be limited. The organization's business plan would have been based on multiple assumptions as to sales, profit margins, and the like. Any significant slippage can create problems. Potential technological change can be equally if less immediately troublesome. Advancing technologies can make equipment obsolete. Longer-established and, presumably, financially stronger competitors can capitalize on such changes to put start-up organizations at a competitive disadvantage. Systems analysis thus suggests that the paper clip manufacturer is most likely to experience problems originating in the economic and technological suprasystems.

IN SUMMARY

Contemporary organizations are caught up in an era of change that apparently will continue for years if not decades. Pressures on organizations reflect those experienced by stakeholder groups as they attempt to cope with changes occurring in the same environments that create difficulties for organizations. Organizations are being called upon to embrace social as well as economic goals under terms of a new, still evolving, social contract. They are being forced to sacrifice a modicum of productivity to maintain legitimacy.

The underlying issue has been called social responsibility. The term is ambiguous in all respects, even to the question of the nature of socially responsible activities. One point, however, has become clear: organizations are being called upon to contribute directly to the good that society expected to be derived when the states agreed to create corporate entities.

Concurrently, organizations are being held to new standards of accountability. They are expected to be, and most are attempting to be, open and forthcoming concerning their operations. These conditions require new and different communication systems originating in strategic planning processes and designed to ensure appropriate organizational conduct as well as efficient message delivery. Communicators progressively are becoming more involved, in other words, in determining the quality of the realities that will support the messages they transmit in behalf of clients or employers.

Communicators are no better prepared to discharge the responsibilities of such roles than are organizations to comply with new standards of social responsibility. Neither managers nor communicators are well-educated for contemporary circumstances. Communicators too often lack adequate knowledge of business and management while managers usually are ill-equipped concerning the human aspects of their enterprises.

Organizations nevertheless must cope with the dynamics of contemporary society by minimizing tension, avoiding conflict, and quickly resolving disputes by assuring fair, equitable treatment to all of the parties. Methods through which tension and conflict can be anticipated and remedied will be described in Chapter 3.

ADDITIONAL READING

Anshen, Melvin. *Corporate Strategies for Social Performance*. New York: Macmillan, 1980.
Drucker, Peter F. *The New Realities: In Government and Politics / In*

Economics and Business/In Society and World View. New York: Harper & Row, 1989.

General Motors Corporation. *General Motors Public Interest Report, 1989.* Detroit, MI: General Motors Corporation, 1989.

Marcus, Alfred A., Allen M. Kaufman, and David R. Beam. "The Pursuit of Corporate Advantage and the Quest for Social Legitimacy," in *Business Strategy and Public Policy*, New York: Quorum, 1987.

"Social Responsibilities of Business Corporations." New York: Committee on Economic Development, June 1971.

3

Tension and Conflict

Organizations' best efforts toward honest and equitable dealings with stakeholders inevitably are inadequate to prevent tension and conflict. Organizational relationships are like family relationships. The most loving families are not free of occasional argument or dispute. Family tension and conflict usually grow out of changes that occur in individuals with growth and maturation. Similar circumstances develop in organizations.

Intergenerational conflict occurs in organizations and families but basic attitudinal differences are more common sources of problems. Organizations and individuals relate to change in different ways. Some create and influence change. Others quickly adjust to change. Still others adapt more slowly, while some are resistant.

Resistance to change more often is seen in passive than active form. Habit and inertia are strong among individuals and organizations. Both tend to cling to the status quo although complexity compounds resistance to change in organizations.

Organizations' relationships with stakeholder groups are more complex than family relationships because organizations are more vulnerable to outsiders' claims. The illegitimate child at the family reunion is readily rejected and ejected without fear of consequences. Claimants to organizational "inheritances" are another matter. They demand immediate social performance in the face of a still-evolving definition of social responsibility. Ambiguity compounds claims that may or may not be legitimate but nevertheless exist and must be dealt with.

Contemporary organizations, as a result, find themselves caught up in confrontations with groups that Chicago public relations consultant Philip Lesly (1984) has categorized as advocates, dissidents, activists, and zealots. Advocates propose organizational action

concerning something they believe in, Lesly says. Dissidents take issue
with organizations over policies or causes. Activists exert pressure in
behalf of one or more causes and occasionally move from one cause to
another. Zealots are single-minded advocates of individual causes for
which they will accept only their own solutions.

Drucker (1989) suggests that contemporary conflict in organizations arises largely out of a new pluralism. The new pluralism, he
suggests, creates new social, community, and political responsibilities;
new rights and responsibilities for organizations; and new roles and
functions for government. Inevitably, the new pluralism also creates
conflict, and communicators in organizations thus find themselves
dealing more and more with conflict management. Conflict management creates new responsibilities for communicators and redefines
their interests. Conflict management also requires that communicators
adapt traditional communication methodologies to meet new challenges
and opportunities.

RESPONSIBILITIES AND INTERESTS

Contemporary conditions are casting communicators in new roles
and investing them with new responsibilities. The new pluralism,
changing definitions of social responsibility, and traditional competition for resources all contribute to these circumstances. Harold Burson
(1974), chairman of Burson-Marsteller, Inc., one of the nation's leading
public relations counseling firms, specified the obligations of organizations and their communicators in these terms:

1. A corporation cannot compensate for its inadequacies with good
   deeds. Its first responsibility is to manage its own affairs profitable.
2. Corporate social responsibility defies precise definition. We know
   a socially responsible company when we see one, but we can't
   completely describe it ahead of time.
3. We should not expect a corporation to adopt a leadership role in
   changing the direction of society. The corporation simply was
   simply not designed for that role.
4. Most of the pressures on corporations stem from two developments: the growing conflict between individuals and large
   institutions,and the compression of time.
5. The public relations function must separate issues from fads and
   work out a timetable for the corporation's response and adjustment.

6. In planning for social change, the role of the public relations executive is critical. He must judge which issues are real and which are merely fads, and he must help decide when the corporation should start to make reforms in policy.
7. The public relations executive has four major roles. He must be the corporate sensor, the corporate conscience, the corporate communicator, and the corporate monitor.
8. The corporation must communicate to, and convince, the public that it is indeed being responsive to the changing expectations of socety and that it is not merely stalling for time. (234)

Burson's seventh point is especially significant. He sets out four roles of equal importance. The traditional communicator role is one of the four, neither more nor less important than the others. As sensors of social change, communicators are responsible for monitoring organizational environments, identifying issues that portend good or ill for the organization, and helping management prepare to cope with the changes involved. As corporate monitors and consciences, communicators are responsible for examining organizational policies and activities—existing and proposed—identifying inequities, and bringing them to the attention of senior managers.

These tasks are not easily accomplished. Each requires that communicators correctly perceive environmental trends and prospective impacts on organizations and stakeholder groups. Having successfully gained this objective, communicators are called upon to complete another, more difficult assignment: ensuring that information they obtain is considered throughout the organization in establishing objectives, developing strategic plans, and conducting day to day operations.

Finally, communicators must act in their own interests and those of their organizations. Communicators' moral and ethical obligations are equally important to their organizations and their careers. Personal and organizational obligations are not in ethical or moral conflict. Reputations are durable and long-lasting. Truthfulness and honesty make winners of practitioners and organizations in the worst of circumstances.

These conditions, coupled with communicators' relatively strong backgrounds in the social sciences, often cast them in the role of conflict resolution specialist. The nature of relationships between organizations and stakeholder groups makes the role a natural one. Communicators constantly attempt to balance diverse stakeholder and organizational interests; to assist employers or clients in concurrently meeting economic and social obligations.

ORIGINS OF CONFLICTS

Tension and conflict between organizations and stakeholders grow out of differences in perceptions of emerging and long-standing issues. Only rarely are the relationships involved free of tension. Organizations and consumers arguably are wholly at peace only momentarily as sales representative and customer shake hands over sales agreements. Tension between unions and organizations ebbs and flows with contract renewal cycles. The same relationships prevail between organizations and regulatory agencies.

Communicators inevitably are caught up in efforts to relieve tension and prevent conflict. Accomplishing these objectives requires understanding the relationships involved. They are not the sort of "good guy–bad guy" or "your team–my team" relationships depicted in fairy tales, paperback novels and athletic competition. The prevalence of competitive mythology does a disservice to organizations and executives dependent on functional relationships.

The root problem is the competitive, "winner–loser" mentality that prevails in domestic society. Organizations are vulnerable to what might be called the competitive syndrome because they are populated by individuals who have been socialized by competitive behaviors in work and play from birth to maturity. Anticipation of conflict, no matter how fraternal, often is a sort of self-fulfilling prophecy. Fulfillment supports the "us against them" mentality that tends to produce progressively rougher play in athletics. Organizational roughness can lead quickly to adversarial mental sets that institutionalize conflict with stakeholders.

These conditions have been spawned by social, psychological, and economic pressures exerted on individuals and organizations through social changes. The United States of the 1980s was far different than that of the 1880s, and the trends that produced the change continue to mold individual and social priorities. The trends include changes from:

- Agrarian to industrial economies.
- Rural to urban societies.
- Close knit to diffused families.
- Children as economic assets to children as economic liabilities.
- In-home recreation to out-of-home recreation.
- Home-developed to church-developed religion.
- Patriarchal to democratic authority.
- Women working for survival to women working for security.
- Permanent marriages for security to temporary marriages for social purposes.

The list could continue but the basic point by now should be made. The world has changed and is changing. Organizations and individuals have no choice but to adapt to change.

Worker Conflict

Tension and conflict between workers and employers has been indigenous to domestic society since the dawn of the industrial age. The transition from agriculture to industry brought radical change in labor patterns. Many who had been self-employed in agriculture came reluctantly and resentfully into industry. In factories and plants, they encountered sweat shop and plantation mentalities that led to physical as well as mental conflict.

The riots and sit-ins that launched the union movement in the United States produced an adversarial tradition that persists today in most organizations. The impact of the adversarial tradition is compounded by economic competition inherent in contemporary organizations and individuals. Whether profit or not-for-profit, organizations are characterized by on-going competition within and across stakeholder groups.

Competition within stakeholder groups occurs among workers, supervisors, and managers. Members of each group are in competition with one another for intrinsic and extrinsic rewards. All seek higher wages, more benefits, and greater recognition. They also compete for perquisites and promotions.

Workers, supervisors, and managers are equally competitive with one another, economically and otherwise. Managers and supervisors compete for resources to enhance careers and because enlarged responsibilities usually are accompanied by greater rewards. They are equally competitive where power or authority are at stake. Fundamental organizational change in the United States often has been frustrated by managerial and supervisory unwillingness to yield authority.

Tension and conflict become endemic in the conditions described above, and these conditions are not likely to change in the foreseeable future. Much of the conflict can be eliminated and tensions can be reduced, however, where organizations (a) deal fairly and equitably with workers at all levels and (b) take care to see that organizational behaviors are perceived as fair and equitable.

Consumer Conflict

Similar tensions and conflicts persist between organizations and consumers of their products or services. Organizations' relationships with consumers, like those with their workers, have evolved over time from a set of practices that have ranged from competitive to exploitative. Caveat emptor—"let the buyer beware"—long was the primary standard for commercial transactions in the United States. Consumers were victimized by false weights, sharp traders, and circus promoters to a point at which every product and service was suspect. Vestiges of this pattern persist today to an extent sufficient to perpetuate skepticism if not suspicion among consumers. Buying an automobile, for example, is viewed by many as comparable to negotiating a mine field.

Economic competition would continue, however, even if these conditions did not prevail. Consumers are engaged in a constant search for the best deal in a combination of price, service, and other factors. Underlying motivational factors support a number of consumer organizations and several magazines that regularly publish evaluations of products and services.

Consumers' continuing efforts to obtain the best deal are countered by vendor efforts to achieve the highest possible profit levels. This trend is evident in marketing strategies designed to invest products and services with intangible values through brand names, endorsements, or otherwise. Tension and conflict, as a result, are indigenous to vendor-consumer relationships. As is the case in employee–employer relationships, tension and conflict can be limited only through fair and equitable behavior.

Vendor Conflict

Organizations' relationships with vendors historically have been more varied than those with consumers and employees. Organizations traditionally have attempted to play off one vendor against another in the same manner consumers use in seeking out the best deal. The two situations are quite comparable. While few recognize the similarities, managements attempt to exploit vendors in the same way that consumers seek economic advantage in dealing with organizations. The only differences between the two situations are a matter of formality. Consumers shop for the best deal on products or services. Organizations depend on competitive bidding to drive down prices. Negotiations may replace formal bidding processes where professional services are involved but the objective and the net result presumably are the same—lower costs.

Vendor relationships depart from the prevailing pattern in only two circumstances. The first has occurred historically where demand outstrips supply, as can be the case when new products are introduced outstrips supply, as can be the case when new products are introduced or during periods of rationing. The second is of more recent vintage, developing where customers ask vendors to provide more than products or services. Manufacturers in recent years have asked for "just in time" deliveries to permit reductions in inventory levels. Vendors also are often asked to handle billing procedures by computer to ease buyers' paper handling burdens. Vendors accommodating to these changes presumably are rewarded with more durable relationships but definitive evidence is lacking.

Other Conflicts

Conflicts with workers, consumers, and vendors occur in almost every organization. Few organizations, however, are fortunate enough to be able to limit their relationships to those three groups. Publicly owned organizations are involved with stockholders and financial analysts. Health care organizations must deal with physicians. Not-for-profit organizations often are deeply involved with members, donors, and other beneficiaries. A variety of regulatory agencies are a part of the life of almost every organization.

Tensions develop between managers and stockholders in publicly owned corporations over allocation of resources, especially profits, among stakeholder groups. Managers find themselves pulled in different directions by stakeholders while attempting to maintain some semblance of balance among groups. Physicians' relationships with hospitals are no less a problem. While providing doctors with facilities that enable them to generate substantial incomes, hospitals exercise almost no control over physician behavior toward employees, visitors, and others. Not-for-profit organizations usually are at the mercy of funding sources ranging from individuals and corporations to foundations or governmental agencies. Their managers nevertheless must balance the demands of these groups against those of employees and others.

Tension and conflict result wherever the interests of competing groups come together. They occur wherever group interests fall short of being identical. Identity of interest occurs rarely and briefly in human and organizational experience. Individuals, organizations, and nations are alike in that they usually form only transient alliances to deal with specific problems. ". . . And they all lived happily ever after" is as much a fairy tale in day-to-day life as in children's nursery rhymes. Communicators, as a result, must be prepared to anticipate tension and conflict.

CONFLICT ANALYSIS

Analytical skills necessary in anticipating conflict are not difficult to master, but more than skill may be necessary where communicators become engaged in conflict resolution. Personal stature and reputation are invaluable to those seeking to resolve conflict of the sort associated with most communication problems. Origins of potential conflict are readily seen in terms of stakeholders' interests. Those interests necessarily are in potential conflict with one another. Each group's needs and wants can be satisfied only at the expense of other groups. Equitably balancing those interests—ensuring that pain and pleasure are equally distributed among stakeholder groups—is one of the primary challenges of strategic planning.

When strategic decisions have been made, communicators must convey them to all stakeholders in a manner that all will understand. Understanding minimizes dissatisfaction, provided that intervening factors do not distort messages and create conflict. Successful message delivery therefore requires an understanding of the manner in which conflict can develop.

Elements of Conflict

Conflict between and among stakeholders usually is a product of tension generated by one of three elements: decision-making procedures, interpersonal or intergroup relationships, and the substance of specific decisions. More than anything else, however, potential for conflict is a function of pre-existing circumstances, conditions, attitudes, and opinions.

Tensions that signal the onset of conflict do not occur by chance. They are produced by the prior experiences of the parties and their resulting predispositions toward one another. Where past performance tells party A that party B is reliable; that the organization deals honestly, openly, and equitably with stakeholder groups; little tension is likely to develop early in connection with any issue. Party B may request additional information. Assurances may be necessary to eliminate latent concerns that party B's interests may be sacrificed to the benefit of party C. Where provided on a timely basis, however, such assurances tend to be accepted, eliminating tension that otherwise might escalate into conflict. Patterns of past performance thus determine initial reactions to most issues. Reactions are governed more by the experientially established reputations of those involved—individuals or organizations—than by the nature of specific issues.

While relationships are primary generators of tension and conflict, procedures used in sensitive situations also can become involved.

Human experience in tension and conflict-laden situations demonstrate that relationships and procedures are at least equal to substance as conflict generators. Procedurally generated problems most commonly arise over decision-making processes. Those left out of decision-making processes are most likely to protest and resist proposed solutions to any problem. The reverse is equally true. Those involved from the outset in problem solving seldom are disposed to challenge the results. They become committed to solutions through participation in problem solving processes.

These conditions militate toward including communicators in organizational strategic planning. Tension and conflict can be prevented or eliminated only where relationships and procedures are treated as delicately as substantive issues. Human feelings, as Carpenter and Kennedy (1988) have pointed out, are as important as technical factors. Decisions are made and battles fought by emotional and irrational human beings rather than coldly logical computers. Problem solving undertaken by technical means alone almost inevitably produces more conflict than the process is designed to eliminate.

Sorting Out

Beyond the involvement issue, tension and conflict—existing or potential—are amenable to analysis in human terms. Emotions, perceptions, and needs are the most common sources of difficulty. Emotions are usually triggered by prior experience with individuals or organizations, or by their reputations. These elements contribute to individuals' perceptions of issues and lead to preliminary conclusions, appropriate or otherwise. Needs may be substantively important but usually are secondary to emotions and perceptions in creating conflict.

Problems must be understood in human context in order to be resolved. Assumptions and stereotypes are deadly. Those who would resolve conflict and eliminate tension must first sort out the emotions, perceptions, needs, and potential cross-purposes of individuals or groups involved. The process is time consuming but productive. Sorting out should begin early, before potential problems become issues. The process can be productively applied, however, at any point in a continuum that can extend from strategic planning to crisis management.

Conflict resolution requires caution. Nowhere is haste apt to be more wasteful. Success is produced through a series of steps undertaken with caution and care:

1. Defining the problem in a manner acceptable to all parties.
2. Establishing mutually acceptable negotiation procedures.

3. Identifying each party's interests and positions.
4. Developing a complete range of alternative solutions.
5. Engendering agreement on a solution.
6. Implementing the solution.

RESOLVING CONFLICTS

The six steps listed above seem to suggest that conflicts are readily resolved. Only occasionally, where parties continue to communicate and where their positions have not become hardened, is this the case. Progress toward resolution requires functional relationships. The parties must be willing to work toward solutions by exchanging information. They must be willing to enter into agreements and fulfill their commitments.

Conflict often deteriorates to levels at which communication is difficult if not impossible. As emotional involvement intensifies, parties stop talking in much the same manner that occurs where individuals become entangled in emotional disputes. Communication then may be avoided as distasteful, or out of suspicion that the process may weaken previously adopted positions. Processes tend to become complicated where these conditions develop. Those involved often argue their positions and convey information through third parties—intermediaries or the news media. Media involvement can produce further deterioration as communication consists more and more of claim and counter-claim; charge and counter-charge.

Defining the Problem

Disputes between individuals and organizations are more complex than they appear. Arguments readily take on lives of their own, especially where individuals' personalities become involved. Parties to disputes too often permit conflicts to become matters of personal honor rather than organizational issues to be rationally resolved. Where this is the case, the origins of disputes literally can become lost in the "me against him (or her)" atmosphere that quickly develops.

The futility and wastefulness of protracted disputes ultimately becomes evident to the parties. Communicators or others attempting to manage the conflict at this point can prepare to intervene. Intervenors often are communicators because communicators frequently deal with tension and conflict. Communicators spend much of their careers seeking equitable, mutually acceptable resolution of issues so complex as to defy simple solutions.

The starting point in the resolution process requires agreement by the parties as to the nature of the issue. Agreement is not hard to achieve where the nature of an issue is known and mutually acknowledged. Additional disputes readily can arise, however, over efforts to isolate issues. The origins of long-standing disagreements often are not clearly remembered, even by the principals. Attempts to identify causes of conflict in these circumstances can compound original disagreements.

Problem definition processes, for these and one other reason, usually begin with extensive discussions with all parties. The remaining reason is most important: success is achieved most rapidly and satisfactorily where parties to a conflict design the process by which it will be resolved as well as the ultimate solution. To encourage this process, those seeking to assist in resolving conflict should provide the minimum guidance necessary rather prescribed solutions. Even the appearance of pressure, as readily can occur where intervenors attempt to sell solutions, can produce suspicion and delay.

Establishing Procedures

Formal, step-by-step procedures seldom are used in conflict resolution other than where the parties are subject to contractually enforceable mediation or conciliation processes. Where used, these processes often come into play relatively early in the conflict, before the parties have experienced sufficient inconvenience or losses to convince them that resolution is in the interests of all involved.

These conditions commend an informal initial approach to resolution followed by as formal a set of procedures as the parties consider appropriate. Involvement of third parties who might be tempted to follow their own agendas should be avoided in most cases. Participation by attorneys should be avoided at all costs. Other than where employed on full-time bases by the parties, attorneys' economic interests are better served by conflict than resolution.

Communicators usually should plan on two preliminary conferences with each party. Preliminary conferences should be oriented solely toward defining the problem. Complete information concerning the conflict should be solicited from each of the parties during the first set of conferences. Results then should be analyzed to identify any substantive conflicts over the facts of the matter. Subsequent conferences should be oriented toward clarifying factual discrepancies. Preliminary conferences should produce two outcomes. The interests of the parties should be precisely defined and differences in their perceptions of the problem should be identified.

Identifying Issues

The interests of the parties, unfortunately, are only part of the fabric of the typical conflict. As conflicts develop, the parties take positions that can be influenced by any number of extraneous factors. Positions can be taken out of pride or anger, or for almost any other reason. Parties to an issue at times adopt extreme positions in full knowledge that they will not get all they want. Their opening positions are taken for bargaining purposes. Where publicly assumed, however, opening positions can determine the direction of bargaining regardless of the nature of underlying issues.

The parties' positions, under these conditions, can assume the same stature as the original problem. Positions can become realities separate from original issues. Because they often are composed of a mixture of vanities, resentments, anxieties, desires, public pronouncement, and face-saving strategies, positions are poor beginning points from which to resolve conflict. Positions tend to limit potential solutions.

The parties' interests tend to be more reasonable than their positions. Interests almost always are different but seldom are mutually exclusive and, as a result, need not necessarily be in conflict. Potential for resolution grows as parties to a conflict recognize that their interests may be amenable to joint satisfaction.

Carpenter and Kennedy (1988) suggest a three-step process that has been known to produce early resolution of conflict. First, ask each party to list what it considers the elements of a good resolution to the conflict. Second, ask each party to list those elements they think the other parties need in a satisfactory resolution. Then, post all the lists for all to see.

Defining Options

Exposure to each other's lists tend to broaden parties' perspectives as to what constitutes potentially satisfactory resolution of their conflict. At minimum, the lists prompt a near limitless number of "what if" questions, stimulating the thinking of all involved and necessarily bringing them closer to understanding each other's positions. As a result, the parties necessarily move closer to agreement on a solution.

Maintaining flexibility should be the primary objective of the resolution process in its early stages. Each and every feasible solution should be enumerated and considered if only to demonstrate that no preconceived notions or hidden agendas are in play. Flexibility requires that alternative plans be carefully thought out. Additional alternatives often evolve as issues are discussed and relationships between and among the parties begin to change. Conflict resolution processes are designed to encourage changes in relationships.

Reaching Agreement

Flexibility of the sort described above is critical to the conflict resolution process but problems nevertheless can occur. Any number of alternative plans prompted by resolution efforts may appear feasible as the process progresses, and none should be discarded out of hand. The resolution process is equally capable, however, of generating unforeseen difficulties. Negotiation is a dynamic process in which the unexpected can and will occur.

Change may develop in the positions of the parties, in their behaviors, and in their willingness to move forward. Change in each of these areas can occur in pendulum-like fashion, and those attempting to resolve conflict must be prepared to move forward under any and all conditions.

Implementing the Agreement

Agreements that resolve conflict can best be achieved and implemented, according to Carpenter and Kennedy (1988), by managing the conflict resolution process through the following steps.

I. Plan preparation
   A. Conflict analysis
   B. Strategy design
   C. Program development
II. Program implementation
   A. Adopt procedures
   B. Educate parties
   C. Develop options
   D. Reach agreements
III. Carry out agreements
   A. Establish monitoring systems
   B. Work out details
   C. Renegotiate where necessary
   D. Handle violations (67)

While the process is important to conflict resolution, each of three elements involved in conflict are critical: the parties and their spokespersons, the substance or characteristics of the dispute, and the procedure or procedures most amenable to use in conflict resolution. Each element must be carefully weighed by those seeking resolution.

The parties to a conflict usually are more numerous than they appear. Parties, in the sense that the term is used above, refers to stakeholder groups rather than individuals although individuals ultimately become involved in most disputes as spokespersons for organizations. Most disputes also involve two sets of parties: primary parties directly involved and secondary parties whose interests may be impinged upon by the terms of settlements undertaken by primary parties. The nature and predispositions of groups and individuals involved are important because they influence the extent and nature of the options that may be open to those seeking to resolve the conflict.

The dispute itself arguably is more important from a conflict resolution standpoint than the parties. Does the dispute arise out of real conflict or from misunderstanding? If the conflict is real, is it superficial or fundamental to the interests or beliefs of the parties? Do public positions that have been taken radically limit potential for resolution, and have those positions become issues in and of themselves? All factors considered, what functional alternatives for resolution really exist?

Resolution procedures are more a function of the nature of the parties and their predispositions than any other factors. The nature of the resolution process must be acceptable to both sides. What is acceptable may change from hour to hour and day to day, depending on practical constraints, legal entanglements, emotional commitments, and other factors. All of these must be considered by those who would understand and/or resolve conflict.

IN SUMMARY

The bulk of the problems with which communicators deal arise out of conflict. Conflict can result from internal or external events and trends, and especially from changing public perceptions and expectations of organizations. Social responsibility, as the thrust of the latter changes have come to be known, has created new ground rules for organizations.

The changes involved are a product of social evolution in society from agrarian to industrial, rural to urban, patriarchal to democratic, and otherwise. These and associated changes have created mounting tensions between organizations and their primary stakeholders—workers, owners, and consumers. Each of them is seeking an ever-larger share of the wealth that organizations create.

Ability to analyze these tensions and to eliminate conflict are at the heart of contemporary communication practice. Six steps are involved:

1. Defining the problem in a manner acceptable to all parties.
2. Establishing mutually acceptable negotiation procedures.
3. Identifying each party's interests and positions.
4. Developing a complete range of alternative solutions.
5. Engendering agreement on a solution.
6. Implementing the solution.

The process is more complex than it appears. Progress toward conflict resolution requires functional relationships between the parties or, at minimum, a willingness to proceed toward resolution of their differences. At their low points, conflicts often deteriorate to a level at which communication is difficult.

Defining the problem is necessary regardless of the extent to which relationships have deteriorated. The parties must agree on the nature of the issue before any progress can be achieved toward a solution.

With agreement as to the problem, the resolution process then can proceed to establishing step-by-step procedures to be used in eliminating the conflict. Informal discussions usually are an appropriate beginning point. These talks enable third parties to propose functional approaches acceptable to both sides.

The first formal step toward conflict resolution involves identifying issues. This element is more complex than it appears because parties to a dispute often take extreme positions for tactical or other reasons. Even in these circumstances, however, identifying issues is a prerequisite to defining alternative solutions. One or more of the solutions then becomes the basis for an agreement—formal or informal—to resolve the conflict.

ADDITIONAL READING

Ajzen, Icek, and Martin Fishbein, *Understanding Attitudes and Predicting Social Behavior.* Englewood Cliffs, NJ: Prentice-Hall, 1986.
Andriole, Stephen J., ed. *Corporate Crisis Management*, Princeton, NJ: Petrocelli, 1985.
Blau, Peter M. *Exchange and Power in Social Life*, New Brunswick, NJ: Transaction Publishers, 2nd ed., 1989.
Burson, Harold. "The Public Relations Function in the Socially Responsible Corporation." In Anshen, Melvin, ed. *Managing the Socially Responsible Corporation.* New York: Macmillan, 1974.

Carpenter, Susan L., and W. J. D. Kennedy. *Managing Public Disputes*. San Francisco: Jossey-Bass, 1988.

Drucker, Peter F. *The New Realities: In Government and Politics / In Economics and Business / In Society and World View*. New York: Harper & Row, 1989.

Greenwood, William T. *Issues in Business and Society*, 3rd. ed. Boston: Houghton Mifflin, 1977.

Hovland, Carl I., I. L. Janis and H. H. Kelley. *Communication and Persuasion*. New Haven, CT: Yale University Press, 1953.

Lerbinger, Otto. *Managing Corporate Crises: Strategies for Executives*. Boston: Barrington Press, 1986.

Lesly, Philip. *Overcoming Opposition: A Survival Manual for Executives*. Englewood Cliffs, NJ: Prentice-Hall, 1984.

4

The Message Trap

Problem solving in communication involves several risks. Perhaps the most pervasive and dangerous among them is generated by a strong predisposition among communicators to think first of mediated messages and only afterward of the many other variables involved. The result is what might be called a "ready, fire, aim syndrome" that often compounds communication problems.

Problems develop more or less naturally among individuals steeped in traditional approaches to journalism or communication. They occur as messages are designed and transmitted without regard for communication or social environments. Communication environments encompass more than is taught in schools of journalism and communication. The world of messages does not end with mediated and interpersonal forms of communication. In addition, communication is part of a larger domain of social exchange. Information is one of several coinages used in transactions among individuals, and between individuals and organizations.

Neither of these concepts is apt to gain significant attention in journalism or communication studies, but each creates limitations on communicators' ability to meet organizational needs. Perhaps the greatest barrier is created by courses of study leading inadvertently to a prevalent belief that problems can be solved by transmitting messages. No concept is farther from reality. Messages do not solve problems. Communicators do not solve problems. Individuals and organizations *can* solve problems, but the solutions necessarily are complex. Moreover, they require functional knowledge of two constructs often neglected in journalism and communication.

The first of those constructs deals with the domain of communication and defines the process as involving relationships among audiences, media, and larger social systems. The second construct, called social exchange, comes from the realm of sociology and deals with the full range of transactions between and among individuals and organizations—emotional, physical, material, and monetary, as well as informational.

THE DOMAIN OF COMMUNICATION

The communicator's world is—or should be—more complex than it appears. Communicators' tasks fall into two basic categories: preventive and remedial. Where on-going, preventive communication efforts produce salutary relationships between organizations and stakeholders, remedial needs are few. Most communication needs arise out of perceptual problems and are readily resolved. The remainder, growing out of conflicts in the interests of the parties, are more demanding.

In each case, the relatively narrow perspectives of academics and practitioners instead tend create barriers to successful resolution of communication problems. Traditional communication studies focus almost exclusively on mediated and interpersonal communication. Most deal primarily with an input-output or information-processing model in which input involves disseminating information and output consists of anticipated responses. Information-processing is the predominant theoretical construct in the primary communication disciplines: advertising, marketing, sales promotion, and public relations. None of these disciplines, unfortunately, has reached substantially beyond the information processing model to embrace and apply a more comprehensive and more cohesive approach to communication.

Developing a more cohesive model and more productive communication systems requires a broader conceptualization of communication. More importantly from a disciplinary standpoint, managing the resulting system requires change in contemporary communication structures and techniques. The need for change becomes apparent, however, only where practitioners look beyond those traditional communication models that imply passivity in audiences. Audiences are not passive. Their members engage in multiple series of transactions among themselves and with near limitless sets of organizations. The relationships involved necessarily are unstable. Each is influenced by prior transactions and anticipated future transactions. Few traditional communication models anticipate this level of complexity.

The passive audience problem has been attacked by developers of two alternative approaches, one labeled the "uses and gratifications theory" and the other a "dependency model" of mass communication. Uses and gratifications focuses on consumers rather than messages and assumes that mass communication audiences are active, goal-oriented, and selective in media use. The media are taken as competing with other sources of need gratification. The mass media effects model model, developed by Melvin L. DeFleur and Sandra J. Ball-Rokeach (1982), takes a broader approach. The authors propose integral relationships among audiences, media, and larger social systems. Their primary variables include:

- Social systems, varying in degree of structural stability.
- Media systems, varying in number and centrality of information functions.
- Audiences, varying in degree of dependency on media information.
- Effects, cognitive, affective, and behavioral.

Adequacy of Models

Save for the dependency model, which rarely is accorded a great deal of attention in academic or professional circles, the concepts described above fail to adequately explain the communication process. Explanations of information processing fall short in defining the terminology involved, especially the word "source." Because most discussions of information processing involve academics and students in interpersonal or mass communication, source is taken to be an individual, organization, or mass medium. Individuals, organizations, and mass media may indeed serve as sources, but messages are more readily and frequently transmitted in other ways, and those ways often are neglected in professional practice and academe.

The broader approach embodied in the Ball-Rokeach and DeFleur (1982) mass media effects model, for these reasons, can add substantially to one's understanding of the word communication. The model links societal systems and media systems to one another and, more important, to audiences (p. 280). "It is through taking these sets of variables into account individually, interactively, and systemically that a more adequate understanding of mass communication effects can be gained," they declared. The mass media effects model in Figure 4.1 suggests that individuals respond to messages originating in society and in events as well as in the media.

A Broader View

The mass media effects model reflects all the complexities of communication. Two features of the model are most significant. First,

Figure 4.1
Mass Media Effects on Individuals: An Integrated Model

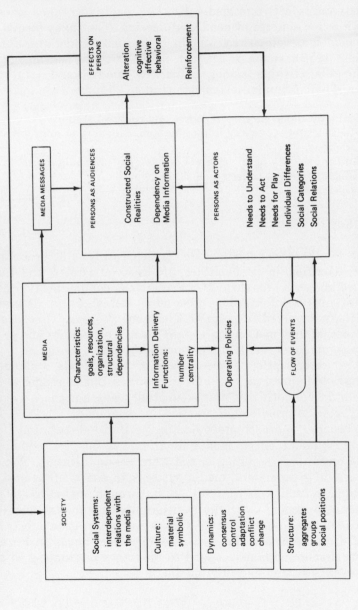

Source: From *Theories of Mass Communication*, Fourth Edition, by Melvin L. DeFleur and Sandra J. Ball-Rokeach. Copyright © 1989 By Longman Publishing Group. Reprinted by permission of Longman Publishing Group.

the model defines the extent to which messages flow from nonmediated sources, especially from contemporary events and from society. Second, the model underscores the fact that humans interact with, rather than merely react to, message sources.

Mediated communication is but one of five primary sources of information. More important, mediated communication usually is least credible among them. Humans respond more strongly to interpersonal than to mediated communication. They react most strongly to realities; to the quality of products and services; to the "user friendliness" of those organizations that offer those services in the market place. They react to what might be called "tangible communication." Tangible communicationencompasses all messages delivered by the attributes of products, services and those who provide them.

Examined from a communication perspective, decisions to acquire or adopt products, services, or points of view are influenced by several types of messages. Some messages are conveyed by the environments organizations create for the manufacture, distribution, and delivery of goods and services. Other messages originate with individuals who populate those environments. Still others are conveyed by products, services, or concepts that organizations offer for sale or adoption. The remaining messages consist of mediated information; information that may be disseminated broadly through mass media or narrowly through selective media.

Purchase or adoption decisions, then, are influenced by:

- *Environmental* communication, consisting of messages conveyed by the characteristics of environments created by organizations for the delivery of products, services, or concepts.
- *Behavioral* communication, consisting of the behaviors of organizations in shaping products, services, or concepts, and in the behaviors of their personnel in developing and delivering those products, services, or concepts.
- *Qualitative* communication, encompassing all of the attributes of the organization's products, services, or concepts.
- *Interpersonal* communication between prospective "buyers" and *all* others, including peers and other users as well as vendors and their representatives.
- *Mediated* communication, consisting of messages delivered through one or more of the print, electronic, and hybrid media available to professional communicators.

The five forms of communication vary in efficiency and effectiveness. Environmental, behavioral, and qualitative communication are more credible than the interpersonal or mediated varieties. Quality of merchandise or services, behaviors of organizational personnel, and the characteristics of environments in which consumers encounter them, are determinants of consumer behavior. These factors govern, in fact, whether or not consumption ensues.

Interpersonal or mediated communication over time can be made to approach the effectiveness of the environmental or behavior, but only where messages are consistent across types of communication. When Toyota and Nissan introduced luxury cars in the United States in 1990, for example, hundreds were purchased before floor models ever arrived. Consistent environmental, behavioral, and qualitative communication made the companies' mediated and interpersonal messages credible among recipients, who responded accordingly.

While earned only over time and through consistent effort, credibility is easily lost and, once lost, is doubly difficult to regain. As Toyota and Nissan earned consumer support, General Motors, Ford, and Chrysler were losing ground. Their mediated claims were overpowered by histories of contrary qualitative and behavioral realities. By the late 1980s, independent research showed the "Big Three" had regained much of the ground that had been lost in product quality. They remained burdened by a credibility problem of monumental proportions that did not appear amenable to short term resolution.

NARROWNESS IN DEFINITIONS

Credibility problems of the sort encountered by domestic auto manufacturers need not be discouraging to communicators. Pragmatically, in fact, the reverse should be true. Understanding the phenomena involved leads to a conclusion favorable to, but mildly troublesome for, communicators. The favorable aspect: consumers and other message recipients can be conditioned to respond to signals. The troublesome factor: more than mediated and interpersonal communication are necessary in the conditioning process.

Quality

The role of quality in shaping perceptions of organizations is less than adequately understood among communicators. Too many have become convinced by contemporary mythology that excellence is essential to success. Marketplace conditions demonstrate otherwise. Economic success is not determined by quality of products or services. Products can be economic successes regardless of quality, provided they are equitably priced and accurately portrayed.

Consider, for example, the common paint brush. Paint brushes are available in many quality categories and in a broad range of prices.

Where price and quality are consistent, no one can be considered best. Some are better suited for one type of paint than others. Differences in customers are even more important. Professional painters buy brushes of superior quality and are as concerned with durability as with price. Many do-it-yourselfers, in contrast, use brushes rarely and find cleaning them distasteful. The professional's best brush thus is relatively expensive but durable while the do-it-yourselfer's best often is inexpensive and expendable.

Expensive and inexpensive paint brushes can be equally desirable and equally successful, provided they are accurately identified and appropriately priced. Consumers receive conflicting messages only where inexpensive brushes are sold at high prices supported by inaccurate claims of durability. Where messages conflict, retailer and manufacturer credibility suffer. Consumers then are conditioned to look elsewhere when they next need paint brushes.

Inadvertent message conflict is more prevalent than intentional deception but can be more destructive of consumer confidence. Many auto makers, for example, have suffered large economic losses where quality claims have been defeated by product quality or behavior. General Motors' Chevrolet Corvair, Ford Motor Company's Pinto, and Volkswagen of America's Audi are among the more memorable examples. The Corvair's problems were documented in Ralph Nader's *Unsafe at Any Speed* (1965). The Pinto's tendency to burst into flame when hit from the rear triggered a number of law suits. Audi was plagued by uncontrollable acceleration. The Corvair and Pinto were withdrawn from the marketplace, but Audi continued to limp along, its sales depressed by fallout from earlier problems. Sound communication strategy required that the manufacturers withdraw their products at great expense, or acknowledge their problems and lead in searching for solutions.

Behavior

The auto manufacturers' problems arguably were as much behavioral as qualitative. Pragmatically, both factors were involved. Audi especially had claimed to market a highly reliable automobile, and had priced the product accordingly. Ford's difficulties with the Pinto predated the company's "Quality is Job One" slogan but nevertheless conflicted with corporate quality claims. General Motors' efforts to discredit Nader rather than acknowledge the Corvair's problems added considerable impetus to the consumer movement in the United States. When realities came into conflict with quality claims, the companies elected to deny the realities. Denial is a behavior, but prospective organizational behavior problems are broader in scope.

The role of organizational behavior in communication is reminiscent of an old childhood chant: "Sticks and stones will break my bones, but words will never hurt me." Behaviors are the sticks and stones of organizations. Messages transmitted through the actions of organizations and their personnel overpower all others. Where consistent with messages originating in other sectors, behavioral messages are the ultimate proof of organizational sincerity and commitment. Where inconsistent, behavioral messages are devastating. They demonstrate the insincerity—perhaps the duplicity—with which the organization fashioned mediated messages—those delivered through print or electronic media.

Supported by near perfect performance, "absolutely, positively overnight" put Federal Express in a position to command premium prices among overnight delivery services. The U.S. Postal Service's less costly Express Mail system, in contrast, was hampered in gaining market share despite lower prices by the organization's reputation for inconsistent service. IBM, in similar manner, maintains exceptional employee relationships by living up to a "no layoff" policy in the face of fluctuating market conditions. General Electric's Answer Center is equally strong in maintaining consumer relationships.

For other companies, ill considered performance has produced organizational disaster. Exxon's lethargic response to the Gulf of Alaska oil spill in 1989 is exemplary of the destructive potential of behavioral messages. The company was perceived as unresponsive, uncaring, and irresponsible and the impression was reinforced during subsequent incidents of a similar nature. A. H. Robins' handling of the Dalkon Shield intra-uterine contraceptive device and Nestle's response to criticism of the company's infant formula distribution system, also were exemplary of behaviors and mediated messages in conflict. In each case, the organization was the loser.

Big losses such as those of Exxon, Robins, and Nestle overshadow the thousands—perhaps millions—of small but collectively important losses suffered daily by all organizations as the result of individual behaviors. Insensitive or uncaring conduct by receptionists, sales personnel, bank tellers, and others drive away legions of patients, clients, and customers at immeasurable cost. Few of those involved bother to complain. The remainder "vote with their feet" and, more importantly, never hesitate to tell friends and neighbors of their experiences.

The result is a destructive chain reaction of considerable length. A few organizational personnel transmitting negative behavioral messages each day arm those legions of once-loyal patients, clients, and customers with "horror stories" that become topics of cocktail party and over-the-fence conversations. No amount of mediated communication can withstand the impact of such on-going assaults on organizational reputations.

Environment

The boundaries of behavioral communication, unfortunately, can be no more precisely defined than those of product or service quality. The term environmental communication refers to messages transmitted by environments organizations create for consumers and employees. Environments can be indoor or outdoor. The term encompasses factors such as temperature and lighting as well as cleanliness, comfort, safety, and security.

Organizational behaviors shape environments and individual behaviors compound the positive or negative impacts of environments, clouding the boundary between environmental and behavioral communication. Environmental communication, as a result, can be viewed as encompassing two groups of components. The first group consists of the attributes of surroundings in which organizations place consumers or employees. The second consists of psychological influences exerted by the behaviors of the organization or its personnel within the environment.

Consider, for example, the factors that influence the attractiveness of building interiors. Heating and air conditioning, lighting, and cleanliness always influence occupants' attitudes. So do a broad range of comfort and safety factors that vary in importance with building type. Floor, wall, and window coverings and the comfort and attractiveness of furnishings influence the opinions of office workers and visitors. Noise, airborne emissions, and similar variables play the same roles in buildings devoted to manufacturing or distribution. Other factors may be equally important in laboratories and other special-purpose facilities.

Comfort and attractiveness seldom are the only sources of environmental messages, however, because environments are populated by organizational personnel who communicate through their behaviors. The potential influence of personnel on the results of environmental communication is considerable. Salutary behaviors induce positive responses from consumers or other visitors amidst marginal surroundings. Negative behaviors destroy the communicative effectiveness of attractive surroundings.

Successful organizations ensure consistency in the content of messages they transmit to stakeholders. Organizations that seek to be perceived as caring demonstrate concern through environments and employee behaviors, quality of products or services, and mediated messages. Such organizations are especially careful to make no promises they can not fulfill and to fulfill every promise made— virtually regardless of cost. Delta Air Lines, generally recognized as one of the nation's best by passengers and personnel alike, quietly changed advertising slogans, for example, to conform to uncontrollable air traffic conditions in the late 1980s. The old slogan, "Delta is ready when you are," implied an on-time departure promise that Delta could not keep. The new slogan: "We love to fly, and it shows." Only through this sort of commitment to message consistency can organizations rationally expect communication efforts to produce desired results. Absent total commitment, harmony in messages deteriorates, with predictable results.

Successful Communication

Delta and a relativey few other organizations are coming to realize that successful communication produces disproportionately large rewards. Successful communication occurs where organizations' messages are consistent across all channels of communication. The organization's mediated messages say, "We've got a good product." Product quality supports that message. The organization's personnel are as helpful and attentive as claimed in its advertising. The stores are clean and comfortable, substantiating management's commitment to the firm's customers. And consumers reciprocate with that increasingly rare attribute known as loyalty.

Some in advertising and marketing have attempted, with limited success, to define, analyze, and quantify what has been called brand loyalty. The term is misleading, and much of the effort has been less than optimally productive, because the several factors at work are both more and less than loyalty.

Loyalty implies a faithfulness that extends beyond product or service quality. Consumer faithfulness to brands, products, services, or organizations is not a product of loyalty. Continuing consumer commitment is produced by perceived superiority in brands, products, services, or organizations. Rather than being generated out of blind loyalty, then, commitments are based on value or, more precisely, added value.

Value, in turn, is created by the attributes of (a) products, services, or concepts, and (b) the organizations or individuals proffering those products, services or concepts. It follows, then, that *durable* perceptions of value are created only by behavioral, environmental, or qualitative communication. Mediated and interpersonal messages usually can do no more than call attention to products, reinforce perceptions, or lead to confirmation by inducing message recipients to expose themselves to other forms of communication—behavioral, environmental, or qualitative.

Organizations can logically and productively respond to these conditions in only one way: with consistent messages emanating from all sources. Where messages are inconsistent, change is essential. Content must be changed to make messages consistent with reality or reality must be altered to conform to messages that organizations want to send. In other words, messages must be adjusted to reflect realities or realities must be changed to validate messages. Nothing less, over time, will suffice. Qualitative, behavioral, and environmental communication ultimately prevail regardless of mediated and interpersonal support.

As with individuals, what organizations do is more convincing than what they say. The quality of their products and services ultimately overcomes the most persuasive advertising campaigns. Credibility is shaped by the extent to which organizations deal honestly and openly with stakeholders. And the extent of their concern for those stakeholders is demonstrated most convincingly—or persuasively—by the environments that organizations create.

Product quality, like truth, ultimately becomes known, with or without formal communication efforts. Honesty and dishonesty usually become apparent, and the nature of environments is apparent to all. Each factor contributes, in positive or negative fashion, to organizational communication efforts.

Communicators must deal with these realities although they seldom wield sufficient power or influence to change them. Inferior products ultimately produce declines in sales. Misleading statements destroy credibility, and neither consumers nor employees will long tolerate inhospitable environments. These conditions obligate communicators to speak out; to counsel senior management concerning potential missteps that can lead to organizational disaster.

Behavior and Communication

Design and development of communication efforts—programs, campaigns, special events, and crisis responses—are limited by the organizations involved. The bulk of communication is generated by the environments, behaviors, and interpersonal exchanges organizations create or endorse. Much of the communication may be unintended but absence of intent does not detract from effectiveness. Comfort, cleanliness, courtesy, helpfulness, and other attributes of organizational facilities and personnel speak loudly to stakeholders.

Messages delivered through mediated communication are at the mercy of those originating elsewhere. Ideally, mediated messages support and reinforce those delivered by environments, behaviors, and individuals. Where messages conflict, the mediated seldom are believed. Inconsistencies attract attention and raise questions about organizational integrity.

Communicators preparing to develop organizational programs, campaigns, special events, or crisis response strategies therefore thus must first determine the extent to which:

1. The organization is what it says it is.
2. Organizational realities reflect fair and equitable treatment of all stakeholder groups.
3. Senior management is prepared to rectify inequities and create the sort of realities necessary to support strong communication efforts.

The nub of the problem is simple. Communicators must be armed with valid appeals in order to apply reason and understanding in persuasion. They must be equipped to respond *both* honestly and convincingly to the unspoken question that properly arises wherever and whenever persuasion is applied: "What's in it for me?"

Consumers must be given adequate reasons to buy and, having bought, sufficient reasons to return and buy again. The reasons may be expressed in quality and durability, or in value for value received. They may include comfortable environments, courteous personnel, and efficient service after the sale. But they must be real rather than figments of copywriters' imagination.

The same principles apply where workers are involved. The average worker in the United States has been estimated to produce at about 60 percent of capacity. Organizations that want more must be prepared to offer more, in bonuses, fringe benefits, time off, or otherwise. Having made such offers, organizations must deliver where workers respond.

Vendors may be asked to meet "just in time" delivery schedules, rigorous quality control standards, and burdensome paperwork requirements. Prompt payment and similar courtesies probably will be necessary, however, to induce consistently acceptable performance.

The list could go on at length but the basic point by now should be well-made: Appeals to reason and understanding must be supported by organizational performance. Failure to perform destroys credibility and any hope of inducing desired behavioral response.

EXCHANGE AND RELATIONSHIPS

The roles of behavioral, environmental, and qualitative communication are more readily understood where they are examined in keeping with the model of mass media effects developed by DeFleur and Ball-Rokeach (1982). Taken in conjunction with social exchange theories advanced by Peter M. Blau (1964) and George C. Homans (1961), the mass media effects model provides an appropriate analytical tool for communicators. The works of Blau and Homans, moreover, leads logically to a new dimension in communication focusing on relationships rather than relations.

The significance of the mass media effects model rests on the linkages it establishes among primary components. Society, media, messages, individuals, and contemporary events all influence behavior. Models designed by Blau and Homans further indicate that exchanges between individuals and organizations are essentially transactional in nature. This construct in turn suggests that communicators should be as concerned over relationships as the exchanges that shape them.

The word relations has appeared most frequently in mass communication in tandem with employee, consumer, shareholder, and vendor. In each case, the term is commonly used to describe a set of communication activities, most of them media oriented and based on the demonstrably tenuous information processing model. Social exchange theory, as developed by Blau and Homans, suggests a more complex reality requiring more sophisticated management strategies.

Relationships and Communication

Communication programs are rooted in organizations' planning processes, especially in strategic planning. A strategic plan is a blueprint designed to assist an organization in proceeding from where it is to where it wants to be. Organizations' strategic plans usually are established in five-year time frames and deal in long-term goals and objectives. Goals and objectives usually are expressed quantitatively in terms of market share, revenue, or profit. Achieving goals and objectives invariably requires inducing specific groups of people to behave in predetermined ways.

Groups whose behaviors are important to organizations include consumers, employees, owners, vendors, and media, although others may be involved as well. Inducing shareholders (owners) in publicly owned corporations to behave as organizational managers desire, for example, often requires that the organization engage the attention of securities analysts, brokers, and others whose actions influence investor behavior. Influencing not-for-profit organizations may require conveying information to their boards or benefactors. Where governments are involved, the owners are taxpayers and organizations may have to become involved in the political process.

These conditions result in communication programs consisting of multiple, stakeholder-specific subprograms. The communication programs of for-profit corporations, for example, almost always include consumer relations, employee relations, investor relations, and vendor relations programs. Not-for-profit organizations may substitute donor relations and beneficiary relations for the investor and consumer components of the for-profit program. Each program is designed to induce a mutually beneficial behavior among members of the stakeholder group involved.

Relationship Roles

Consumer-, employee-, investor-, and vendor-oriented program components are ill-named in terms of contemporary society. Today's consumer relations program, for example, would be more accurately called a consumer relationship program. Relationships, rather than relations, are the key to organizational success in contemporary society. The two words are quite different. Relations long has been appropriately applied as a synonym for communication. Organizations' traditional, mediated communication programs could be appropriately identified as consumer communication, employee communication, and so forth. Traditional, mediated communication alone is inadequate, however, to develop and maintain functional relationships with stakeholders.

Relationships involve commitment as well as communication. Communication is a transient phenomenon that arguably occurs more often in unilateral than bilateral form. Relationships, in contrast, are implied in the integrated mass media effects model defined by DeFleur and Ball-Rokeach (1982), and implicit in the work of Blau and Homans. Where communication may persuade, social exchange builds relationships and commitments. Commitment on the part of stakeholder groups, although rarely recognized as such, is the essence of organizational success. Committed workers tolerate the boss's "bad day." Committed customers forgive the occasional product defect. Commitment creates the same tolerance toward organizations that it creates among humans.

Commitment is what keeps customers coming back even if prices are not always the lowest or if service occasionally is less than the best. Commitment ensures the loyalty of subordinates even when the boss makes an occasional mistake in evaluating performance, or granting raises. Commitment induces shareholders to hold their stock even if the last quarter's results were poorer than expected. And commitment produces continuing support from vendors even when the company's purchase fail to grow as anticipated. Commitment binds organizations and stakeholders in the same manner as families and their members.

Committed organizations work hard to ensure that stakeholders share in their successes—economic and otherwise. In the economic sector, rewards are allocated to workers in wages and bonuses; to owners as profits or dividends; to vendors in increased purchases; and to consumers in new and improved products. Recognition and other forms of reward also are equitably allocated, with predictable results.

"The" organization becomes "my" organization. All involved establish a form of psychological ownership that works to mutual benefit. Workers "go the extra mile" to produce products and services that command premium prices that are willingly paid for the level of quality the organization delivers. Premium prices generate greater revenue to fund greater rewards and enhanced product development efforts, both leading to still greater sales. Commitment, in other words, feeds on itself, and validates the thesis advanced by management theorists who contend that there are no stable organizations. Organizations, they declare, are dynamic entities constantly changing—for better or worse.

Nonrelationships

Relationship building in organizations also is preferable to conventional management practices for another reason. Problems once solved by committed individuals, or by committed groups and organizations, tend to remain solved. In the absence of relationships, or in adversarial circumstances, the reverse tends to be true. Old problems reoccur. Ancient animosities are nurtured.

At best, uncommitted consumers shop constantly for lower prices and/or higher values. In the absence of loyalty to vendors or manufacturers, products and services tend to become commodities sold in a sort of continuing auction. Competition among vendors drives prices downward to a point at which profits are marginal. Organizations suffer economically and, ultimately, so do all of their stakeholders. At worst, uncommitted consumers are affronted by the behaviors of cut rate organizations' uncaring personnel, or by the absence of amenities, and never return.

Circumstances can be even worse where workers, vendors, or shareholders are involved. Uncommitted workers tend to be lackadaisical in attendance and performance. Employers' costs and product quality suffer accordingly. Uncommitted vendors may or may not deliver the quality that organizations require and, where quality is maintained, may not deliver on timely bases. Uncommitted shareholders tend to sell at the first sign of decline in profits, and stock prices suffer accordingly.

The benefits of relationships, and the risks that attach to uncommitted stakeholders, occur regardless of the nature of organizations. Public office holders are unlikely to be elected to second terms where voter support erodes. Charitable organizations flounder where contributors find themselves unappreciated. Unions self-destruct where leaders are unresponsive. Manager and executives in each case are apt to find themselves caught up in unending problem-solving cycles. Their circumstances resemble those of a juggler attempting to keep a half dozen plates spinning on as many slender poles. Just as the last plate starts spinning, the first needs attention. Then, the second slows to a point where it is about to fall. As the juggler respins the second plate, the third begins to wobble. Problems, in like manner, can occur again and again. Solutions tend to be transient in the absence of relationships.

Strong relationships will not eliminate all problems. They will, however, render organizations relatively immune to problems of the sort produced by lack of confidence, trust, and loyalty, or by suspicion, distrust, and disloyalty. These circumstances demand that organizations and their communicators take a longer-term view of stakeholder groups. Organizations' dealings with stakeholders almost universally are becoming a "pay me now or pay me later" proposition. Organizations can deal honorably and equitably with stakeholders today or pay the price of distrust and disloyalty at some future date or dates.

Relationships At Work

Strength of relationships, or the absence of relationships, contributes to organizational communication needs. Strong relationships, established and nurtured through programs that embrace social exchange theory, render organizations relatively immune to the day-to-day crises that bedevil their less socially responsible counterparts.

What might have been two troublesome problems for Federal Express Corporation (FedEx) in 1989, for example, became non-events because of the company's strong relationships with news media and employees. The first incident involved an "expose" by the television program *20/20* of the company's handling of high security packages for the federal government. FedEx's reputation for honest dealing with the media made the 20/20 segment one of the program's least remembered. "We had only one media call afterward," FedEx spokesperson Armand

Schneider told colleagues later, despite the "pack instinct" for which journalists have become notorious.

The second challenge involved employee relationships. Federal Express recently had acquired Flying Tiger Airlines, whose pilots were members of the Air Line Pilots Association (ALPA). FedEx pilots were non-union. A National Labor Relations Board election was called to determine whether all FedEx pilots should be represented by the union. ALPA was defeated. Some 2,000 pilots, about half of them formerly with Flying Tiger, were eligible to vote. Fewer than 725 union votes were cast. Federal Express' loyalty had been reciprocated. In fact, it had attracted the support of about 25 percent of the former Flying Tigers.

Outcomes of this sort, involving issues that can become crises or requiring extensive communication efforts, usually are determined more by the nature and strength of underlying relationships than by any other factor. In these instances, Federal Express had developed strong relationships with news media representatives and pilots based on open and truthful communication. Neither reporters nor their editors apparently were disposed to follow 20/20's lead, and FedEx pilots voted not to exchange their mutually beneficial relationship with the company for inherently adversarial collective bargaining.

The nature of pre-existing relationships between organizations and stakeholders, for these several reasons, determines the magnitude of challenges communicators face in designing and implementing communication plans, programs, campaigns, special events, and in crisis response efforts. Armed with the sort of credibility that Federal Express enjoys, ambush journalism and union organizing campaigns fell short of becoming major challenges to the company's communication staff. Similar circumstances would have been more troublesome to most organizations.

The primary difference between Federal Express and other organizations is the strength of the relationships between FedEx and the company's personnel at all levels. The FedEx commitment to people is based on Chairman Fred Smith's now-proven thesis that such commitments will be reciprocated as workers deliver quality services that can be sold at premium prices to the benefit of all involved.

Federal Express backs its commitment to personnel with an employee communication budget in excess of $60 million annually. The funds involved are committed to a two-way communication system second to none in corporate America. The system is committed to the thesis that communication is a social process through which ideas, concepts, and emotions are exchanged between individuals and/or organizations.

The notion of *exchange* is the most important concept in the paragraph above. Communication is essentially transactional, regardless of the manner in which thoughts are transmitted. The nature of communication, and the nature of human behavior, therefore are most readily understood in two frameworks, one sociological and the other originating in communication. The sociological concept has been labeled "social exchange theory," and suggests that most human and organizational behavior is essentially transactional. The two-way symmetrical communication model advanced by Professors James E. Grunig and Todd Hunt (1984) suggests, however, that the transactional model is equally applicable in communication.

SOCIAL EXCHANGE THEORY

The transactional view of human events is embodied in social exchange theory as elaborated by Homans and, later, by Blau. Each deals primarily with interpersonal transactions, but their concepts are equally applicable to organizations, especially from the communication perspective.

Homans, Blau, and other advocates of social exchange theory adopted a number of principles from economics, psychology and other disciplines in developing their concept. In a 1986 introduction to a second printing of his 1964 work, Homans emphasized the breadth of exchange theory in these words: "Once social norms are known, conformity needs no further explanation. What does require explanation is the broad spectrum of social interaction that is permitted but not required by social norms"(xvi). Homans borrowed heavily from behavioral psychologist B. F. Skinner and from basic economics. He redefined economic man, however, to encompass the nonmaterial gratifications that often motivate behavior.

Social exchange theory is built around three premises:

1. Individuals tend to behave in ways that produce benefits for them, material or psychological.
2. Demand or need for a benefit declines as supply and/or availability increases.
3. Social benefits obtained are contingent benefits. They occur where something is provided in exchange.

Social exchange theory thus focuses on benefits derived from social transactions. Volumes have been written on the topic (see Additional Reading) but most contemporary writings are based on the work of Homans and/or Blau.

Homans' Social Organization

Homans (1961) undertook to explain patterns of social organization with five axioms:

1. Behaviors rewarded in the past are apt to be repeated.
2. Likelihood that behaviors will be repeated increases with the frequency of past rewards.
3. The more valuable the reward, the more often the behavior will be repeated.
4. The value of rewards declines with the frequency at which they recently have been received.
5. Likelihood of angry response increases with disadvantages created by inequitable behaviors.

Homans later added a derivation significant to communicators: the value of a behavior to an individual is governed by the extent of the benefits derived.

Although less than obvious in reading, Homans' axioms encompass intangible as well as tangible rewards. Conformity, self-respect, group membership, high rank, and similar factors that motivate behavior all can be part of exchange equations.

Blau's (1989) concept of human behavior involves rewards whose values can vary from one transaction to another and whose value cannot be expressed precisely in terms of a single medium such as money. He points out, however, that the ambiguities that surround values exchanged are a "substantive fact, not simply a methodological problem" (88). Blau's assumptions as to individual behavior:

- The likelihood that a behavior will occur is governed by the anticipated benefits involved.
- Series of exchanges lead to reciprocal obligations that guide subsequent exchanges.
- Negative behaviors tend to increase with violations of reciprocal obligations.
- Behaviors are progressively perceived as less valuable and are less likely to occur where assurance of rewards is high.
- Norms of fair exchange become increasingly common as exchange relationships become better-established.
- Negative behaviors increase in proportion to the extent that norms of fairness are violated.
- The more stable and balanced are some exchange relationships between parties, the more likely other exchange relationships are to be come unbalanced and unstable.

The applicability of these concepts to communication should be apparent, especially where communicators pause to examine them in terms of specific organization-stakeholder relationships.

The works of Blau and Homans, taken in concert, suggests that organizational success in dealing with stakeholders ultimately is governed by on-going series of exchanges or transactions, informational and otherwise. Those who would succeed in communication, as a result, must control all transactions or exchanges rather than the relative few that occur by design and through mass media.

Successful exchange through communication, in other words, requires more than messages. Messages are necessary but not sufficient. Sufficiency arises out of environments, behaviors, and qualities of products or services. Faced with a problem, the communicator's first concern must be with substance rather than messages. The question is not "What should we say," but "What must the organization do?" What terms of exchange, in other words, should messages propose?

IN SUMMARY

Preoccupation with creating and transmitting messages can create problems for communicators. Successful communication requires a broader focus. Communicators must be sensitive to potential inconsistencies in messages that vary in origin and credibility. They also must understand the transactional nature of the communication process and the role of communication in social exchange.

Narrow perspectives conveyed by academics and practitioners too often create barriers to problem solving in communication. The process encompasses more than interpersonal and mediated delivery mechanisms, as reflected in the mass media effects model of communication developed by Melvin L. DeFleur and Sandra J. Ball-Rokeach (1982). Their broader approach encompasses social systems, media systems, audiences, and effects as well as communication channels, and suggests that individuals respond to messages from diverse sources.

The DeFleur and Ball-Rokeach model defines the extent to which messages originated in non-mediated sources and stresses the extent to which humans interact with those sources. Their behaviors are influenced by environmental, behavioral, and qualitative as well as interpersonal and mediated communication. Environmental messages are transmitted by the characteristics of the environments organizations create. Behavioral messages are delivered through the behaviors of employees as well as organizations. Qualitative messages are generated by the attributes of products and services. Consistency among these messages is critical because durable perceptions of value are created primarily through environmental, behavioral and qualitative messages. Mediated and interpersonal communication usually can accomplish little beyond calling attention to products, reinforcing perceptions, or inducing recipients to expose themselves to other forms of communication.

These concepts are most readily understood where examined in light of social exchange theories advanced by Blau (1964, 1989) and Homans (1961). Their work focuses on the transactional nature of contacts among and between individuals and organizations and produces a shift in communication focus. Social exchange theory suggests that communicators concentrate their efforts on developing relationships rather than on transmitting information through programs oriented toward stakeholder relations. Where communication may persuade, social exchange builds relationships and commitments that lead to mutual benefits.

Social exchange theory redefines B. F. Skinner's concept of economic man to encompass the nonmaterial gratifications that often motivate behavior. Those nonmaterial elements more often than not are the primary coinage of communication. Conformity, self-respect, group membership, high rank, and other motivating factors all can be part of social exchange.

ADDITIONAL READING

Anshen, Melvin. *Corporate Strategies for Social Performance.* New York: Columbia University Press, 1980.

Bedeian, Arthur G. *Organizations: Theory and Analysis.* Hinsdale, Ill.: Dryden Press, 1980.

DeFleur, Melvin L., and Sandra J. Ball-Rokeach, *Theories of Mass Communication.* 4th ed. New York: Longman, 1982.

Blau, Peter M. *Exchange and Power in Social Life.* New York: Wiley, 1964.

_____. *Exchange and Power in Social Life,* 2nd ed. New Brunswick, NJ: Transcation Publishers, 1989.

Grunig, James E., and Todd Hunt. *Managing Public Relations,* New York: Holt, Rinehart and Winston, 1984.

Hall, Richard H. *Organizations: Structure and Process.* Englewood Cliffs, N.J.: Prentice-Hall, 2nd. ed., 1977.

Homans, George C. *Social Behavior: Its Elementary Forms.* New York: Harcourt, Brace & World, 1961.

Homans, George C., and David M. Schneider. *Marriage, Authority and Final Causes: A Study of Unilateral Cross-Cousin Marriages.* New York: Free Press, 1955.

Littlejohn, Stephen W. *Theories of Human Communication*. 3rd ed. Bemont, CA: Wadsworth, 1989.

Nader, Ralph. *Unsafe at Any Speed*. New York: Grossman, 1965.

Rice, Ronald E., and Charles K. Atkin. *Public Communication Campaigns*, 2nd. ed. Newbury Park, CA: Sage, 1989.

Rosenberg, Morris, and Ralph H. Turner. *Social Psychology: Sociological Perspectives*. New York: Basic Books, 1981.

5

Meeting Information Needs

Volume and accuracy of available information are the primary governors of success in communication. Knowledge of organizations and their stakeholders governs communicator ability to build salutary relationships and respond to day-to-day problems. Knowledge is applied in designing and implementing communication projects and in assessing the results of communication efforts.

Two types of information are required. One category consists of all information communicators use in fashioning messages designed to produce change in stakeholder attitudes, opinions, and behaviors. The other consists of data that serve as direct or indirect indicators of change in attitude, opinion, or behavior. The first category can best be described as planning information while the second consists of measurement information.

The two types of information may be separate and distinct but always are related. Both are required throughout the communication process since measurement or assessment systems, like messages, must be fashioned before communication begins. Assessment requires special attention where communication is intended to produce change in attitude or opinion rather than behavior. Behavior can be measured with relative ease. Change in attitude and opinion are more difficult to quantify. Measurement is necessary to enable communicators to fine tune longer-term efforts and to assess outcomes. These factors can be measured directly only with difficulty and at considerable expense. Indirect measures of results can be used, but successful use requires prior agreement by communicators and their employers. Both must accept the validity of indirect indicators in order to eliminate potential disputes over outcomes. Criteria for success must be precisely defined, in other words, before communication begins.

With agreement on measurement techniques communicators can plan their information gathering to achieve three objectives. The first is information about the organization and its stakeholders necessary to project development, including designing messages and selecting delivery mechanisms. The second is feedback information; data about stakeholder reactions that may suggest change in messages or delivery systems during the course of the project. The third is assessment data; information concerning those agreed-upon factors that are to be used to measure results.

No single information-gathering technique is adequate to satisfy all needs. Some techniques are applicable in several areas but none is universally productive. Experienced communicators seek information about organizations by examining stakeholder groups, industries in which organizations function, and environments in which they operate. The information involved is vital during several steps in the communication process. Planning and assessment have become as information intensive as message development and delivery.

PROBLEMS AND NEEDS

The ways in which communicator information needs are met vary with problems at hand. Where leisurely planning is possible, as in program development, extensive statistical data of known validity usually are required. Valid data often are available only at considerable expense in time and dollars. Accurate statistics therefore tend to be supplanted by more readily available information from other sources as time pressures compound. Campaign and special event planning typically is undertaken under more pressure than program development. Crises create even greater time pressures. Communicators are forced to act on the basis of progressively inferior information as time limitations grow more stringent.

Communicators skilled in developing organizations' communication plans are relatively well-prepared to handle programs, campaigns, special events, and crisis response systems. Data acquired during planning and program design can be beneficially applied in campaign and special event planning. Information used in other communication applications usually is equally applicable in crisis response situations.

Communication careers typically involve communicators first in planning and programming and subsequently in campaigns, special events, and crisis response efforts. Informational needs are most readily examined in keeping with the plan-program-campaign-special event-crisis response sequence. Needs in each case can be analyzed in two ways. Communicators first specify types of information they need and then identify alternative sources for each type of information.

Needs are relatively consistent across plans, programs, campaigns, special events, and crises. All needs relate to organizations with which communicators work, to environments in which organizations function, and to stakeholder groups with which organizations are involved.

Needs can be filled in one of two ways: by using existing information or by creating new information. The former approach is faster, less expensive, and usually preferable but access to existing information is limited in some circumstances. Political parties, for example, may share information internally but individual candidates and their managers rarely are so generous.

Communicators' informational needs in any given situation can be assessed by examining three factors:

1. The problem at hand, whether it involves a plan, program, campaign or special event, or crisis response system.
2. The nature of the organization involved, its functions and its stakeholders.
3. The types of information that can be successfully applied in the given situation.

ORGANIZATIONAL NEEDS

Types of information applicable to specific communication problems are limited most frequently by two factors: time and money. Willingness to allocate dollars usually increases as time factors become more pressing. Few organizations invest in sophisticated, on-going survey research in support of communication planning or programming, but budgets tend to increase when crises develop. The pattern reflects human tendencies to spend lavishly on cures while neglecting prevention. Communication should be considered even more a "pay me now or pay me later" function than maintenance of machines. Damaged stakeholder relationships are more costly and more difficult to repair. The short-term profit orientation of senior managers nevertheless encourages remedial rather than preventive communication systems. Prevention-oriented systems deal primarily in planning and programming and, to a lesser extent, in campaigns and special events. Other systems, by default, deal in serial crises.

Types of Information

Information applied in developing and maintaining communication plans and programs is drawn from multiple sources in keeping with diverse organizational relationships. Communicators are concerned with organizational stakeholders and the environments in which stakeholders and organizations function. Environmental conditions influence relationships between organizations and stakeholders. Communicators therefore monitor environmental events, trends, and issues in order to:

1. Anticipate how they may influence stakeholders.
2. Define alternative organizational responses and make recommendations to senior managers.
3. Communicate organizational positions and the content and consequences of organizational decisions to stakeholders.

These steps—and the information they require—are identical regardless of communication situation. Informational needs are consistent whether communicators are dealing with programs, campaigns, special events, or crises. Information availability and quality vary, however, from one situation to another.

Programming Information

Communication plans and programs are designed to engender and maintain strong, functional relationships between organizations and stakeholders. Accomplishing this objective requires that communicators maintain current information about:

1. Attitudes toward and opinions of the organization among stakeholders.
2. Events, trends and issues that may influence attitude and opinion toward the organization.

The latter category is more complex than it appears. Second-, third-, and fourth-order results flowing from events and trends can be as important as immediate consequences. Nuclear power plant shutdowns arising out of the anti-nuclear movements of the 1970s and 1980s, for example, will produce power shortages and higher electricity rates (second-order result) during the 1990s. Ultimate outcomes may include renewed interest in nuclear power and enhanced consumer interest in more efficient lighting equipment and home appliances (third-order results).

Novices in communication often are taken aback by this sort of reasoning. Students long have accused professors of wanting them to "know everything." That's not quite the case. What is necessary is sufficient basic knowledge to create sufficient insight into organizational operations to permit logically tracing the results of events or trends. Those in the appliance industry, for example, well understand relationships among electric rates, efficiency of equipment produced, and value of that equipment in the eyes of prospective purchasers.

Relationships, in fact, are what communication is all about. Communication planning and programming are equivalent to relationship management. They deal with developing and maintaining ongoing, distortion-free transactions and information exchanges between organizations and stakeholder groups.

Assessment Information

Measuring the results of communication is no less complex. Assessment requires a precise answer to a complex question: To what extent did messages sent in the course of the communication effort produce desired results? Complexity develops because communicators are interested in the extent to which results were produced by messages delivered. Results, in and of themselves, are inadequate to justify continuing the massive expenditures that organizations invest in communication efforts. Significant percentages of total sales of many products, for example, occur with or without attendant product publicity programs. Such programs can be justified economically only where additional sales are adequate to support expenditures involved.

Results of communication can be measured directly or indirectly. Assessment can be accomplished by using existing or new measuring devices. Decisions by organizations and communicators as to types of measurements to be used usually are governed by levels of precision required and costs involved. Costs are lowest where existing indicators can be used but indirect measurement usually is relatively imprecise.

Consider, for example, an organization's decision to attack employee morale problems through a campaign using multiple behavioral and environmental changes and several mediated communication channels. Morale levels could be measured indirectly by tracking absenteeism, tardiness, and turnover rates, or directly, through employee surveys. Sophisticated survey research techniques would be necessary to determine whether the employee newspaper was more productive than a supervisory training program or a new worker recreational facility in producing observed results.

Assessment efforts must accomplish two objectives. First, they must produce data that demonstrate results to the satisfaction of senior managers or clients. Requirements vary among members of these groups. Communicators therefore must come to agreements with clients or superiors before programs begin in order to later provide the information they require.

Assessment techniques designed to determine the relative efficiency of media and messages are more important to communicators. Communication efforts can be fine tuned as they proceed only to the extent that communicators can obtain accurate information (a) as to the ability of media to convey messages and (b) recipient responses to those messages. Employers and clients often are unwilling or unable to fund research necessary to provide such information. These conditions are not insurmountable barriers, however, because considerable information is available for the asking through environmental assessment and otherwise.

ENVIRONMENTAL ASSESSMENT

Communication programs are built on informational foundations. The foundations are essentially similar regardless of the type of communication process. Plan, program, campaign and special event development, and crisis response planning require much the same information.

Most information is obtained through two long-used processes recently labeled "environmental assessment." Environmental assessment is accomplished by scanning organizational horizons for events that may signal the start of significant trends and by monitoring the development of resulting trends.

Environmental assessment is undertaken at individual and organizational levels. Organizational assessment or trend-watching processes deal with organizations' primary stakeholder groups: consumers, workers, and owners.

Trend Watching

Trend watching involves tracking events and the levels of attention they receive in the mass media, and can be conducted formally or informally. Trend watching assumes that information is an agent of change and movement, and that change and movement can be understood by monitoring information flows. Content analysis techniques perfected in formal research may or may not be applied in trend watching. Formal monitoring systems usually involve content analyses. Informal, and more frequently used, approaches may involving nothing more than regular reading of a set of media oriented to the needs of specific professions, businesses, or industries.

Most trend watching deals with a set of primary information flows including:

- National and international economies
- The sector in which the organization operates
- Products/services used in and/or produced by the sector
- Contemporary and emerging issues in the sector
- Environmental issues
- Human issues

Sector trends. Within information flows, trend watchers often focus their attention in one or more of several subsectors: general, technology, labor, human values and concerns, family trends and institutions. Each sector encompasses a set of factors that can influence organizational interests. Virtually every trend watcher monitors the state of the economy, expansion in human knowledge, international influences on domestic economies and societies, and pervasive trends such as urbanization and cultural homogenization. Trends in other sectors often tracked include:

Technology—The role of research and development, accelerating product maturation rates and limitations imposed by finite natural resources.

Labor— The national shift in emphasis from manufacturing to service and information industries, increasing popularity of second careers and midlife changes, and progressive deterioration in the work ethic.

Values/concerns—Decline in traditional authority, growth in consumerism and the maturation of diversity as an explicit value.

Family trends—Changes in family formation, marriage, divorce and life styles; improvements in nutrition and longer life; decline in the significance of rites of passage; and growth in the aging component of the population.

Institutional factors—Bigness in government, bureaucratization of institutions, public participation in institutional decision making, accountability on the part of those in public endeavors, and demands for social responsibility.

All of these and many other factors can be monitored with varying degrees of formality by trend watchers. Trend watching remains a relatively informal information-gathering technique. Competitive intelligence processes have become more formalized, however, and now include systematically gathering and analyzing all available information about organizations. In-house sources, competitive and trade sources, published information, and third parties all are enlisted in the process. Each of these categories includes a long list of prospective information sources.

Alternative techniques. Information in the competitor and trade sector, for example, might be obtained by direct inquiry, observation, visits, speeches, company publications, news releases, investor information, advertisements and promotional materials, help-wanted advertising, trade and professional organizations and their publications, and trade shows. Published and government sources include bibliographies, directories, periodicals, clipping services, and government and university sources. Computer databases of various kinds are the fastest-growing source of competitor and trade data. Third-party sources include customers, suppliers, other competitors, journalists, consultants, unions, financial analysts, advocacy groups, and research organizations.

Competitive intelligence readily can be extended to individuals within organizations. Public records alone can provide considerable information. Access to an individual's name and age, for example, can enable a researcher to obtain copies of his or her driver's license application. The address on the application can lead to real estate and mortgage records, and so on. Far more information is readily available on most individuals than any of them realize.

Personal Systems

Personal information systems parallel those used in trend watching, applying monitoring and tracking techniques to identify significant incidents and follow developing trends. Most personal systems are designed to monitor mass media, disciplinary media, and business or industry media that deal with client or employer concerns. Professional and academic media dealing with client or employer activities often are added to personal media lists.

Mass media. Professional communicators often read two to three newspapers daily, at least one of them published in their home communities. The others are apt to be *The New York Times*, which provides exceptional coverage of emerging socioeconomic and technical issues, and *The Wall Street Journal*, which focuses on business. Many also read *Business Week* and *Industry Week*. Local and regional business newspapers and magazines often are also on professionals' reading lists.

Disciplinary media. Many professionals also read both academic and professional journals and newsletters in communication and its subdisciplines. Public relations practitioners, for example, might read *Public Relations Review* and *Public Relations Research Annual*, written primarily for academics, as well as *Public Relations Journal* and *Public Relations Quarterly.* Some also scan publications such as *Communication Abstracts* and *Journalism Abstracts* to ensure that they miss nothing of importance.

Industry media. The term industry media refers to business and professional publications written for communicators' clients and employers and for organizations' stakeholder groups. Automotive industry reading, for example, might include publications serving the tire, glass, steel, and plastics sectors as well as others oriented to the financial community, organized labor, and the like.

Organizational Systems

Larger organizations often maintain internal library services that prepare information digests for managers. Similar services may be provided by so-called issues management units but issues managers usually confine their efforts to the few contemporary issues deemed most important to the organization. Larger communication consultancies maintain information services for internal use and, at times, as a service to clients.

Communicators often establish information-gathering systems in their departments where organizational resources are lacking. Communication departments should have access to all necessary publications as well as one or more computer data bases.

Communicators' personal information networks frequently are more productive than organizational systems. Formal systems in larger organizations usually are organized to meet the needs of disciplines other than communication. Communicators then must turn to less formal organizational resources, including records maintained for internal monitoring and in compliance with regulatory requirements.

STAKEHOLDER ASSESSMENT

Success in developing communication plans, programs, campaigns, special events, and crisis response systems also requires information about organizational stakeholders. Primary stakeholders, in most organizations including consumers, personnel and owners, are most important. In publicly owned corporations, the owners are stockholders. Prospective stockholders and members of the financial community whose attitudes and opinions influence corporations and their securities usually are considered primary groups as well. Information concerning competitors also may be important.

Communicators are most interested in group demographic and sociographic characteristics and in group members' perceptions of the organization and its products or services. These variables can be measured directly or indirectly. Direct measurement, through surveys or other forms of original research, is time-consuming and relatively expensive, especially when undertaken on continuing bases, as should be the case. Survey results are similar to financial statements. They are "snapshots in time"; accurate depictions of conditions prevalent on the day the data were gathered. Changing conditions render data obsolete and, in many ways, dangerous. These circumstances encourage communicators to use data regularly collected for other purposes to establish demographic and sociographic profiles of primary groups and monitor attitude and opinion within groups. Considerable information is available within organizations that can be used for these purposes. Primary stakeholder groups, in fact, largely can be identified and monitored by analyzing existing data.

Employees

Perhaps no group is as well-documented as organizations' workers. Most documentation maintained to satisfy regulatory requirements, for example, is valuable to communicators. Human resources department and regulatory compliance office records contain demographic and sociographic data on organizational personnel. Age, sex, race, occupation, income level, and numbers of dependents are readily obtained. Occupational data also provide indirect indicators of educational level where that information is not separately maintained. Addresses or U.S. Postal Service ZIP codes recorded as part of addresses can be used with data from the U.S. Bureau of the Census to create further insights.

Many human resources departments also conduct exit interviews with personnel who are resigning or have been discharged. Analyses of records of those interviews also can be enlightening.

Additional information is available through sales and marketing departments, especially where company products are relatively costly and warranties must be registered. Warranty cards usually are used by sales and marketing units to obtain information about consumers that is equally helpful in other departments.

What about morale? Information concerning worker attitude and opinion is readily inferred from payroll data. Absenteeism, tardiness and turnover rates are valid indicators of morale, although figures can not be considered good or bad in absolute terms. A three percent absenteeism rate, for example, may be relatively high in manufacturing facilities populated primarily by males but low in largely female offices. Tracking data over time is another matter. Month-to-month and year-to-year figures are valid indicators of improvement or deterioration.

Numbers of customer complaints, volume of defects reported by quality control personnel, numbers of disciplinary cases, and the extent to which worker appeals procedures are used also are indirect measures of morale. Types of indicators vary with organizations and the products or services they offer but exist in ample numbers in all organizations.

Consumers

Information about consumers is almost as easily obtained as data about personnel, and is equally important. Consumers, like workers, no longer can be considered an expendable resource.

Behavior is the best indicator of consumer opinion of organizations. Customers vote with their feet. So do students, patients, clients, and members of any other group in which (a) dissatisfaction prevails and (b) alternatives are within reach. Voters in some jurisdictions have been known to respond to what they perceive to be less-than-satisfactory government by moving across city, county, or state boundaries.

Conditions of this sort threaten the welfare of organizations in contemporary demographic circumstances. Population growth is slowing rapidly in the United States. Zero growth is expected by the turn of the century. By 2010, barring radical change in childbearing or emigration patterns, the population will be in decline. These conditions deny organizations the luxury of alienating consumers. Organizational success requires that consumer dissatisfaction be remedied.

Identifying and solving problems requires that consumer attitude, opinion, and behavior be monitored directly and/or indirectly. Perhaps the best indicator of consumer satisfaction is turnover, a factor easily measured in organizations that maintain transaction records.

Consumer attrition can be monitored by periodically calculating ratios of new customers to old. Numbers of consumers and average transaction size ideally should be consistently increasing. Numbers of complaints at minimum should remain stable in relation to numbers of consumers and/or transactions.

Demographic and sociographic characteristics are more difficult to analyze among consumers than among workers. Exceptions to this rule occur only where customers complete "registration cards" to activate product warranties or where marketing survey data are available. Consumers usually provide requested information despite the fact that much of it is designed primarily to meet marketing needs. Marketing departments usually are not overly reluctant to share summaries with members of other communication disciplines.

Stockholders

Although more difficult to monitor than consumers, organizational owners or stockholders also require attention. Stockholders, like workers, can "vote with their feet," selling their holdings and driving down stock prices as they move dollars into what they consider better investments. Depressed security prices, in turn, can limit organizational ability to raise funds.

Since stockholders are influenced by analysts, brokers, media, and others in the financial community, financial communication efforts usually encompass these groups as well. Analysts often get special attention because of the weight their recommendations carry with institutional investors, pension fund managers and others whose securities purchases and sales can influence market prices.

Stockholder tracking is difficult because considerable stock is held by brokers for customers. Customers, moreover, may elect to have their identities concealed from companies whose shares they own. Direct contact with such stockholders then is limited to financial reports and proxy statements distributed through brokers. Monitoring can consist of little more than tracking sales volume in listed securities. Monitoring nevertheless is important because sudden change in activity levels may signal potential takeovers as well as economic problems.

Analysts and brokers are more readily identified. Their recommendations usually are published and serve as indicators of the financial community's perceptions of the organization. Some organizations monitor brokerage house recommendations and analysts' reports. The strengths of analysts' evaluations rests in their relative objectivity. That objectivity is impaired only by limits on available information.

The sum of analysts' opinions concerning major players in an industry is especially valuable to communicators seeking insight into environmental trends that may influence organizational destinies.

INDUSTRIAL PERSPECTIVES

While organizations and their primary stakeholder groups are of primary concern to communicators, industries in which organizations function are almost equally important. Problems or opportunities that develop in the economy or in industrial or business sectors involve all organizations. None can escape, whether opportunities or problems are involved. Aggressive organizations seeking to capitalize on opportunities may succeed or fail. Those that succeed gain market share at competitors' expense. Those that fail usually lose market share.

These conditions require that communicators monitor commercial or industrial sectors in which clients or employers are involved. Developments that may influence organizational access to and use of resources are especially important. Raw material and energy problems can be troublesome in manufacturing. Manpower shortages can be equally damaging to service organizations. Legislative and/or regulatory change can produce difficulties for any organization.

Information enabling communicators to monitor industrial and business sectors is most readily obtained from three sources. First and most accessible are business, trade, and professional organizations that serve the fields in question. Second, and only slightly less accessible, are the records of regulatory and administrative components of government at all levels. The third source consists of several sets of media that are accessible but demanding in terms of monitoring and data analysis.

Organizational Information

Business, trade, and professional associations can provide near-limitless information about commercial or industrial sectors in which their members operate. Many associations are membership groups whose primary purposes are educational or informational. They are dedicated to enhancing members' productivity by meeting their informational needs.

Many needs are met through industry surveys designed to assess collective intentions as to plant and equipment investments, work force expansion, and other indicators of the relative health of the industry and its members. Some surveys go so far as to assess the extent of technological progress that members are experiencing. Others are oriented toward forecasting sales on annual or seasonal bases.

The stature of membership organizations in members' eyes encourages accurate responses to surveys. Such responses generate more reliable results than might be obtained from other sources. Data involved can be of special interest in assessing the progress of individual organizations in relation to their competitors. Is market share going up or down? Is the company keeping pace in modernizing plant and equipment as rapidly as competitors? Relatively precise insights into these and other questions often are most readily obtained through pertinent industry reports.

Governmental Information

Governmental sources often can be almost equally helpful where industry data are lacking. Information obtained from regulatory and bureaucratic bodies usually is accurate but may become available too late to be of maximum benefit. Governmental bodies usually make summary reports on annual or fiscal year bases. Data for one fiscal year may not be available until late in the ensuing year. Slowness in reporting can limit usefulness of industrial production data, for example, in making sales forecasts for ensuing years.

In other cases, governmental data can be highly valuable. Several of the nation's larger corporations have obtained competitors' proprietary information by obtaining copies of bids they had submitted to federal agencies. The Freedom of Information Act requires that such information be made public.   Regulatory agencies are another source of valuable information. Reports filed by inspectors for the Occupational Safety and Health Administration or Environmental Protection Agency can produce insights into competitors' products and production processes. Consumer Product Safety Commission, Food and Drug Administration, Interstate Commerce Commission, Federal Communication Commission, Securities and Exchange Commission, National Labor Relations Board, and other records can be equally informative. Reports vary in importance with the nature of industries in which communicators are involved but nevertheless deserve attention.

Almost no organization today is unregulated. Regulation exists in varying degrees at municipal, county, and state as well as Federal levels. Agencies at the several levels, in addition, often exchange information, making data available from multiple sources. Information from regulatory agencies often can help communicators in assessing the accuracy of data obtained within their organizations. Information concerning consumer attitude and opinion, for example, often is available from consumer protection agencies. Individual cases may be of little interest but volume of complaints against specific organizations or types of products can signal potential problems or opportunities.

Planning and zoning records, corporate charters, business licenses, and other data maintained by administrative and regulatory agencies also can be helpful in specific circumstances. Government today reaches into every corner of organizational life, creating paper trails of almost infinite length and breadth. Records involved usually are subject to so-called "sunshine laws." Although enacted at the urging of news media, resulting statutes open most governmental records to any citizen.

Mediated Information

Sunshine laws have created more information sources for communicators than for the media. Mass media information is intended for mass audiences. Mass audiences seldom are sufficiently interested in individual organizations or industries to induce editors or program directors to provide information in the depth that communicators require.

Other media are available, however, that provide information in varying quantity and quality. These can best be categorized as general business or industrial media, industry or sector specific media, and academic journals. Each group can contribute to communicator knowledge of organizations and industries they serve.

General media. The commercial and industrial communities of the United States and most other nations are served by a number of "general business" publications. Most significant among them in the United States are the *Wall Street Journal*, a five-day-a-week newspaper, and several magazines. The magazines include *Business Week, Industry Week, Barron's, Forbes*, and *Fortune* at the national level and a host of regional and state publications. This media sector also is populated by a number of newsletters including the several Kiplinger letters, securities market letters, regulatory letters, and so forth.

Industry-specific media. Newsletters and magazines have proliferated in recent years and now serve almost every business or industry. In basic industry, for example, there are publications dealing with raw materials, fabricating techniques, and finished products. These are supplemented by specialized publications for almost every discipline involved in associated organizations. In the typical manufacturing organization, executives in purchasing, engineering, research, traffic, manufacturing, marketing, sales, and distribution each are apt to have their own journals. Occupationally-specific publications also may be available in larger industries, such as food, housing, and pharmaceuticals. Food distributors and retails are so numerous and their interests are so diverse that each group is served by different publications.

Academic publications. Similar circumstances prevail in the academic world, which supports publications that can be of as much interest as business or trade journals. These conditions are most prevalent among the professions, including the several communication disciplines. The journals of the Public Relations Society of America and International Association of Business Communicators, for example, are no more important to communicators than *Public Relations Review*, *Public Opinion Quarterly*, or *Management Communication Quarterly*. The latter journals deal with research and theory directly and immediately applicable in communication practice.

Research journals in metallurgy, physics, or biology may be less immediately applicable in commercial or industrial settings. Few would argue, however, that organizational managers or their communicators can afford to neglect new knowledge being developed through basic research. The properties of a newly developed steel alloy, for example, can create manufacturing advantages for those who know about them, and disadvantages for competitors.

INFORMAL RESEARCH

Beyond organizations' walls, be they corporations or communication agencies, is a world of information available from multiple sources. Sources range from conventional and electronic libraries to business, trade and professional associations, news services, and governmental agencies. These sources are the domain of informal research, where information can be quickly assembled on any topic of contemporary interest.

Informal information resources have grown so large that books could be written on how to obtain information pertinent to specific communication problems. Only an overview and an admonition can be provided here. The admonition: Success in resolving communication problems almost always is governed by communicator ability to find and apply information. The best informed party to an issue, in other words, is apt to win the battle for the public mind. Information can be obtained from an almost unlimited number of sources. The sources vary in accessibility and range from local and regional libraries to distant computer databases.

Libraries

The word library traditionally applied to buildings housing collections of books. Too many today continue to think of libraries exclusively in those terms. What has come to be known as the information explosion has forced libraries to change in ways that render them more valuable to communicators. Most have been forced to limit acquisitions by economic and space considerations. The books published each year continue to increase in number and importance with the growth of human knowledge. No traditional library can hope to keep pace. What no one library can accomplish, however, has been achieved by groups of libraries through interlibrary loan programs.

Interlibrary loan programs have produced circumstances in which no library is local. Community libraries instead have access to the collections of other libraries across the nation, enlarging their value as resources for communicators. Books not locally owned usually can be obtained in three to five days at little or no cost.

Educational collections. More extensive collections, especially on scientific or technical subjects, often are found at colleges and universities. These institutions also are linked to one another and to local libraries by loan programs. Schools that grant master's and doctoral degrees maintain unusually complete libraries in disciplines in which they offer graduate study.

Libraries also are usually linked to one or more of the several thousand computer databases that are supplanting periodical collections as favored sources of information. Nexis, Dialog, ERIC, and other databases usually are accessible to librarians who perform searches for students and, in many cases, are accessible to students as well. Research librarians skilled in using specific databases can be especially helpful. Their knowledge of search strategy design can save hours of on-line time and resulting expense.

Privileges available. While many assume the contrary, college and university libraries often are open to professionals and residents of local communities. A day or two may be required to process requests for user privileges but most libraries permit visitors immediate access to their collections short of removing books from the premises.

After privileges have been granted, college and university libraries often permit use of computer database terminals. Access to catalog computers usually can be gained by modem-equipped microcomputers, enabling communicators to determine whether specific resources are available before visiting libraries.

Private libraries maintained by professional, business and trade associations are less accessible but may be more valuable. Communicators usually gain access through their own professional groups. Access to others' professional libraries often can be arranged through clients, employers, and trade or business associations with which they are involved. Professional, business, and trade association libraries usually contain substantial amounts of specialized knowledge otherwise available only on similarly specialized college university campuses.

Governmental Documents

Many colleges and universities also serve as repositories for collections of governmental publications. Federal documents, especially those originating in the Department of Commerce and Bureau of the Census, often are valuable to communicators. Census data include precise demographic and sociographic profiles of neighborhoods by U.S. Postal Service ZIP code. Available data includes age, educational, occupational, and household information as well as economic statistics.

Equally valuable information is available, and may be accessible by computer, from federal and state regulatory agencies. Almost all organizations and some stakeholder groups today are regulated by government. Federal agencies commonly encountered by organizations include the Securities and Exchange Commission, Occupational Safety and Health Administration, National Labor Relations Board, Environmental Protection Agency, Interstate Commerce Commission, and Consumer Product Safety Commission.

Available information. The list could go on at length. Almost every organization is regulated by one or more public agencies. Most agencies' records are open to the public or must be made accessible on request. Their potential value is almost beyond belief. Consider how much information about the paper clip manufacturer discussed earlier that you could have for the asking. By making requests of the agencies listed above you could quickly determine:

- The initial ownership and capitalization of the firm and any substantive changes since the date of founding.
- Results of any OSHA inspections of the plant or competitors' plants.
- Records of any labor problems in the plant or in the industry.
- Financial information about unions that have organized or threaten to organize the plant.
- The nature of any environmental difficulties in the plant or industry.
- Safety records of corporate motor vehicles and those of competitors.
- Details of product safety problems.

Additional data. Further information could be obtained from comparable state, county, and local agencies that regulate the company because most of their records also are public. So, too, are the corporate and financial records of nonprofit corporations and lobbying groups. Most pressure groups organize as nonprofit corporations to make supporters' donations tax deductible. Their political action committees file regular financial reports and all lobbyists are required to register and provide names of their clients, often at state as well as federal levels.

Governmental information seldom is needed but can be highly valuable in specific circumstances. Communicators assisting clients in resisting labor union organizing efforts, for example, often find unions' annual reports to the Department of Labor—including officers' wages and expense accounts—to be most helpful.

Computer Resources

Some governmental information is available to communicators by modem-equipped microcomputer. Many federal agencies are making large portions of their computer files accessible to the public. Some are being opened to comply with open record laws but most are opened to reduce time agency members spend in responding to information requests.

Access to governmental computers nevertheless represents a small part of the total information accessible through electronic databases and computer utilities. The latter terms require definition. An electronic database is a library of information compiled by an organization and made available, usually at a fee, to any interested party. Computer utilities are electronic services that often incorporate "gateways" through which users can obtain access to electronic databases as part of more comprehensive services.

Electronic databases. Numbers of electronic databases in the United States have been increasing at a near geometric rate. From a few hundred in the early 1980s, these information sources grew to more than 4,000 by 1990 with no end in sight. They range in scope from encyclopedic to profession- or subject-specific.

The best known of the encyclopedic databases include Nexis, Dialog, ABI/Inform, and ERIC. Profession-specific databases include sources such as Medline, which is dedicated exclusively to the health professions. Subject-specific databases include Baseline, which specializes in the entertainment industry.

No two databases are alike. Most include the content of one or more periodicals. Some offer full texts while others provide only abstracts. Some supplement periodical content with academic papers. Some are exclusively on-line services where users must capture information on their own computers. Others offer mail delivery as well.

Computer utilities. Some databases offer alternative access paths for users. All are accessible on a direct basis. Some make files available through so-called "gateway services" and others are accessible through computer utilities. Gateway services play a distributor role in the database world. They buy wholesale subscriptions to individual databases and sell retail subscriptions to consumers. Gateway services are especially attractive to low-volume users. Databases always impose subscription fees and often establish minimum monthly charges, but these charges usually do not apply to gateway service subscribers.

Computer utility features of most interest to communicators often include fast-growing rosters of special interest groups. Special interest group participants frequently are expert in their fields. Many computer hardware and software firms, for example, directly or indirectly support special interest groups composed of individuals who use their products. Questions about products or product applications usually produce detailed responses in a matter of hours.

With rare exceptions, however, neither analyses of information obtained through computer utilities nor use of the other techniques described above provide hard data. Some information may originate with experts in their fields but content is more often anecdotal than statistical. While informative and frequently valuable in communication, such information falls short of providing data necessary to analyze or track developing trends. Formal research usually is necessary to develop that level of precision.

FORMAL RESEARCH

Precision implies hard numbers; data generated through strictly applied principles of scientific research—formal research, as the term is understood by academics and scientists. Formal research can be undertaken in one of two forms: Primary and secondary. The primary form involves basic research; gathering and analyzing data to produce new knowledge. The secondary form involves applying and/or reanalyzing data developed in primary research.

Communicators are too little involved in primary research other than in academic pursuits. While primary research provides the most accurate measures of performance, organizational resources often preclude expensive and time-consuming surveys. Time factors can be prohibitive even if cost were no object. Practitioners usually require research results in a matter of weeks if not days. Time spans in primary research often are measured in months or years.

Some of the nation's largest public relations counseling firms contribute to client and employer willingness to accept less-than-adequate evidence of the results of communication. Ketchum Public Relations, for example, as late as 1990 was merchandising the Ketchum Tracking Model, a computer-based program designed to track and analyze media exposure. Ketchum apparently proceeds on the questionable assumption that messages distributed through the mass media necessarily produce change in recipient attitudes, opinions, and behaviors.

Secondary Research

Limited resources, coupled with the availability of valid data from existing sources, leads communicators to deal more extensively in secondary than in primary research. Secondary research involves reuse of primary or original data for new or different purposes. Re-analysis of Bureau of the Census data to project change in consumer behavior would fall into the secondary research category. So would re-examination of serial Gallup or Roper poll results to identify and project public opinion trends.

More complex analyses of data reported by those engaged in primary research also are common. Such analyses are more frequent in the physical sciences, however, than in communication and the social sciences.

Primary Research

Mass communication long has been said to suffer from lack of a base of primary research. Most theory used in mass communication is derived from other disciplines. Psychology, sociology, social psychology, anthropology, and economics all have contributed to mass communication. Mass communication theory has become a more popular academic pursuit in recent years but relatively few theoreticians have focused their efforts on public relations, advertising, and other relatively narrow subdisciplines.

These conditions are not unknown in younger disciplines and need not be overly troublesome to those engaged in developing and applying mass communication plans, programs, campaigns, special events, and crisis response systems. Practitioners in each area can reap significant benefits, however, from the research published in contemporary literature.

Historical research, consisting of analytical studies of mass communication problems and experiences, can be especially enlightening. Communication efforts that have produced exceptional results—good or bad—are worthy of special attention. Research accompanying or following disasters of various kinds is especially worthy of attention in that such incidents tend to reoccur. Retrospective studies of product tampering and political concealment cases can be equally enlightening. So can conditions surrounding oil and chemical spills, airliner crashes, and the like. Examined dispassionately by historians, cases of these types deserve special attention from practitioners in occupational settings that suggest potential for similar difficulties.

IN SUMMARY

Knowledge is a vital component of problem solving in communication. Bodies of knowledge required vary little with communication tasks. Planning, programming, and developing campaign, special event and crisis response plans require virtually identical knowledge bases. The ways in which knowledge and information needs are met differ, however, from one task to another.

Time and money are the primary task variables. Crisis responses are—or should be—managed in keeping with plans developed in anticipation of such problems. Time pressures are too intense to permit traditional planning. Campaigns, special event, plan, and program development pose different problems. Most campaigns and special events can be designed as far in advance as necessary to meet any reasonable time requirements. Communication planning and programming usually are conducted in annual cycles and create little time pressure.

Economic considerations are another matter. Plans, programs, and special events are controlled by detailed budgets. Campaigns, other than those of the political variety, which almost inevitably produce deficits, also are subject to rigid budgets. Budgets rarely exist for crisis communication but organizations seldom impose spending limitations when confronted with problems of crisis magnitude.

Potential for time problems demands that communicators maintain knowledge of their organizations, of stakeholder groups with which their organizations are involved, and of environmental factors that may influence organizations or stakeholders. Much of the information required is readily obtained through environmental assessment processes developed and maintained by individuals and organizations. Communicators, for example, should monitor media dealing with social and economic trends, with communication, and with employer or client industries. Organizations, in like fashion, should track events and trends that may influence the behaviors of consumers, employees, owners and other primary stakeholder groups.

Information gathered by client and employer organizations, by governmental agencies, and by business and trade associations is highly valuable in monitoring environmental trends. This information is readily supplemented through informal and formal research. The informal, once confined to traditional libraries, now extends to a host of electronic data bases through which detailed information is readily available on almost any conceivable topic. The formal includes primary as well as secondary research. Secondary research, involving analyses of data produced by others to create new insights into organizational environments and stakeholder groups, is more prevalent than the primary variety. Primary research is expensive in time and dollars and only rarely is undertaken in developing communication efforts. Most research in communication deals with monitoring attitude and opinion among stakeholder groups as campaigns progress and crises are resolved.

ADDITIONAL READING

Brody, E. W., and Gerald C. Stone. *Public Relations Research*. New York: Praeger, 1989.

Broom, Glen M., and David M. Dozier. *Using Research in Public Relations: Applications in Program Management*. Englewood Cliffs, NJ: Prentice-Hall, 1990.

Eisenhart, Tom. "Where To Go When You Need to Know," *Business Marketing*, 74 (November 1989).

Robinson, Edward J. *Public Relations and Survey Research*. New York: Appleton-Century-Crofts, 1969.

Settle, Robert B., and Pamela L. Alreck. *Why They Buy: American Consumers Inside and Out*. New York: Wiley, 1986.

Strasser, Susan. *Satisfaction Guaranteed: The Making of the American Mass Market*. New York: Pantheon, 1989.

6

Fundamental Planning Techniques

Productivity in mass communication is limited by two factors: the scope of planning processes and the extent to which communicators are involved in organizational planning. Success in communication compounds when the process begins at senior management levels and organizations "speak with one voice." Too many organizations nevertheless cling to traditional management systems that make communication a secondary or tertiary concern and deny communicators a part in strategic decision-making.

Strategic communication planning occurs where organizations follow models of the sort designed by Professor Melvin Anshen of Columbia University. The Anshen model (1974) is functionally similar to, but organizationally different from, the traditional four-step communication model. The Anshen process consists of seven steps: information gathering, information analysis, pre-planning, planning, assessment, communication, and what might be called management tutoring for spokesperson roles. Other than in the latter sector, Anshen departs from the traditional communication model in sequencing his steps but places the process at the senior management level.

Anshen's information-gathering and analysis steps parallel communication's research phase. His pre-planning and planning steps are comparable to planning in communication. The Anshen assessment and communication stages are identical to those used in communication other than in their sequencing. Close examination of Anshen's thinking reveals, however, that he considers assessment an on-going process.

COMMUNICATION MANAGEMENT

While consistent in many ways with communication's four-step process, Anshen's approach raises questions about that traditional model. Growing complexity in contemporary society and fast-changing needs among communicators' clients or employers suggests that something more is necessary. Satisfying those needs, according to Anshen, requires redefining the communication function to include:

1. Continuing monitoring and evaluation of social attitudes and expectations related to . . . the performance and behavior of organizations.
2. Continuing analysis of (a) the significance of social attitudes and expectations for existing and potential corporate policies or programs, and (b) specific actions that influence the reality and perception of organizational social performance.
3. Developing recommendations to maintain or change company policies and programs, and design of new policies and programs related to social performance.
4. Participating in corporate strategic planning, especially identifying social performance objectives and relationships between social and economic objectives, and developing strategies and programs to accomplish approved objectives.
5. Participating in the assessment of performance against targets and in amending plans and programs as part of continuing planning cycles.
6. Directing design and execution of communication to all relevant publics within and outside the corporation.
7. Preparing senior corporate officers and lower level managers for roles in communicating and interacting with stakeholders.

The Anshen model, then, would reposition communicators in management and involve them in shaping organizational policy and procedure. They would participate in organizational as well as communication policy-making. They would join in shaping environmental, behavioral, and qualitative as well as mediated and interpersonal communication.

Communicators, in Anshen's concept, gain two advantages critical to organizational and communication success. First, they are positioned to ensure consistency in communication. Second, they participate in shaping the exchanges or transactions in which organizations engage with all stakeholders. External pressures slowly but surely are turning organizational emphases toward the Anshen concept.

THE CHANGING PROCESS

Communication planning is changing in response to change in societies and organizations. Pressure for greater organizational responsiveness to stakeholder needs and expectations has produced radical change in traditional communication systems. Planning processes have become more complex, and are initiated earlier in organizational planning cycles.

Change in communication planning, which continues to accelerate, has been driven more by necessity than by far-sighted management. Changing socioeconomic, demographic, and political conditions have imposed unacceptable penalties on organizations that cling to traditional communication mechanisms. Risk created by potential conflict in messages originating from diverse sources has proven especially hazardous. In addition, traditional operational planning processes have proven inadequate to achieve strategic goals.

Emerging communication planning patterns concurrently address strategic and operational concerns although emphases are shifting from operational to strategic. Strategic communication is oriented toward what can best be described as relationship-building. Developing and maintaining relationships or mutual commitments between organizations and stakeholders is the primary purpose of strategic communication programming. Mutual commitment, manifested in loyalty, produces mutual benefits. As Patricia Sellers pointed out in *Fortune* magazines, satisfied employees produce satisfied customers, who spend more money and create more profits to enable the company to further enhance employee satisfaction. The cyclical process feeds on itself and is bi-directional, producing upward and downward spirals with equal ease.

Process Orientation

Strategic communication should address (a) the types of relationships that must exist between organizations and stakeholders if mutual objectives are to be achieved, and (b) the steps necessary to develop and/or maintain those relationships. Relationship building, in turn, is accomplished in keeping with social exchange theory and in light of a single question: What should be the characteristics and attributes of transactions between the organization and its stakeholders? Organizational managements, in other words, must look to stakeholders' needs and desires in designing transactions that will be mutually satisfying; that will contribute to durable relationships expressed in mutual satisfaction and mutual commitment.

Strategic plans are designed to create, maintain, or enhance relationships between organizations and stakeholders. The term relationships, as used here, involves more than is readily apparent. The word implies an on-going series of social transactions. Relationships can be positive, negative or nonexistent. Salutary relationships encourage stakeholders to continue the set of transactions. Negative relationships encourage discontinuation. Absence of relationships creates voids that can be filled by competitors.

The transactional nature of the process requires that the "communication" in strategic communication planning involve more than mediated and interpersonal tactics. Value can and should be added to transactions through other forms of communication. Strategic communication planning deals largely with environmental, behavioral, and qualitative message generators for two reasons. First, change in these areas rarely can be generated within the annual frameworks for which most operational plans are designed. Second, and more important, these changes are not the exclusive domain of communication. Multiple organizational components are involved in environmental, behavioral, and qualitative communication although few organizations deal with these factors in an organized manner. Environmental, behavioral, and qualitative messages are delivered more often by chance than design because these forms of communication rarely are recognized and more rarely are designated as managerial responsibilities.

Mediated and interpersonal messages developed and disseminated under operational communication plans nevertheless tend to succeed only to the extent that they conform to messages emanating from other sources. These conditions demand greater attention to the strategic component of the planning process.

The nature of strategic communication planning requires little of communicators beyond the research necessary to determine how environments, behaviors, and product or service quality are perceived by stakeholders. Senior management decisions then are necessary to address inconsistencies. Mediated and interpersonal communication efforts can be successfully designed only in keeping with known environmental, behavioral, and qualitative messages. These circumstances require close coordination of strategic and operational communication plans.

Strategic vs. Operational

Strategic communication planning is oriented primarily toward developing relationships between organizations and stakeholders that predispose stakeholders toward the organization. Operational communication, in contrast, is action-oriented. The objectives of operational communication are specified as stakeholder behaviors rather than predispositions. Sales, customer turnover, product quality, attendance, and similar outcomes are involved.

The emphases of strategic communication also are broader than those of the operational variety. Strategic communication planners are as concerned with messages transmitted by organizational environments, behaviors, and product/service quality as by interpersonal or mediated means. Much of strategic planning is dedicated to ensuring consistency across messages. Operational communication, in contrast, deals primarily with mediated and interpersonal channels. Strategic communication planners, like their corporate counterparts, take a longer, developmental view of organizational activities. Operational planners are concerned with the ensuing year. The processes often are not mutually exclusive. Most communication staffs are small. The same personnel often are involved in strategic and operational communication planning, and the two processes, as a result, often are blended into one extended effort.

Senior managements may or may not endorse or condone the extra effort required in strategic communication planning. The process is important to communicators, however, in that it illuminates potential problems and pitfalls that can create difficulties as plans are implemented. Generally accepted planning procedures, applicable in all cases, enhance the efficiency and effectiveness of resulting communication activities. Communication inherently is an uncertain process. Any precautions that minimize associated risks for communicators and their clients or employers therefore are worthwhile.

STRUCTURAL ALTERNATIVES

Planning based on the Anshen communication model produces superior results but exacts a price in complexity. Success in planning requires attention to all forms of communication although Professor Anshen was concerned primarily with the mediated and interpersonal. Incorporating environmental, behavioral, and qualitative information sources into strategic communication systems requires something more.

Strategic communication planning logically can be examined as a sort of framework or suprasystem designed to support a comprehensive planning process. The suprasystem must embrace communication in all forms as directed to all organizational stakeholder groups. Logic suggests, as a result, that the communication suprasystem consists of two subsystems dealing with messages and stakeholders.

Message Origins

Messages originate in the five sources identified earlier: environmental, behavioral, qualitative, interpersonal, and mediated. The message subsystem should address all of these sources, and planning should focus primarily on assuring consistency in message content. Quality promised in messages originating in the mediated sector must be supported by messages from the qualitative sector.

The message subsystem thus deals with the attributes of message sources that contribute to communication content. Environmental factors, for example, logically are sorted into interior and exterior categories to deal with both environments created by organizations for employees, customers and others. Internal environmental factors include elements such as decor, lighting, heating/air conditioning, and furnishings. Comparable factors exist in the external area.

Parallel approaches are applicable in dealing with behavioral, qualitative, interpersonal, and mediated communication. Each factor that influences messages *as received by members of stakeholder groups* must be addressed. Organizational and individual behaviors are examined, for example, as to their existing and prospective impacts. Change in policy and procedure may be necessary to alter organizational behavior. Re-orientation and retraining similarly may be required to conform personnel to new performance standards.

The message subsystem extends beyond traditional communication boundaries. Communicators, or others charged with parallel responsibilities, would be assigned responsibility for coherently managing messages that traditionally have been left uncontrolled. Organizations only recently have fully recognized the influences—negative or positive—that environments and behaviors exert. Few have taken steps to coherently manage the messages involved.

Pervasive neglect of messages other than the mediated and interpersonal is a product of traditional organizational management structures. Most organized communication efforts are assigned to one of several established communication disciplines: advertising, marketing, public relations, and sales promotion. None of them traditionally has been involved in nonmediated communication. Most of them, in addition, have been preoccupied in recent years with interdisciplinary competition.

The traditional disciplines, in addition, are strongly stakeholder-specific in orientations and methodologies. Advertising, and the communication component of marketing, are almost exclusively oriented toward consumers and mass media. Public relations embraces a broader set of stakeholders and channels but remains largely confined to the mediated arena. Sales promotion deals primarily with consumers through coupons, contests, and in-store promotions.

These strong disciplinary and media orientations often work to the disadvantage of organizations. Economy and efficiency require comprehensive communication efforts free of interdisciplinary conflicts and cross-disciplinary gaps.

Message Destinations

Organizations need comprehensive strategic planning and something more. Stakeholder-specific communication plans must be developed for employees, consumers, vendors, government, investors, and any other significant groups. Analyses of environmental, behavioral and qualitative factors—impact statements, in a sense—ideally are incorporated into every stakeholder-specific communication plan. In the alternative, environmental, behavioral, qualitative, interpersonal, and mediated communication plans can be designed with components oriented toward each stakeholder group. Planners must assess the potential contribution of each sector to organizational relationships with stakeholder groups. Integrated planning processes of this sort encourage communicators to ensure that mediated messages do not conflict with those originating elsewhere.

Knowledge of stakeholders and message sources enables planners also to ensure that resources are best applied to produce desired results. Resource allocation should be undertaken with one eye on message sources and the other on communication efforts that may be undertaken to achieve specific organizational objectives.

SEMANTIC PROBLEMS

One further step is necessary before planning begins. Communicators must establish uniform sets of labels and definitions for the processes with which they deal. Misleading labels too often are attached to mass communication projects. *Projects* refers to tasks of all kinds, from special events to long-term developmental efforts. Today's presumably more specific but nevertheless confusing labels result from attempts to differentiate between messages used in communication project development and management planning.

Planning methods in communication are almost identical to those used elsewhere. No rational purpose is served in mass communication by using *program* and *programming* as synonyms for *plan* and *planning*. This especially is the case because *program* is as often applied to components of an organization's communication effort as to the sum of those components. An organization's "communication program," as a result, may include a consumer communication program, an employee communication program, an investor communication program, and a vendor communication program. Governmental, media, industry, and other communication programs also are often found in larger organizations. Organizations' communication's programs thus appear to consist of programs, creating no little confusion.

Program, in this book, refers only to stakeholder-specific efforts; to consumer communication, employee communication, investor communication, and so forth. The sum of those programs is called a communication *plan*. More specifically, the sum of organizations' communication efforts will be described in the same terms used in management, as *plans*.

Communication Plans

Communication plans, like organizational plans, are of two types. The more common of the two is the *operational* communication plan. Operational communication plans encompass all of an organization's communication programs. Exceptions occur only where communication responsibilities are divided among operating units. Investor and employee communication, for example, occasionally are assigned to finance and human resources rather than communication departments.

Operational communication plans, designed and implemented in parallel with and in support of organizations' operational plans, usually are established on annual bases. *Strategic* communication plans parallel organizational strategic plans, usually covering five-year time spans. Strategic planning is a relatively new activity undertaken by growing numbers of organizations in response to rapid change in operating environments. Most strategic plans are brought up to date annually as operational plans are developed for ensuing years.

Communication plans—operational and strategic—consist of multiple programs. Programs usually are stakeholder-specific but may be oriented to message types. Communication programs could be as readily managed as behavioral, environmental, qualitative, interpersonal and mediated, in other words, as in stakeholder-specific form. Stakeholder-specific programs ideally consist of message-oriented components in the same way that message-oriented programs would consist of stakeholder-specific components. A consumer communication program, for example, might involve environmental, behavioral, qualitative, mediated and interpersonal components.

Each program consists of sets of strategies and tactics. Strategies are the techniques that communicators use to achieve their objectives. Strategies define the transactions or exchanges that communicators propose to encourage the development of salutary relationships. Strategies are implemented through one or more tactics or message delivery mechanisms.

Strategies and tactics are specified in greater detail as one moves "down the continuum" from strategic plan to operational plan and thence to program and project. Strategic plans, designed by senior managers to guide junior managers, often specify goals but rarely deal in strategies. In similar manner, junior managers may establish goals for subordinate supervisors but leave tactics to their discretion.

Strategies and tactics also are the basic components of other communication efforts, all of them essentially transactional in nature. Programs, campaigns, special events, and crisis response mechanisms all are included, although these terms, like planning, have become progressively less precise as mass communication has become more complex.

Programs

Consider, for example, the communication *program*. The word traditionally has been used in two ways: to refer to the annual operational communication plan and to identify stakeholder-specific components of the plan. Consumer, employee, vendor, investor and governmental communication *programs* are common. Each program consists of a set of activities undertaken over a period of 12 months, and designed to convey information to the specified stakeholder group.

Programs can be distinguished from plans in two ways. While plans deal with multiple stakeholder groups, programs are audience-specific. Programs also are more detailed, specifying strategies and tactics to be used. In most organizations, programs are components of organizational plans, in the same manner that communication programs are components of communication plans. Programs may be separately developed and implemented, however, where communication responsibilities are divided. Employee communication programming, for example, occasionally is assigned to a human resources department rather than to a communication department. The employee communication program then would be a component of the human resources operational plan.

Campaigns

Mass communication *campaigns* are similar to programs in that both consist of strategies and tactics. Campaigns usually are shorter in duration than programs but longer than special events. Membership, fund-raising, and election campaigns are typical. Most campaigns range in duration from weeks to months although national political campaigns can extend from one presidential election to the next. Campaigns can be free-standing, as in the case of a heart transplant fund-raising effort, or they can be embedded in organizations' communication programs, as is the case with annual membership campaigns.

Potential for confusion nevertheless exists, especially since issues managers declared themselves proprietors of a specialized discipline in the early 1980s. Issues managers lay claim to communication efforts that (a) have typical life spans of 18 to 36 months and (b) deal with issues amenable to legislative resolution. Projects of 18 to 36 months in duration usually would be considered campaigns. Other than where "issues" are involved, campaigns are predictable in duration and therefore can be planned in more-or-less leisurely fashion. Campaigns may be cyclical, as in the case of elections and some fund-raising efforts, or episodic, as with a campaign to build a new park or fund an organ transplant.

Special Events

Like campaigns, *special events* may be self-contained or organized as components of programs or campaigns. For organizations such as shopping malls, communication programs may consist of series of special events carried out over a period of months or on year around bases. Special events can be geographically isolated or world wide. They can be casually planned and executed by a single administrator or may require years in development by large planning staffs.

Special events can be as brief and as relatively simple as an awards luncheon and as lasting and complex as a World's Fair or exposition. Events in the latter category can continue for years, especially where planning and preparation time is included. Special events such as World's Fairs, national expositions, and the summer and winter Olympics require more planned communication than most campaigns.

Crisis Communication

Mass communication efforts associated with *crises* differ chrono-
logically from programs, campaigns, and special events. Other than in
crisis communication, implementation always follows planning. Crisis
communication plans, in contrast, are prepared far in advance of
potential crises that may never occur. Crisis communication plans are
developed on contingency bases to minimize the impact of worst case
problems. Crisis or disaster plans are created to guide responses to *all*
emergencies and are necessarily imprecise as a result. Managers
attempt to draft crisis response plans in terms so general as to make
them universally applicable. In the process, they sacrifice the level of
detail necessary to produce best results in handling specific problems.

Crises can develop in any of several forms. Some arise without
warning as natural or environmental disasters of unprecedented scope
or severity. Union Carbide's gas leak in Bhopal, which killed several
thousand, is exemplary of this sort of crisis. Other crises are at least
in part predictable, as was Exxon's mammoth Gulf of Alaska oil spill
in 1989. A spill of similar magnitude had occurred earlier off the coast
of France. The relative sensitivity of the Alaskan environment was the
only significant difference between the two.

Finally, there is the predictable disaster. Predictable disasters
befall organizations that fail to respond to changing environmental
conditions. By the late 1980s, for example, governmental and utility
executives were predicting that energy shortages would spread from
the northeast across the nation through the 1990s. The result may be
economic disasters for organizations that fail to prepare for "brown-
outs" or worse.

Crises are equally likely to occur as self-inflicted wounds of
several varieties. Legislative, regulatory, or other governmental
investigations that reveal illegal or unethical behavior by organizational executives can produce immediate and lasting damage. The
stripping away of organizational secrecy intended to conceal misconduct can be even more damaging. Real or publicly perceived disregard
for the public interest, as in inadequate testing of prescription drugs,
can produce similar conditions.

To summarize, plans, programs, campaigns, special events, and
crisis response mechanisms necessarily are interrelated. Programs are
components of plans. Campaigns usually are planned components of
programs. Special events may be program components but also can be
established as free-standing efforts. Crisis responses are contingent
components of plans or programs, supplanting or supplementing them
when disaster strikes. Crisis response mechanisms are triggered
automatically by disasters and, "for the duration," may supersede other

communication efforts. The extent to which routine activities are supplanted is governed by organizational size and resources. Transnational corporations such as the Dow Chemical Company may be able to marshal internal resources to meet crises without suspending ongoing programs. Most organizations, however, elect to supplement standing staffs with counselors in order to maintain on-going communication operations. Organizations may have communication plans, programs, campaigns, special events, and crisis response mechanisms operating concurrently in circumstances of this sort.

Diversity among activities that communicators are called upon to plan and execute is offset, however, by the fact that planning procedures follow a uniform pattern for most activities. Only crisis communication problems differ significantly from other varieties in that communicators must plan in anticipation of circumstances they will not be able to control. Communication planning in all cases is complex, however, and especially so where those involved adhere to emerging rather than traditional planning criteria.

Plan vs. Planning

The product of planning is a plan or plans—nothing more; nothing less. Organizational and communication plans are road maps; sets of strategies that planners believe will achieve communicators' objectives and organizational purposes. This concept is important because many in mass communication inadvertently sacrifice the structural and functional integrity of plans by concentrating too much on the creative aspects of communication. No volume of messages, no matter how creative, can adequately substitute for the inherent strengths of sound planning.

Planning processes defined by professionals such as Texas Medical Center Vice President Gerald Hickman, produce plans that universally encompass specific steps. These include, at minimum:

1. Developing a statement of purpose or goals defining what needs to be done and why.
2. Listing objectives, or steps that must be taken to achieve specified goals.
3. Assessing environmental factors bearing on problems, including their histories, the nature of groups involved, and group positions on pertinent issues.
4. Defining all assumptions concerning issues, allies, opponents, and outcomes.
5. Developing a critical assessment of plan potential and costs.

6. Establishing policies, procedures and responsibilities for implementation.
7. Determining strategies and tactics to be used in implementation.
8. Assigning tasks to individuals and/or organizational components. (1989, 353)

Planners occasionally will add one or more steps to the planning process but those listed above usually are considered essential. Budgets and production/execution timetables always are necessary, for example, but budgets usually are projected as part of plan assessment and timetables most often are established as tasks are assigned. Most other vital functions—research, implementation and assessment—are undertaken before planning begins or after planning has been completed. There exists, however, one significant exception: establishing the scope of the planning process.

THE PLANNING PROCESS

The planning process applies to all communication activities. Planning is essential to the success of programs, campaigns, special events, and crisis responses. Each requires a plan. Differences in plan development occur only because of ambiguities that confront planners in attempting to anticipate crises. Ambiguities prevent crisis response planners from achieving the level of detail normally incorporated into plans for other communication projects.

Uniformity in planning also is appropriate because the several types of communication projects are essentially similar. Plans, programs, campaigns, and special events vary primarily only in duration, intensity, and level of detail. Crisis responses differ only in that they are activated in response to external conditions rather than on specific dates.

Purpose and Goals

Communication rarely is considered a purpose or goal in the planning process. *Purpose* and *goal* refer instead to organizational purposes and goals, which must be understood before communication planning can begin. Communication purposes and goals are spelled out during planning, and are categorized as strategies and tactics in the second phase of the process. The statement of communication purpose and goals should:

1. Describe the organization's problem and the proposed solution.
2. Specify why the proposed solution is appropriate.

3. Identify stakeholder groups, their interests, and their preferred behaviors.
4. Describe the magnitude of the proposed communication effort.
5. Identify both organizational and communication goals.

While seemingly simple and straightforward, these steps demand more of planners than any other process component. Each requires communicators to reach beyond disciplinary boundaries to ensure that plans will succeed.

Problem and Solution. Problems must be stated objectively. Because most problems involve the perceptions of one or more stakeholder groups, and because perceptions often must be changed, existing perceptions must be known and accurately portrayed. Realities must be described with equal accuracy. Are the organization's service personnel uncaring or do they merely appear to be uncaring? Appropriate information can be obtained from any of several sources (see Chapter 5), but sound planning demands that information be candidly interpreted and reported.

Types and amounts of information available to communication planners vary with circumstances. Strategic communication planners seek guidance in organizations' philosophies, mission statements and strategic plans. They analyze this information with exhaustive data from external sources in developing plans to enhance organization-stakeholder relationships. Relationship-building through strategic communication planning is undertaken on long-term bases. Organizations' strategic plans usually involve five-year projections.

Where strategic communication efforts begin with strategic plans, operational efforts begin with annual plans. Operational programming focuses on current and succeeding years. Communicators analyze two sets of data in developing operational programs. The first set originates in current years' plans and is analyzed in keeping with two questions: What were the year's objectives and to what extent were they accomplished? Both questions are applied to organizational performance and communication performance. The second set of data, originating in plans for the succeeding year, also poses two questions: What objectives have been established by senior management for the organization, and what do those objectives imply as to communication needs?

Adequate delineation of communication plans requires detailed responses to six vital questions:

1. How is the organization perceived by members of key stakeholder groups?
2. How does the organization want to be perceived by those groups?
3. To what extent do perceptions among stakeholder groups match organizational realities?

4. What steps must the organization take to create the realities that management wants stakeholders to perceive?
5. What messages must be transmitted to stakeholders to inform them of the new realities?
6. What channels of communication should be used to transmit those messages?

More crudely put, the questions become: (a) what do we want of them; (b) what do we have do to be deserving of the specified response; (c) what steps must we take; and (d) how do we get the word out?

Appropriateness of goals. The process thus becomes inherently transactional. It involves designing a social exchange, or series of exchanges, between organization and stakeholder group members. Each exchange must be sufficiently satisfying to predispose individuals or organizations involved toward further exchanges.

Solutions inevitably require more than promises—on both sides. Organizations that seek mutually productive relationships must be prepared to address legitimate complaints, whatever their origins. Changes in environments, behaviors, and quality levels may be necessary to create the sort of equitable social exchanges that produce stakeholder loyalty. Where this is the case, those changes must be forthcoming. Communicators can honestly transmit appropriate messages only where deficiencies have been corrected, for only then will organizational performance have created adequate support for those messages.

Mutually satisfactory solutions to problems require equitable social exchanges. Exchanges or transactions must be fair and equitable. Values can be expressed environmentally or behaviorally, through comfortable facilities and attentive personnel or product or service quality, for these are valued organizational attributes. Nothing less than equitable transactions will suffice, however, and strategic purposes and objectives should be expressed in terms of stronger relationships rather than immediate stakeholders' responses.

Stakeholder characteristics. Analyses of goals require attention to stakeholder characteristics. Two sets of attributes or characteristics create behavioral predispositions among stakeholders. The first consists of the nature and strength of their relationships with organizations. The second includes demographic, psychographic, and sociocultural factors often used by sales-oriented communicators.

In keeping with social exchange theory, experience outweighs messages in influencing promises. Recipients tend to believe or disbelieve messages, and to engage or not engage in social transactions based on past experiences. To the extent that organizational welfare depends on serial rather than individual transactions, relationships and strategic communication planning increase in importance. The reputations of retail stores and restaurants, for example, are vital to their success. Every exchange or transaction is critical. The greetings of sales clerks and waiters, the cleanliness and comfort of surroundings, quality of products and services, and after-the-sale support all contribute satisfaction or dissatisfaction.

Relationships usually play a small part, in contrast, in consumer decisions concerning entertainment. Purchases of tickets to carnivals or rock music concerts are influenced more by sociocultural characteristics than other factors. Unsatisfactory social exchanges are of little significance to carnival operators and concert promoters because their shows will not soon play the same community again. Communication planning, in these conditions, is almost entirely operational in nature. Communicators are responsible primarily for persuasively informing prospective ticket buyers of forthcoming events.

The predispositions of stakeholder groups must be considered in the planning process. Potential responses from each group must be identified, and proposed solutions at times must be modified to create mutually advantageous transactions.

Defining the effort. Transactional analyses also serve communicators in making preliminary estimates as to the scope and cost of efforts necessary to achieve specified goals. Planners must submit estimates as to the magnitude of projects, anticipated costs, and expected benefits. Itemizing goals that can be achieved and benefits that will result also helps in organizational decision-making processes. Decisions are made, for the most part, on the basis of cost-benefit analyses. Executives elect to execute those plans that will produce the greatest return on required investments.

Specifying Objectives

When project purposes have been fully defined, planners turn to developing lists of objectives. An *objective* is a statement of a task to be accomplished. The objective statement specifies (a) what activity will be undertaken, (b) when it will be undertaken, (c) by whom it will be undertaken, and (d) what results will be achieved. Objectives *always* must be stated so that benefits are expressed clearly and in measurable terms. Measurability is necessary in order that results can be precisely assessed.

Implementing communication plans requires organization and resources, and more may be needed in specific circumstances. Intergroup alliances, for example, often are necessary to achieve political or legislative objectives. Coalition-building, frequently used in governmental affairs, also is applicable in other activities. Special events rarely can be readily executed without cooperation and support from many individuals and organizations. Effective crisis response plans are even more dependent on the support of public agencies. Those who specify communication objectives therefore always list organizations or agencies whose support or neutrality is necessary to success.

Other resources consist for the most part of organizational support and funding. Organizational support may include assistance from other departments as well as temporary assignment of additional personnel, equipment, and facilities to the communication department for the duration of the effort.

In specifying objectives, planners identify necessary sources of support, internal and external, and define the ways these resources will be used. Definitions must include timetables or sequences of events in adequate detail to enable decision makers to satisfy themselves that the project is practical.

Environmental Assessment

The comprehensiveness of environmental assessment, a process commonly used in a subspecialty of public relations called issues management, commends its use in communication planning. Planners' knowledge of circumstances with which they are dealing must be as complete as possible. The origins of conditions or trends that may produce change in stakeholder attitude and opinion, for example, are as important as improvement or deterioration in those areas. Equally detailed information is necessary concerning issues, organizations, and individuals that may be directly or indirectly involved in problems at hand.

Three elements are critical: accurate information concerning the status of the problem; a history of the problem encompassing individuals and groups involved and the arguments they have used; and an insight into the predispositions of those involved, especially to the extent that those predispositions may bias or prejudice statements or behaviors.

Organizational records, attitude/opinion studies, published information, and insights from involved professionals such as attorneys or accountants all can provide insight into communication problems. Every informational resource, from computer utilities and databases to professional or trade associations, should be used to develop accurate assessments for planners and those who will use their plans.

Examining Assumptions

The road to communication disaster is paved with tenuous assumptions. Disasters can be triggered by any significant difference between expectations and the realities communicators encounter as plans are implemented. Differences can arise in any number of areas that communicators neglect at great peril.

The words, "but I thought they would . . ." well could be engraved on a common tombstone for inept planners. Success and failure in planning, and especially in communication planning, are governed by the accuracy of planners' assumptions.

Those assumptions deal with individuals, organizations, media, and messages. Overly-optimistic estimates as to the attributes of senior managers and their potential behavior "under fire," for example, can produce disasters in news conferences. Assumptions as to the behaviors of senior managers and potential allies can be equally disastrous. Expectations that organizations known for liberal views will behave accordingly have created disasters, for example, for those attempting to establish labor organizations. Assumptions concerning media support often fail to materialize for politician, and speakers' estimates of audience ability to absorb and comprehend complex issues have proven only marginally better.

In general, communication planners are best served by conservative analyses of all assumptions. The same approach is advisable in developing assessments of project potential and, even more importantly, in developing project budgets.

Critical Assessments

The assessment process is based on a recapitulation of all information gathered, all assumptions evaluated, and all costs projected. These factors are synthesized to produce three components of the completed plan:

1. A summary of objectives, environmental data and assumptions.
2. A review of positive and negative factors that can be expected to influence the outcome of the project.
3. An estimate covering
   a. What realistically can be accomplished,
   b. costs involved, and
   c. whether the costs can be justified.

Communicator ability is most tested in evaluating assumptions and rendering judgments as to project potential. Clients and employers do not like to be told that their goals can not be achieved, or can be accomplished only at great expense. They are entitled to planners' best judgments before they commit themselves or their organizations to the considerable expense involved in communication projects, however, and planners are ethically bound to provide those judgments, "warts and all." Failure to protect a client or employer from error can be as damaging to the career of a planner or communicator as to the organization involved.

Policies and Procedures

Recommendations incorporated into the plan also should include operational steps necessary to achieve success. Provision must be made to control communication processes, especially in large organizations and most especially where organizations operate in several locations.

Many organizations' policies are adequate to handle almost any communication project. Others operate on ad hoc bases that can prove troublesome under added burdens. Planners' policy and procedural recommendations, for these reasons, often include critical assessments of existing communication systems and alternatives.

At least three alternatives exist through which organizations can ensure against unnecessary difficulties while communication plans are implemented. Where projects are expected to cover extended periods, internal staffs may be temporarily expanded. Counseling firms also may be called upon to supplement organizational communication staffs. Only rarely can major projects be undertaken without additional resources.

Strategies and Tactics

Finally, the communication plan must deal with communication, specifically the nature of messages and media. Most plans provide considerable detail concerning questions of language, types of strategies—aggressive versus conservative—and communication channels to be used. Strategies and tactics will be discussed in detail in Chapter 8.

Channel selection becomes progressively more difficult as media increase in numbers and their audiences deteriorate in size. Communication plans require recommendations as to whether projects should use paid as well as unpaid media, and as to how specific audiences should be contacted. More and more plans include audience analyses incorporating specific media recommendations.

IN SUMMARY

Planning, and the extent to which communicators are involved in planning, govern the success of organizations' communication efforts. Communication is predisposed to succeed where organizations follow patterns similar to that prescribed by Columbia University Professor Melvin Anshen. Anshen's model is functionally similar to, but organizational different from, the traditional four-step communication process. He positions communication planning at the senior management level but incorporates spokesperson training into the model.

Organizations slowly are installing communication systems patterned after the Anshen model in response to external pressures. Most embrace strategic as well as operational communication planning, orienting the former toward building relationships with stakeholders and the latter toward message delivery. Structurally communication plans can be subdivided into stakeholder-oriented or message-oriented programs. Traditional program design is stakeholder-oriented, with programs designed for consumers, employees, investors, and so forth. Environmental, behavioral, qualitative, interpersonal and mediated components readily can be developed within stakeholder-specific programs. In the alternative, programming can be structured by message source with stakeholder-specific components developed in terms of each message source.

Whichever approach is taken, uniformity in terminology is essential. Logic suggests using the words *plan* and *planning*, strategic and operational, in keeping with traditional business practices. Stakeholder- or message-specific components of plans then are referred to as *programs*. Plans may or may not extend below the program level to specify strategies and tactics, but strategies and tactics always are specified as program components.

Strategies and tactics also are the primary components of campaigns, special events, and crisis communication responses. Campaigns are similar to programs but of shorter duration. They can be free-standing operational units or may be incorporated into plans or programs. Special events usually are of still shorter duration and also can be developed independently or as components of plans, programs, or campaigns. Crisis response mechanisms depart from these norms in two respects. Crisis responses are designed to be implemented in the event of disaster. Programs, campaigns, and special events are developed for implementation on predetermined schedules. Because they must be generic in order to cover every conceivable eventuality, crisis response system designs are not situation-specific. Programs, campaigns, and special events, in contrast, are prepared in complete detail in response to known conditions.

All communication projects require plans, however, and the planning process is designed to produce those plans. Plans are road maps; sets of strategies and tactics that planners believe will achieve specified objectives. They universally involve these steps:

1. Developing a statement of purpose or goals defining what needs to be done and why.
2. Listing objectives, or steps that must be taken to achieve specified goals.
3. Assessing environmental factors bearing on problems, including their histories, the nature of groups involved, and group positions on pertinent issues.
4. Defining all assumptions concerning issues, allies, opponents, and outcomes.
5. Developing a critical assessment of plan potential and costs.
6. Establishing policies, procedures and responsibilities for implementation.
7. Determining strategies and tactics to be used in implementation.
8. Assigning tasks to individuals and/or organizational components.

Followed regardless of the nature of the problem at hand, these steps demand more of planners than any other component of the communication process.

ADDITIONAL READING

Anshen, Melvin, ed. *Managing the Socially Responsible Corporation.* New York: Macmillan, 1974.

_____. *Corporate Strategies for Social Performance.* New York: Columbia University Press, 1980.

Atkin, Charles R., "Mass Media Information Campaign Effectiveness." In Ronald Rice and William Paisley, eds., *Public Communication Campaigns.*. Beverly Hills, CA: Sage, 1981.

Baker, Frank, ed. *Organization PR/Systems: General Systems Approaches to Complex Organizations.* Homewood, IL: Richard D. Irwin, 1973.

Gray, James G., Jr., *Managing the Corporate Image: The Key to Public Trust.* Westport, CT: Greenwood, 1986.

Greene, Charles N., Everett E. Adam, Jr., and Ronald O. Ebert. *Management for Effective Performance.* Englewood Cliffs, NJ: 1985.

Greenwood, William T. *Issues in Business and Society.* 3rd. ed. Boston: Houghton Mifflin, 1977.

Haley, Russell I. *Developing Effective Communications Strategy: A Benefit Segmentation Approach.* New York: Wiley, 1985.

Hickman, Gerald, "Analyzing and Developing a Public Relations Strategy," In Chester Burger, ed., *Experts in Action: Inside Public Relations*, 2nd. ed., New York: Longman, 1989.

Nanus, Burt, and Craig Lundberg, "In Quest of Strategic Planning," *Cornell H.R.A. Quarterly*, (August, 1988).

"In New Decade of Personalized Relationships & Communication, Changes in Techniques, Strategies & Practitioner Attitudes are Predictable: How to Reach Thousands or Millions Personally?" *pr reporter*, (January 1, 1990).

Preston, Lee E., and James E. Post. *Private Management and Public Policy: The Principle of Public Responsibility*. Englewood Cliffs, NJ: Prentice-Hall, 1975.

Sellers, Patricia, "What Customers Really Want," *Fortune*, (June 4, 1990).

Steckmest, Francis W. *Corporate Performance: The Key to Public Trust*. New York: McGraw-Hill, 1982.

7

The Programming Process

The nature and complexity of communication programming are governed by organizational planning processes. All steps necessary to communication planning must be incorporated into communication program development in the absence of an appropriate planning process. Where planning has produced rational bases for social exchange, and where organizations have acted to ensure that environmental, behavioral, and qualitative messages are consistent with proposed interpersonal and mediated messages, programming is readily accomplished. Programming becomes more complex and more difficult in the absence of comprehensive planning. All factors otherwise incorporated into planning (see Chapter 6) must be addressed in developing the communication program.

Where strategic and operational communication plans are completed, programming efforts can be focused on the four-step mass communication sequence: research, planning, implementation, and assessment. Much of the information necessary to that process usually is accumulated and analyzed in the course of planning. Program design and implementation nevertheless are demanding because of continuing change in societies, audiences, and media.

Programs are stakeholder-specific. They specify communication goals and objectives in terms of specific groups, as in the case of consumer communication, employee communication, and so forth. Programs tend to be most cohesive, coherent and productive where they are organized within guidelines of established plans and where they are attuned to the needs of organizations and their stakeholders.

Programs usually deteriorate in effectiveness where they are established and conducted independently of one another. This often is the
case where, for example, the sales department is responsible for
consumer communication and the human resources department
manages employee communication.

Insensitivity to contemporary realities also can create problems.
Successes communicators once enjoyed as corporate cosmeticians have
become progressively more rare due in part to social change and in
part to changing expectations of communication. Communicators'
responsibilities no longer are considered fulfilled with message
transmission. Today's organizations expect measurable behavioral
results among designated stakeholder groups in return for their
communication investments. The results of communication cannot be
adequately measured in media exposure no matter how sophisticated
the measuring system or computer program involved. Employers and
clients count results in sales or votes.

The four-step communication process, as applied in programming,
is more accurately perceived as requiring answers to six questions:

1. What stakeholders are involved?
2. What behaviors are sought of those stakeholders?
3. What messages must be sent to induce those behaviors?
4. What must the organization do to validate those messages?
5. What communication channels will be most efficient in delivering
   the messages?
6. How will results be measured?

These questions reflect communicators' sequential interest in the
three primary variables in the communication process: audience,
medium, and message. Accurate responses are vital to communicator
success. No single variable is most important. Audience characteristics
are as important in message design as in channel selection.

ANALYZING STAKEHOLDERS

Communicator preoccupation with audiences is a logical outcome of
the process. Knowledge of audiences is vital in designing messages and
selecting media to produce the best possible results. No two audiences
are alike. No two will respond equally to the same message, and no
two can be reached in equal numbers by the same media. Small
differences, in addition, can produce major changes in program results.

Audiences or stakeholder groups can be analyzed in any number of
ways. Sophisticated demographic and psychographic analyses are

common in communication subdisciplines such as advertising, marketing and public relations. Individual behavioral tendencies, from media habits to consumption patterns, can be predicted with considerable accuracy by examining group members by age, sex, occupation, place of residence, income level, and so forth.

Issue Analyses

Audiences are most readily analyzed, however, in terms of their interests in issues. A complete and accurate response to a single question usually is sufficient to identify the parties to any issue: What groups' interests are involved? Consider, for example, something as simple as proposed issuance of a retail beer sales permit to a corner grocery. Although varying with the nature of the neighborhood, the issue will engage the interests of:

1. Customers of the sponsoring business and others in the neighbor hood, who may or may not find alcoholic beverages objectionable.
2. Owners of the business, who must be assumed to be seeking greater profits.
3. Employees of the business, who may be concerned over changing clienteles or interested in potential for greater wages.
4. Owners and occupants of residences in the immediate vicinity, who will be concerned over noise and debris.
5. Owners of nearby businesses, whose customers also might be influenced by the noise and debris.
6. Parents of children whose paths might take them past the store en route to and from school.
7. Clergymen who, because of their opposition to the use of alcohol, automatically oppose any increase in retail access.
8. Educators at the nearby school who would be concerned over the welfare of their students.
9. Law enforcement officers who might be called upon to deal with inebriated customers.
10. Members of pressure groups from Mothers Against Drunk Driving to the American Christian Temperance Union.
11. Alcoholic beverage distributors, whose sales and profits would be expected to increase with issuance of the permit.
12. Elected and/or appointed public officials who will have to make a decision on the permit application and whose political well-being may be influenced accordingly.
13. Representatives of regulatory agencies that subsequently would be responsible for monitoring the licensed establishment.

All of these groups are important from a communication standpoint in that their direct or indirect responses to the application will influence the decision of elected or appointed officials who issue alcoholic beverage permits. Office holders tend to behave in much the same manner as voters. Where those who go to the ballot box usually "vote their pocketbooks," officeholders tend to count votes rather than dollars. They usually handle all issues in a manner that will produce the most votes at the next election.

Other Factors

Stakeholder predispositions on specific issues also can deduced by examining the interests of those involved. More information ultimately is needed, however, in selecting communication channels and fashioning appropriate messages. This information can be obtained only through research of one sort or another.

Research in connection with communication problems deals with issues and groups involved. Knowledge of stakeholder interests helps communicators create effective messages. Information about group characteristics provides insights that help in selecting communication channels.

If the store seeking the beer permit is in a neighborhood consisting primarily of young marrieds in low- to middle-income groups, resistance is apt to be lower than in an area dominated by young professionals with children. Communication channels and messages must be adjusted to address the implied interests of the groups involved.

Where issues are more pervasive, as in the environmental sector, even more information is readily available. The objectives, strategies, and tactics of organizations such as Greenpeace and the Sierra Club, for example, have been well-documented by the media. A computer search of any of several databases yields a wealth of information for communicators whose clients or employers find themselves at cross purposes with these organizations. The same is true where employers and unions are in conflict. Considerable information in annual reports to the Federal government is available to any citizen under the Freedom of Information Act.

Significance of Analyses

Knowledge of groups' interests and activities thus leads to helpful information as to their potential behaviors in specific circumstances. Close examinations of group characteristics also can suggest ways in which predispositions may be modified.

Those seeking the beer sales permit, for example, could minimize potential for opposition among specific stakeholder groups in any of several ways. Alcohol might be sold for off-premises consumption only, for example, to address the concerns of parents and educational authorities. An especially rigorous identification system might be installed to ensure that no sales would be made to minors. The off-premises provision also would limit potential for noise, and for debris in the neighborhood. Conditions might be attached to the license application, in other words, that would make the transaction less objectionable to other interested parties.

Potential compromises are important because clients and employers are entitled to communicators' best estimates as to the extent to which campaigns can succeed. Communicator accountability for results also militates toward candid assessment of success potential.

SPECIFYING BEHAVIORS

Accountability implies that results of communication must be measurable. More important, accountability demands that success must be defined before implementation begins. Communicators and their employers must agree as to what is to be accomplished, and as to definitions of success.

Goal setting involves applying research results in negotiating definitions of success. In the beer permit case, for example, research might demonstrate that success is unlikely unless the applicant makes concessions as to sales hours, off-premises consumption, and buyer identification. A communicator retained by the applicant then would have to make it clear that no amount of communication is apt to produce a permit unless the concessions are made—unless the proposed transaction is modified.

The same rationale prevails in election campaigns. Popular misconceptions notwithstanding, many political campaigns are not expected to produce victory. Incumbents may be too well-entrenched. Challengers may be too inexperienced. The timing may be wrong. Communicators on losing sides can "succeed," however, where the communication objective is defined as a predetermined percentage of the vote, or enhanced name recognition for a political novice intent on preparing for a second campaign rather than winning than the first. These steps are especially important where program development is undertaken in the absence of a comprehensive communication plan. Communicators then must accomplish two objectives in specifying behaviors. They must define transactions that social exchange theory suggests will produce desired results, and then negotiate definitions of success based on proposed transactions.

Defining Transactions

To achieve objectives, communicators assume ombudsman roles in defining transactions to be incorporated into messages for stakeholders. The process can be demanding in the absence of a communication plan. Programmers then must specify (a) the behavioral outcomes they expect to achieve and (b) the conditions they consider prerequisite to achieve those objectives. Both sides of the social exchange must be clearly defined.

Consider, for example, a communication program designed to reduce absenteeism, tardiness, and turnover rates among company personnel. The fact that those indirect indicators of morale are high suggests underlying problems. Research would demonstrate the extent to which underlying dissatisfaction has been created by environments, behaviors, quality of leadership, or other factors. Other than in rare cases where problems are perceived rather than real, communication alone will not produce results. Change in employee behavior can be prompted only through change in the on-going series of transactions between the organization and its personnel. Improvements in wages, benefits, supervision, working conditions, and other factors may be necessary.

Only when proposed exchanges have been modified can communicators fashion messages sufficiently persuasive to produce change in employee behavior. And only when employees behave as specified will communicators be considered to have achieved their objectives.

Producing Results

To produce results acceptable to managers or clients, then, communicators couple research to analytical and negotiating techniques to define and win acceptance for fair and equitable transactions. Research in this case would have required a series of steps:

1. Employee surveys to determine causes of unsatisfactory transactions that were producing poor performance.
2. Negotiations with organizational managers to change transsactions (policies, procedures, behaviors), making them more acceptable to personnel.
3. Communicating the revised terms to employees.

Only when these steps are completed can behavior be expected to change, and only then will the communication process have succeeded.

Two further points must be made concerning definitions of success. First, definitions must be precise. Ideally, they should be expressed numerically, in percentages or raw numbers. "Reduced absenteeism" is more ambiguous than "a 20 percent reduction in absenteeism." After-the-fact disagreements over program success are unlikely where management agrees in advance that a 20 percent reduction in absenteeism will constitute "success."

Second, success must be measurable in economic terms. A single question is involved: Will anticipated benefits be adequate to justify costs? The programming process requires that budgets be prepared with sufficient precision and detail to permit decisions based on costs and benefits. Budgets, as discussed in more detail in Chapter 11, also are required in developing campaign and special events. Budgets are rarely developed as components of crisis response plans because of their inherent ambiguities.

MESSAGE CONTENT

While programs and budgets are necessary in communication, success and failure ultimately are governed more by message content than any other factor. The words "success," "failure," and "message content," however, require careful use. Short-term success and long-term disaster too often are joint products of mediated or interpersonal messages where content conflicts with messages from other sources.

Conflicting messages can produce desired responses while destroying potential relationships. That's precisely what happens where products fail to perform as promised, where employers fail to fulfill promises to employees, or where organizations fail to meet implied or explicit commitments to the public welfare. It's as easy in communication as in medicine to have a successful operation and a dead patient.

Organizational reality—environmental, behavioral, and qualitative—creates the essence of messages. Manufacturer action alone, in the form of product quality, design, price, and other factors valued by consumers, can create the "best deal" for auto buyers. Communicators can embellish realities with appropriate language but messages *never* should mislead recipients.

Successful communicators produce behavioral responses by using only those appeals that will be validated by organizational performance. Unfulfilled promises—implied or implicit—destroy the effectiveness of subsequent communication. Failure to use every appeal validated by performance, on the other hand, weakens potential for stakeholder response. These conditions require that communicators pursue one of three basic strategies in program development.

1. Shape organizational environments and behaviors to create realities that will support proposed messages.
2. Fashion messages that reflect the organization as it exists regardless of whether those messages will produce desired stakeholder behaviors.
3. Make sufficient changes in the organization and/or its products or services validate messages of sufficient strength to produce required behaviors.

Communicators have two responsibilities in connection with these options. First, they are obligated to provide their best estimates as to what behaviors are necessary to induce desired response. When management decisions have been made, communicators are further obligated to present only the resulting reality—nothing more and nothing less—in messages to stakeholders. These standards—especially the latter—are not always easily followed. There remain in the business community too many senior managers whose fields of vision extend only to the bottom line for the current quarter.

Developing message content in a programming situation may be accomplished with considerable difficulty or relative ease. The process is easily completed where comprehensive planning already has addressed matters of social exchange and message consistency. Otherwise, these tasks must be completed during programming.

Message Development

Messages should call attention to the most attractive attributes of environments, behaviors, and products or services. More specifically, messages should reflect relative advantages that every organization enjoys in one or more of those areas. Messages should underscore areas in which sponsoring organizations excel.

Developing messages from masses of available information is not an easy task, especially for communicators employed by organizations involved. Employees too often are caught up in the cultures and mythologies of organizations they serve. Their perceptions then become so distorted as to be valueless in assessing organizational attributes for communication purposes.

Breaking out of perceptual traps is not difficult, however, for those committed to best serving employers. Communicators must avoid being overly socialized. They must maintain emotional detachment at all costs. "My country right or wrong" may be an admirable manifestation of patriotism but, "my organization right or wrong" implies professional malfeasance. Communicators must see their organizations from the perspectives of consumers and competitors. They must recognize and accept relative strengths and weaknesses in order to adjust messages accordingly.

Capitalizing on strengths and minimizing the impact of weaknesses is accomplished in one of two ways. The first, as described in Chapter 6, involves deliberately creating advantages and incorporating them into proposed transactions. The alternative, probably more often used, involves identifying and exploiting organizational strengths and competitor weaknesses.

"The competition" may be nothing more than inertia on the part of target audiences, but "strengths and weaknesses approaches" are always applicable. They apply in competitive circumstances and they apply in media selection, as discussed below. Innovative communicators find ways to overcome communication as well as message barriers.

Laziness and lack of originality are the primary barriers to identifying strengths and weaknesses. The information communicators require always is available through research, but usually can be obtained more easily and economically merely by asking. Organizational strengths and weaknesses almost always are known. Design and development, engineering and quality control department personnel almost invariably are well aware of relative product quality in manufacturing organizations. Those who do the selling are equally knowledgeable in sales-oriented organizations. They deal with the relative attributes of their products and those of competitors on day-to-day bases. They must overcome reality-based as well as perceptually-based disadvantages in order to meet sales quotas.

Sales and marketing departments are informational gold mines for communicators. Every organization has a sales or a marketing department under one name or another. In a professional association, it's the membership department. In a charitable organization, it's the fundraising unit. In a governmental agency, it's the group responsible for legislative relations. Everyone is selling something, and those who do the selling have the competitive information that communicators require.

That information is important because it's the heart of what those in sales and marketing call the "unique selling proposition." That's the attribute or benefit available only through the product or service offered by the communicator's organization. Each such attribute or benefit can be fashioned into a "superiority statement" that becomes the heart of mediated messages. Superiority statements are demonstrably honest claims that serve as foundations for ethical and effective selling messages. They are statements that (a) cannot be successfully countered by competitors and (b) provide powerful inducements to recipients to behave as sponsors require. No more than a few such

statements are needed. Often, and especially in advertising, only one
is necessary.

Reducing a message to the precise phraseology necessary for a
specific medium, given an honest statement of superiority, is a
relatively easy task. The message must be expressed in terms
meaningful to the audience and suitable to the medium. Brilliance is
not only unnecessary but undesirable. Potential for successful
communication declines where prospective consumers pause to marvel
over the verbal adroitness of copy writers. Time spent preparing such
written or verbal pearls usually is better expended in ensuring that
the prerequisites to successful communication are met.

PREREQUISITE ACTIONS

Fair social exchange and message consistency are the primary
prerequisites. Both must be established before communication
programs can be successfully implemented. Inequitable or otherwise
unacceptable realities that threaten successful completion of social
exchanges or transactions must be changed before mediated and
interpersonal communication begin.

In the employee communication situation discussed above, working
conditions would have to be corrected and supervisory behaviors
changed before a communication program could succeed. The same
approach is necessary regardless of the stakeholder group involved.

Communication is doubly difficult where behavior over time has
created pervasive distrust. Domestic auto manufacturers in 1990
demonstrated total misunderstanding of this concept. Their claims to
be "building cars just as good as the Japanese" were pitted against a
decade-long record of technical inferiority and customer dissatisfaction.
The claims may have been true. If they were, insufficient time had not
elapsed to permit their being validated through consumer experience.
If they were not, and reports from objective testing organizations
suggested this was the case, the ultimate result would be still further
losses.

Honesty is prerequisite to long-term success in communication. If
reality makes honesty unacceptable, reality must be changed to
validate the messages that organizations want to send. The auto
makers' claims were contradicted by independent quality assessment
reports. The result, in all likelihood, was further deterioration, rather
than improvement, in the manufacturers' reputation for quality.

These conditions underscore communicator need for message
consistency. Reality today is such that it would be only slightly

exaggerating to say that communication serves largely as an accelerator, drawing attention more rapidly than otherwise would be the case to good and bad alike. Good and bad products ultimately succeed or fail on their merits. Mediated communication can do little more than speed up the process.

The dynamics of contemporary market places nevertheless encourage extensive use of mediated communication. Those unaware of products or services are unlikely to buy. That fact, coupled with incremental profits that develop with increased patronage, generate a rising volume of communication, mediated and otherwise.

More and more organizations nevertheless are spending larger percentages of their resources on maintaining existing relationships than in attempting to build new ones. Their efforts are based on the premise that it's easier (and more profitable) to keep a customer happy (i.e., to maintain a salutary relationship) than to find a new one (i.e., create a new relationship). Why else would a mail order company, having rectified an error, expend the time and effort necessary to send an individually typed, personally signed letter of apology to a customer? That process is standard procedure for Norm Thompson, (a Portland, Oregon catalog marketer), even when transactions are so small that the cost of a letter turns a small profit into a loss.

Most in merchandising long ago found that it's easier to sell additional products or services to existing customers than to establish new accounts. That circumstance, coupled with the fact that the population of the United States is approaching zero growth, encourages more personalized communication. Relationships are growing progressively more valuable.

COMMUNICATION CHANNELS

The changing nature of mass media and their audiences, more than other factors, are driving communicators toward alternative communication channels. Three major trends are involved. Media audiences are deteriorating in size. The informational content of the media is being supplanted by entertainment-oriented material. Finally, media audiences are better-educated and more discriminating in their use of information.

The nature of these phenomena is important to communicators seeking to convey information effectively and efficiently to diverse populations. Audience declines are a product of media proliferation that developed in two stages. First, numbers of media serving specific communities and audience segments multiplied. Then, new media sprung up to compete with the old.

Change in media content has been less obvious but is no less real. Media executives competing for readers and viewers defend a content emphasis trend away from information and toward entertainment. They argue that content is shaped to meet reader and viewer standards; that they are merely responding to market conditions. The market, however, consists of generally better-educated readers and viewers who more often find cause to question mass media credibility. Collectively, these circumstances produce erosion in mass media efficiency and drive communicators' continuing searches for alternative channels.

Media and Audiences

Change in audiences has been produced by increases in numbers of media outlets in print and electronic sectors. While daily newspapers declined in number, weeklies increased. Advancing technology spawned *USA Today*, and enabled the *The Wall Street Journal* and *The New York Times* to move into national distribution. At the same time, numbers of magazines increased sharply. The mass circulation magazines of the mid-1900s went into decline but specialized magazines grew explosively in number. Annual net increases in numbers of magazines totaled more than 300 for much of the second half of the century.

The same patterns prevailed in the electronic sector, especially in television. Television networks first encountered competition in major markets from independent stations. Cable systems then came into being, and where consumers suddenly had 30 to 50 rather than three to five or six channels at their disposal.

In each case, average audience size declined. Daily newspapers lost circulation. A shakeout in magazines developed in 1990. And the major television networks that once commanded 90 percent of their markets were happy to share 30 percent among them. In addition, as the new century dawned, there was developing what *American Demographics* senior editor Blayne Cutler (1990) called "the fifth medium."

On-line interactive information and entertainment is "a new medium . . . that may be more powerful than newspapers, magazines and television put together," Cutler wrote in 1990 (24). Combining facsimile, computer, answering machine, stereo, and videocassette recorder technologies, the new medium will enable merchants to offer merchandise, make the sale and arrange for payment in their customers' homes.

These conditions will demand even greater precision in message delivery. One daily newspaper and two of three network television stations once were sufficient to deliver the bulk of a market population to advertisers. These same media now count fewer than half of the residents of the typical community among their audiences. The results are evident in the explosive growth in sales promotion. More and more advertisers are retaining sales promotion agencies in addition to advertising agencies to manage a growing volume of coupons, in-store promotions, and other message delivery systems.

Complex Choices

The primary question communication programmers encounter, in light of these conditions, is simple: What medium will do the best job? The answer is complex. The best medium is the medium that reaches the greatest percentage of the target audience. Since most communication programming deals with relatively narrow audiences, traditional mass media rarely are communicators' first choices.

Few communication programs are directed toward the entire population of any community. Their targets are smaller groups such as consumers, employees, vendors, and owners. Communicators are concerned not only with reaching those groups, but with reaching the highest possible percentage of group members. Given those parameters, consumers are most easily reached in stores they patronize or through media that attract narrowly defined socioeconomic groups. Employees are most readily reached on the job. Vendors and owners can be contacted most easily by mail or through the financial media.

Channel selection thus has become one of the most demanding and creative aspects of mediated communication. Thousands of media exist. Most are readily accessible, but considerable knowledge is necessary to identify the most effective among them. And even when selections have been made, questions arise as to whether personalized communication techniques might be preferable.

Personalized techniques. Personal communication efforts are based in part in opinion leader theory, which suggests that five types of influencers—role models, opinion leaders, power leaders, cheerleaders, and celebrities—can facilitate the communication process.

Networking and organizational development are perceived as equally powerful. Opinion leader lists, networking charts and organizational development techniques all can be useful in employee relations, consumer relations and community relations, according to *pr reporter*, an industry newsletter edited by practitioner Patrick Jackson.

Mediated techniques. The same principles apply, however, in mediated communication, especially were "media" is broadly defined. Most individuals are members of multiple organizations—vocational, avocational, civic, religious, and so forth. Each organization is served by one or several media ranging from computer data bases to newspapers, newsletters, and magazines.

These specialized media almost always are granted greater credibility by those who use them than are the mass media. More important, their content is more thoroughly and more regularly digested. If your audience consists of public relations practitioners, for example, and especially if you are most interested in those at the cutting edge of that profession, you will probably reach more of them through *pr reporter* than through any other medium. You'll reach more practitioners through *Public Relations Journal*, the monthly membership magazine of the Public Relations Society of America, but the society membership includes more novices than senior practitioners.

MEASURING RESULTS

The importance of media selection processes is underscored by continuing change in the methods through which the results of communication are measured. Early communicators managed to evade accountability by claiming that results could not be accurately measured. Pressure for accountability continued to grow through the late 1900s, however, and communicators retreated from their earlier positions.

Their next line of defense consisted of systems that measured volume of delivered messages. Tracking systems such as clipping services were used to produce "evidence of success" for clients and employers. Communicators extrapolated from clippings and broadcast news "mentions" to numbers of readers or viewers reached on the basis audience data used in advertising. The extrapolations assumed that messages were received, assimilated, and acted upon.

The appearance of the microcomputer perpetuated the tendency to equate message exposure to recipient behavior. Application software that enabled communicators to track "placements" and calculate exposure levels proliferated. More sophisticated systems could be programmed to monitor length of articles or duration of broadcast exposure; "positions" of these items in publications or newscasts; and numbers of critical information points covered. Aggressive promotion of such "tracking systems" obscured their inherent inability to measure anything more than message exposure. Some aggressive publicists went so far as to establish fees based on media exposure. Other than in coupon redemption, however, there remained no accurate system through which results could be measured. Mounting pressure from clients and employers nevertheless is resulting in more precise measurement of outcomes.

Alternative Strategies

At least two imperfect alternatives can be used in demonstrating successful communication. The first involves relatively time-consuming and costly research procedures using one of several survey techniques. The second involves using a measurable although indirect indicator of success. The options are imperfect in that neither provides direct evidence of the efficiency or productivity of communication. They are quite serviceable, however, in that they provide quantitative measures of results and require that success be defined by the parties involved.

Agreement as to what constitutes success enables the parties to objectively determine after the fact whether success has been achieved. In the employee communication campaign designed to reduce absenteeism and tardiness, for example, the prescribed 10 percent reduction is success by definition.

The only alternative is survey research conducted in one of two ways. One option involves measuring change in attitude and opinion among message recipients. The other requires measuring change in behaviors. The former approach is preferable from a communication standpoint in that attitude and opinion are more easily measured through survey techniques. Data on subject-reported behaviors are more apt to be distorted.

Potential Traps

Neither of the approaches described above will prove that a communication program, and that program alone, produced measured results. Both will demonstrate that change has occurred, however, and achieving specified objectives usually satisfies employers and clients.

Absence of agreed-upon definitions of success, in contrast, can be risky. Disputes over credit or blame, which are quite common in organizations, are more readily resolved before they develop than afterward. Where success has not been defined, such disputes tend to be damaging to all involved.

IN SUMMARY

Communication programming can be simple or complex, depending in large part on underlying communication plans. All of the steps necessary to strategic, and operational communication planning must be completed as components of the programming process where communication begins at the program rather than the plan level. Given appropriate communication plans, programming is stakeholder-specific and, in most organizations, yields a set of programs oriented toward primary constituencies. Consumer, employee, vendor, investor, and governmental communication programs are most common.

Communication programmers proceed with the process by addressing six critical questions:

1. What stakeholders are involved?
2. What behaviors are sought of those stakeholders?
3. What messages must be sent to induce those behaviors?
4. What must the organization do to validate those messages?
5. What communication channels will be most efficient in delivering the messages?
6. How will results be measured?

Question 1 requires that programmers define the group or groups with which they are dealing in considerable detail. Socioeconomic, sociographic, and demographic analyses are commonly used to induce the greatest possible insight into the nature of each group.

Question 2 requires that the objectives of the program be specified; that programmers state precisely what behaviors they will attempt to induce in the groups involved.

Question 3 addresses motivational factors as well as messages. Programmers must decide how to appeal to the interests of stakeholder groups if messages they design are to produce desired responses.

Question 4 arguably is the most significant of the six. Organizational reality must support every message. Messages are essentially transactional, and the organization therefore must determine what it is prepared to offer in each contemplated social exchange.

Question 5 usually is readily answered by re-examining information gathered in response to Question 1. Media usually can be found that will effectively and efficiently deliver messages to any group. Communicators nevertheless are challenged to identify those that best balance efficiency, effectiveness, and economy.

Question 6 deals equally with the concerns of communicators and their employers or clients. Methods through which program effectiveness will be assessed must be specified before programs are implemented. The process is relatively straightforward where outcomes can be defined in numbers of votes of incidence of absenteeism or tardiness. Results are more difficult to quantify, however, where a program might be oriented toward greater consumer acceptance of a product or service.

Ambiguous objectives must be clarified and reduced to quantitatively measurable terms if communicators are to adequately guard against ex post facto disputes as to whether programs succeed. Where accomplishments are not readily measurable, communicators can agree with clients or employers as to mutually acceptable evidence of success.

ADDITIONAL READING

Anshen, Melvin, ed. *Managing the Socially Responsible Corporation*. New York: Macmillan, 1974.
_____. *Corporate Strategies for Social Performance*. New York: Columbia University Press, 1980.
Brody, E. W. *Public Relations Programming and Production*, New York: Praeger, 1988.
Bucholz, Rogene A., William D. Evans, and Robert A. Wagley. *Management Response to Public Issues: Concepts & Cases in Strategy Formulation*. Englewood Cliffs, NJ: Prentice-Hall, 1985.
Cantor, Bill. *Inside Public Relations: Experts in Action*. New York: Longman, 1984.
Cutler, Blayne, "The Fifth Medium," *American Demographics*, June 1990.
Haley, Russell I. *Developing Effective Communications Strategy: A Benefit Segmentation Approach*. New York: Wiley, 1985.
Haynes, Jim, "How to Win Friends and Influence Management with a Communication Game Plan," *Journal of Organizational Communication*, no. 2, 1978, pp. 15-17.
Heitpas, Quentin, "Planning," in *Experts in Action: Inside Public Relations*, Bill Cantor, ed. New York: Longman, 1984.
"In New Decade of Personalized Relationships & Communication, Changes in Techniques, Strategies & Practitioner Attitudes are Predictable: How to Reach Thousands or Millions Personally?" *pr reporter*, January 1, 1990.
Nager, Norman R., and Richard H. Truitt. *Strategic Public Relations: Models from the Counselors Academy*. New York: Longman, 1987.

8

Communication Campaigns

Communication campaigns differ from programs primarily in focus and level of detail. Campaigns begin where programs end. Where programs spell out organizational objectives in terms of stakeholder groups, campaigns specify the strategies and tactics that are used in achieving those objectives.

Campaigns also may differ from programs as to the time spans they cover. Programs usually are designed on annual bases. Most campaigns are of shorter duration. A majority deal with social issues and fund-raising efforts of various kinds but a significant minority are political in nature. State and local political campaigns usually span several months although national campaigns can span a number of years.

Communication campaigns have existed for centuries. In their earliest domestic incarnations, before the Civil War, communication campaigns were word-of-mouth affairs. They were conducted by special interest groups or associations concerned with social issues. Mass media became involved between the Civil War and the turn of the century, first in support of the associations but later in their own right. Many media appeared more interested in building circulation than in the social causes they addressed.

Early communication campaigns prodded the federal government into legislative involvement on many social issues. The Interstate Commerce Act of 1887, the Pure Food and Drug Act of 1906, and the Child Labor Act of 1916 were precursors of campaign-driven legislation in the civil rights, occupational, and environmental sectors.

Contemporary campaigns encompass a broader range of activities. Campaigns over emerging social issues, from poverty and homelessness to abortion, are prominently and consistently displayed by today's media. Many nonprofit organizations, from the American Red Cross to groups dedicated to eradicating specific diseases, link membership and fund-raising campaigns to contemporary problems. Social issues occasionally are supplanted or supplemented by the political, especially during quadrennial national election campaigns. More rarely, post-disaster fund raising or one of thousands of repetitive fund-raising campaigns temporarily capture media attention.

THE NATURE OF CAMPAIGNS

The term "communication campaign" is difficult to concisely define. The meanings of the words can be established with relative clarity, however, by examining them from several perspectives. Campaigns can be analyzed as to their intentions, as to strategies applied in their development, and as to steps usually involved in their execution.

Understanding communication campaigns also requires that they be examined from strategic and developmental standpoints. Most campaigns are based on three strategic approaches, and all follow relatively consistent developmental processes.

Campaign Categories

Communication campaigns can be sorted into categories in several ways. Campaigns almost always are designed to influence beliefs or behaviors. Sought-after responses may be immediate or long term, but belief and behavior remain the primary objectives. Campaigns designed to encourage development of mass transit, or to discourage use of agricultural chemicals, fall into the long-term category. Campaigns launched for fund-raising purposes, or to influence voters, usually are intended to produce responses in days or weeks.

Campaigns also can be defined in terms of sponsors' intentions, or by the processes involved. Many campaigns are designed to establish social control, as in the case of the several that developed around the abortion issue. Others resemble a sort of journalism, consisting of efforts to gain influence by manipulating mass media. Efforts by religious groups to conform television programming to their standards of morality are exemplary of the latter sort of campaign.

Finally, campaigns can be differentiated by the nature of their intended benefits. Some campaigns are launched to generate individual benefits while others are designed to create group or collective benefits. Those who advocate national health insurance programs, for example, are intent on providing individual benefits, while campaigns by energy conservation advocates would benefit communities or societies.

Strategies and Risks

Communication campaigns, as the foregoing suggests, essentially are adversarial in nature. Most are "us versus them" efforts whether the goal is a city council seat or funds for a kidney transplant. Adversarial campaigns are fought on three fronts and involve an equal number of stakeholder groups. Campaigns are designed to (a) reinforce the commitments of supporters, (b) influence the undecided, and (c) raise doubts among opponents.

Differences among objectives require different but consistent messages. Differences in audiences, and in communicators' knowledge of audiences, also may suggest that different media be used in message transmission. Well-managed campaigns can achieve objectives by dealing successfully with different groups, messages, and media, but not without risk.

The adversarial nature of campaigns encourages a mental set that creates risks for workers and the causes to which they are committed. Commitment leads to emotional involvement that compounds as campaign climaxes approach. Committed campaigners caught up in the emotions of the moment come to view their efforts in the manner attributed to Green Bay Packer football coach Vince Lombardi, for whom winning was "not everything, but the only thing." The mental set involved encourages workers to go beyond moral and ethical boundaries they otherwise might observe.

Developmental Processes

While campaigns can depart from planners' established designs for any number of reasons, better-designed plans usually incorporate three separate and aptly labeled phases: pre-implementation, implementation and post-implementation. The bulk of the planning effort is concentrated in the pre-implementation phase. Implementation requires that the plan be followed; the process and its effectiveness be monitored; and adjustments made where necessary or appropriate. Post-implementation is dedicated to a post-mortem to assess (a) the extent to which objectives were achieved and (b) the manner in which the campaign might be replicated on a cost-effective basis. The three phases follow the basic patterns applied in developing communication programs.

Pre-implementation involves eight steps:

1. Defining objectives
2. Cataloging resources

3. Conducting formal and informal research
4. Cataloging campaign assumptions
5. Assessing success potential
6. Formulating policies, strategies and tactics
7. Preparing materials
8. Organizing and scheduling campaign tasks

Implementation involves three processes that are more readily stated but more demanding than the pre-implementation steps. Implementation requires continuous campaign monitoring. Formal research techniques are used to assess stakeholder responses. Media, messages and occasionally strategies may be changed as research data are analyzed. Managers hope that little more than "fine tuning" will be required but major changes may be necessary in response to competition or environmental developments.

Post-implementation requires detailed review of pre-implementation and implementation stages with special attention to the cost and effectiveness of each campaign component. Post-implementation enables planners to learn from successes or failures and enhances the effectiveness of subsequent campaigns.

The three-phase concept is invaluable in campaign planning but creates a potentially fatal pitfall. The three-step construct implies that campaigns are more or less mechanical in nature. Nothing is farther from the truth. Campaigns require instinct, talent, and insight on the part of planners during every step in their development and implementation.

THE PRE-IMPLEMENTATION PHASE

Success or failure in campaigns usually is determined during pre-implementation. Careful preparation is necessary to ensure success. Given total preparedness, failure usually occurs only through ineptitude in adjusting to changing circumstances. Care in executing pre-implementation processes can not guarantee success, but success is rare where pre-implementation efforts are inadequate or inept.

Extensive lists of tasks that must be accomplished during pre-implementation vary with the nature of specific campaigns. Several tasks are critical, however, regardless of the nature of the effort. They include setting objectives, defining audiences, selecting media, developing messages, establishing strategies and timetables, and preparing budgets.

Setting Objectives

Initial steps in pre-implementation are more complex than they appear. Establishing objectives in communication programs is a relatively straightforward task. The process is made more difficult in campaigns by several potential limitations and variables. Campaign resources, for example, always are limited and may not materialize. Promised donations to political campaigns can be especially elusive. Campaigns also may involve multiple independent groups whose efforts can be coordinated with difficulty if at all. Resource and organizational problems thus compound planning processes otherwise similar to those used in programming.

The first step toward defining objectives is an analysis of the problem at hand. Objectives vary with the nature of campaigns. Some campaigns are purely financial. Others measure success in pints of blood donated, numbers of students immunized, or numbers of smokers who kick the habit. Campaigns that deal in behavioral change are more complex than those whose results can be expressed in dollars or votes. No amount of education will produce increases in immunization levels, for example, where the primary barrier to action is limited access rather than lack of information.

Successful planning requires understanding the nature of problems and the reasons they exist. Goals may be expressed as changes in immunization rates, as in the case above, but objectives may have to be defined in terms of transportation or satellite clinics if the campaign is to succeed. No amount of communication will serve where a bus is required.

After objectives have been specified, planning processes must be focused on target audiences, defined behavioral responses, and available resources. Resources in campaign planning are not identical to those involved in communication programming. Where programming is based on organizational budgets, campaign planning may involve much more. Resources can encompass other organizations and their personnel, funding, and materials.

Availability of external resources varies with the nature of the effort, as demonstrated by the "strange bedfellow effect" often seen in the political arena. Election campaigns attract human and economic resources from individuals and organizations with diverse political interests. Religious and illicit liquor interests, for example, traditionally find themselves in agreement on referendum questions relating to alcoholic beverage. Immunization campaigns also can attract support from parent, academic, health, and governmental groups.

Volume of resources available is critical to campaign success. Campaigns usually are designed, as a result, to engage the interests and support of as many stakeholder groups as possible. Campaign objectives must be specified accordingly. These circumstances require early analyses of potential alliances and their prospective contributions to overall strength.

Cataloging Resources

When campaign objectives have been specified and potential alliances or coalitions are known, planners develop tentative lists of resources—economic, human and otherwise. The objective of the listing process is two-fold. Potential for success is governed by the effectiveness with which resources are applied rather than the sum of resources available. Effectiveness and efficiency are products of organization. The listing process serves as an early step toward organization.

Cataloging resources requires that campaign organizers examine all potential sources of support and assistance. The process is as productive internally as externally. Organizations seeking legislative relief, for example, often find they can enlist employees, stockholders, and vendors in support of lobbying efforts. Legislators track sentiment among constituents by tallying mail received for and against specific issues—and often vote accordingly.

Cataloging is best accomplished through detailed responses to two questions. First, what other organizations might be involved in a campaign in support of shared interests and, second, what resources might be obtained from these organizations or elsewhere? Some interested parties may offer nothing more than information, as in the case of trade associations, but information can be vital in union organizing campaigns, hostile takeover attempts, and similar situations. Others groups may provide personnel, material, and other tangible resources. Materials or services obtained through borrowing or donation need not be purchased, and dollars involved can be reallocated to other purposes.

Conducting Research

Information gathering, through formal research or otherwise, is critical to campaign success. Needs vary with campaigns, but accurate information is essential. Research or information gathering processes often begin even before the campaign's pre-implementation phase. In political situations, for example, campaigns rarely start until prospective candidates and their staffs have obtained and analyzed all available information to assess potential for success.

Information is especially important in adversarial situations. Outcomes of union organizing campaigns often can be influenced through skillful use of information about unions involved. Considerable information can be obtained from reports unions are required to file with the federal government. The files of state governments and of business or trade associations also can yield valuable data about organizing tactics and other union behaviors. The same principles apply in business. Most corporate raiders are well-known, for example, and their tactics have been dutifully recorded by the financial media.

Communicators preparing for campaigns find it helpful to obtain and catalog all available information about organizations and issues with which they expect to be involved. Where organizations are known to have strong leaders, information about their personalities, habits, and predispositions also can be helpful. Recent histories of organizations and issues can be especially helpful in validating or invalidating the implied or implicit assumptions on which campaigns are often based.

Cataloging Campaign Assumptions

Information produced through research serves as a screening device to eliminate unwarranted assumptions that can endanger communication campaigns. Many otherwise well-designed campaigns have failed because planners failed to confirm the assumptions on which their strategies were predicated.

Risks associated with unwarranted assumptions are most often demonstrated in the political arena. Many would-be public officials have been frustrated at the polls by voter tolerance of what appeared to be damaging behavior by incumbents. The same type of problems develops in union organizing campaigns. Unions' traditional assumptions concerning workers were repeatedly proven ill-founded during the 1980s.

Unions' difficulties were produced by environmental changes that influenced worker attitude and opinion. The same sort of phenomena threaten the unwary at every turn. Those who read newspapers are prone to assume that others continue to read them, for example, although circulation data demonstrate that readership continues to decline.

Assumptions often are necessary as to (a) campaign stakeholder groups, (b) motivational factors that may influence them, (c) the manner in which those factors should be incorporated into messages, and (d) the channels through which messages should be transmitted. To the extent that time and resources permit, every assumption should be identified and validated. Where validation is impossible, communicators must proceed with caution. Logic demands that unsupported assumptions be discarded for planning purposes.

Assessing Success Potential

Estimates of success potential calculated during the campaign design process are doubly risky because they are based on the sum of the assumptions involved. Problem potential varies with the nature of assumptions. Those dealing with resource availability can be especially troublesome. The absence of expected resources can cripple a campaign from its inception.

In many cases, and especially in political campaigns, estimates of success potential may be manipulated for campaign purposes. The relative status of candidates during campaigns always is a closely guarded secret. Candidates, campaign managers, and key strategists may be aware of the results of on-going polling but workers are deliberately isolated from reality. Favorable realities presumably might encourage workers to relax their efforts. Where realities are unfavorable, workers might become discouraged. Conventional political wisdom in either case suggests that while knowledge is power, ignorance in the ranks is bliss.

The same sort of secrecy can prevail at lower echelons in membership or fund-raising campaigns. Many managers, for example, time progress reports to coincide with meetings that serve as campaign "pep rallies." Alternatively, good news may be hoarded for use at times when media exposure is apt to be most extensive. The rationale may be less manipulative than in the political setting but the results are the same.

Policies, Strategies and Tactics

While secrecy in handling sensitive information may serve campaign objectives, efforts to obscure or mislead are impractical where policies, strategies, and tactics are involved. In campaigns, to an even greater extent than in programs, behaviors deliver the strongest of messages. Interpersonal and mediated messages are effective only where consistent with behavior. Inconsistencies detract from campaign effectiveness. These circumstances require that messages reflect behaviors. Fund-raising efforts succeed over time, for example, only where charities perform as promised. Required reports to regulatory bodies that contradict promises to contributors can be devastating.

Strategic and tactical decisions in most campaigns do not revolve around ethical issues. Most deal instead with matters of timing. Timing is vital where elected offices or other political goals are at stake and is almost as important in other campaigns. Most fund-raising efforts, for example, are designed to enable organizations to proceed with specific projects. Efforts to preserve historic buildings or protect endangered wildlife usually are equally deadline oriented. Preservationists and environmentalists often are moved to action only as time-oriented threats appear in one form or another. Campaigns, for these reasons, usually are designed to produce predetermined numbers of votes or dollars, or to accomplish other objectives, by certain dates.

Most strategists, because of temporal and psychological factors, seek to generate increasing momentum through the course of campaigns. Strategies are developed to build excitement as target dates grow closer and, in the process, motivate volunteers to maximum effort at the critical moment. The objective always is to peak at that point, be it the day of the fund-raising victory celebration or the day of election. That objective is so important that many campaigns—especially political and fund-raising—are orchestrated to ensure that success will be within grasp and that appropriate milestones can be reached as planned.

Political campaigns rarely begin unless candidates and managers believe they have a real chance to succeed—in the current campaign or in a future effort. Fund raisers establish goals in a manner that assures they will be reached, or almost reached. Morale is more readily maintained where goals are close at hand. Discouraging words are avoided at all times.

Bringing campaigns to successful conclusions by having them peak at specified times requires orienting strategies and tactics toward that goal. Events, activities, and accompanying mediated communication are timed with exquisite care to ensure that momentum builds toward the grand finale, be it an election, an "over the top rally," or some other concluding event. Other than in these respects, campaign development parallels the program development process described earlier. Behavioral outcomes among stakeholders may be more precisely described but close attention must be paid to messages and media if group members are to respond as desired.

Building Coalitions

Many of the strategies and tactics used in campaigns, especially in the political and governmental sectors, are contingent on communicator or organizational ability to establish coalitions or alliances on the basis of mutual interest. Coalition building is a function of enlightened self-interest. Coalitions and alliances form because the parties recognize that their combined strength is necessary to achieve individual objectives. Coalition building, however, is no easy task.

Developing coalitions requires exceptional communication skills. Coalition and alliance builders must maintain open channels of communication with all parties to the issues with which they are involved. The philosophies or positions of the parties should have no bearing on open communication. The coalition- and alliance-building process also entails:

- Reaching agreements with other parties to the issue on those objectives toward which you can work together. This usually means concurrently setting aside those points on which agreement can not be reached.
- Identifying and neutralizing those who, while not potential allies, can be induced to take no position on the issue at hand.
- Learning the positions of all parties to the issue and, in the process, informing them of your organization's position. This process arms communicators to refute opponents arguments and develop an internal consensus with allies concerning joint positions.
- Organize members of alliances and coalitions, allocate responsibilities in keeping with resources, and coordinate the parties effort to achieve optimal results.

Coalition-building often ultimately requires that communicators become involved in negotiation, compromise, and grass roots organizing. The extent to which communicators must negotiate and conclude compromise agreements varies from one organization to another but the processes are essential in forming beneficial alliances.

The coalition-building process also requires identifying and contacting those individuals and organizations who, while not prospective allies or coalition partners, might be induced to remain neutral.

Preparing Materials

A near-limitless number of communication channels can be used to deliver campaign messages. Selecting appropriate channels involves the same techniques applied in other situations with one exception. The escalating nature of campaigns requires greater-than-usual emphasis on timing. The bulk of messages conveyed during campaigns is crowded into their closing weeks and days, but all must be in readiness far in advance.

This emphasis on early preparation means that most of the time and effort dedicated to campaign communication is expended before stakeholders are aware a campaign is in progress. Campaigns require preliminary research to assess stakeholder attitude and opinion toward the candidate or organization. Motivational factors must be identified and messages specified before communication channels can be selected and materials developed.

Channel selection is controlled by several factors. Budgetary constraints and variation in developmental flexibility often are primary among them. Many campaigns are developed on the basis of projected budgets rather than dollars in hand. Selecting communication channels is contingent on the availability of funds. Only as funds are received can they be committed to fund preparation of television commercials and other materials. Developmental time requirements then become the governing factor. Where inadequate time remains to produce elaborate brochures, simpler versions may have to be substituted.

Developmental schedules, in addition, must include time to test and revise materials and complete field arrangements. Field arrangements, which can include paid field staff as well as neighborhood offices and support facilities, often can be put in place only as resources become available. The extent of field facilities often limits the campaign's ability to develop large corps of volunteer workers and this factor, in turn, can influence channel selection for mediated communication. Time for testing is important regardless of media and message selections. Risks involved in committing large percentages of available resources to media that may or may not reach specified audiences, and to messages that may or may not prompt desired responses, are too great to be tolerated.

Organizing and Scheduling Tasks

Critical time and budget factors require that campaign scheduling be handled with surgical precision. The process involves tracking multiple time lines—the schedules under which events are organized and materials are produced. Bringing in a national figure such as a federal cabinet member to speak at a victory dinner or a campaign kick-off, for example, may require that arrangements be completed more than a year in advance. Commitments must be obtained from the speaker, from the owners or operators of the facility in which the event is to be conducted, and, perhaps, from others as well.

The opening of a new corporate headquarters can involve a series of events conducted over a period of weeks for different stakeholder groups. Associated logistical challenges, ranging from souvenirs and hotel accommodations to media kits and media room arrangements, can be monumental. Tasks of this sort once were undertaken by organizing "war rooms," with schedules and sub-schedules written on wall-sized chalkboards. Most planners today substitute powerful microcomputers and sophisticated planning software for chalkboards but the management tasks involved have not changed.

The primary planning challenge is to deliver finished products on schedule. Producing the most attractive possible brochure may require taking photos of flowers in bloom months in advance of an anticipated winter delivery date. Arrangements for large numbers of distinguished guests requires that their individual and, occasionally, idiosyncratic needs be determined and met. The process can encompass interminable negotiation with one or several hotels, caterers, and others. The overall objective is simple although probably unattainable: to be able to sit back and relax during the event or campaign as every vendor and participant performs as requested.

THE IMPLEMENTATION PHASE

Since what can go wrong will go wrong, campaign implementation is as important as pre-implementation period. Three primary functions are vital in addition to tracking the thousands of details that always require attention. The three are on-going monitoring, evaluating effectiveness, and fine tuning. The implementation phase in campaign management in many ways is similar to child rearing. You know what you want to accomplish, and that it can be accomplished, but you've got to "stay on top of it" from hour to hour and day to day.

Campaign implementation is so demanding that consultants who specialize in campaign management often abandon all other pursuits for the duration. Labor relations consultants frequently live on clients' premises during the weeks preceding worker elections supervised by the National Labor Relations Board. Their efforts during those weeks are dedicated to the monitoring, evaluating, and fine tuning of campaign functions.

Monitoring and evaluating involves tracking the progress of the campaign based on earlier-established measuring techniques (see Chapter 5). Methods involved can be formal or informal but accurate data on attitude and opinion among pro, con, and undecided elements in target populations is essential. Much of the monitoring in political campaigns is accomplished through continuous polling on local, regional, and national levels. The monitoring process is applied to the effectiveness of media and messages as well as to the campaign as a whole.

Research by advertisers and agencies and by candidates and managers over many years has demonstrated that monitoring and fine tuning can make the difference between victory and defeat in political campaigns. These conditions have resulted in mounting investments in polling and other research to arm managers with data necessary to fine tuning.

Fine tuning refers to small but important changes in campaign direction that may be found necessary as data are analyzed. Managers attempt to maintain sufficient flexibility to change strategies as necessary. New strategies may require changes in messages and media, and all must be accomplished within demanding time schedules.

Campaigns differ as to purpose but the basic strategies described above always are applicable. Only the intensity with which strategies are applied varies from one set of circumstances to another. Fund-raising efforts, for example, are less critical than presidential election campaigns. Fund-raisers in some respects operate under more stringent economic restraints than political campaigners. Fund-raising expenditures are limited, legally or otherwise, to fixed percentages of collections, and those involved usually allocate relatively little for research conducted while campaigns are in progress.

THE POST-IMPLEMENTATION PHASE

While limiting research expenditures during campaigns, fund raisers and others who engage in repetitive campaign cycles are as involved in research as their political contemporaries. Lack of resources merely shifts research efforts to periods between campaigns when data can be analyzed at a more leisurely pace and plans for ensuing campaigns can be adjusted accordingly.

Much of the post-implementation phase of campaigns is dedicated to analyses of this sort, all oriented toward assessing achievement and examining the cost and efficiency of strategies and tactics. The political or economic importance of campaigns makes analytical processes complex.

Assessing Achievement

The assessment process is designed to provide precise responses to several questions. What did the campaign accomplish in relation to objectives established at the outset? Were monetary objectives achieved? Did the candidate get elected? By what margins? With whose support? What strategies and tactics proved most productive? Which messages and media triggered the strongest responses?

The latter questions are more important than the former. Successful campaigners look at their efforts as learning experiences as well as win-lose situations. Extensive campaign post mortems are oriented toward the future rather than the past. They are designed to equip managers to produce better results in subsequent campaigns. Those involved recognize the errors—their own and those of others—that inevitably occur in pressure situations.

Cost and Efficiency

Communication professionals are most interested in those aspects of campaign post mortems that deal with cost and efficiency; with the manner in which resources were committed and with the results of those commitments. Cost and efficiency in communication refer to the extent to which attitude, opinion, and behavior were influenced by messages. These factors seldom can be measured with the precision communicators would prefer.

Stakeholder groups targeted in communication campaigns usually are subjected to multiple messages delivered through a variety of channels. Only rarely, through careful analyses of message content and distribution records, can communicators differentiate among message and media affects. Greater insight can be achieved where campaigns are more or less repetitive. In union organizing fund-raising efforts, for example, communicators can compare messages, media, and results across campaigns. Resulting data may be less than wholly comparable but nevertheless can be enlightening. The process often produces insights that may enable communicators to enhance cost/efficiency ratios in ensuing campaigns.

BEYOND MECHANICAL GUIDELINES

All of the steps listed above are necessary, but may or may not be sufficient, to campaign success. Communicators who have "been through the wars" in campaigns ranging from political and financial to those essentially issue-oriented (see Chapter 10), offer considerable worthwhile advice. Some is new; some not so new. The not-so-new consists largely of military maxims.

"The best defense is a good offense," for example, is a proven principle that serves communicators well regardless of the nature of the campaigns in which they become involved. In the political arena, an accelerating series of attacks uninterrupted by defensive moves can devastate the opposition. Attacks also attract media attention while defensive explanations rarely are sufficiently newsworthy to offset attack-oriented headlines. The same sort of strategy serves well in corporate takeover battles, in union organizing campaigns, and in other purely adversarial, win-lose situations. Conditions are more complex where opposing forces ultimately can accept a middle ground.

Whatever the campaign, and whatever its objectives, basic advice from those who have "been there before" is worthy of close attention. Among most often heard admonitions are these:

1. Know your opponents and what they are doing. Do your research homework (see chapter 5). Be especially sensitive to what opponents are telling the news media and others who may constitute centers of influence. Conversations with reporters often are unplanned, and casual comments can reveal a great deal as to the opposition's future plans.
2. Avoid overconfidence. Those most certain that their positions and strategies render them impregnable are most often defeated. Arrogance breeds disaster. No matter how good things look at the moment, heed the wisdom of legions of political campaign managers: "always run scared."
3. Plan carefully and follow your plan. Never change your direction on the basis of incomplete information, published reports, or rumors. Double and triple check all information from third parties.
4. Seize and maintain the informational initiative whether news is good or bad. If it's good, get it all out. If it's bad, get it all out faster. Recognition among the media that you run an open campaign; (i.e., that you tell the truth even if it hurts), is your best defense against any efforts to deceive on the part of your opponents.
5. Handle information from a media perspective as you pursue an aggressive communication policy. Preempt criticism by quickly accepting blame for problems that may arise, even when the fault evidently is not wholly yours. In the process, you establish the context of any public argument to your benefit.
6. Be candid and open under any and all circumstances. Candor and speed in disseminating information, even when the news is bad, helps recipients reach more rational, objective judgments. Reticence and slowness essentially yield the field of battle to opponents.
7. Don't hesitate, when your standard approach is candor and openness, to delay where necessary. Occasional delay in releasing information is acceptable to insure accuracy or to protect negotiations in progress. Never let reporters blackmail you by declaring that they'll "go with the story" whether or not you comment.
8. Cast your opponent in the "bad guy" role whenever and wherever you can honestly achieve that objective. Unions are expensive for

their members, for example, and workers should be constantly reminded of that fact during organizing campaigns. Perpetrators of hostile takeovers rarely wear white hats from the standpoint of the public and rationally can be cast as raiders or buccaneers.

9. Always be accessible to media representatives. Accessible means more than merely having a warm body at a telephone. The individual at the end of the line must be (a) knowledgeable and (b) authorized to speak for the organization. Use cellular telephones, beepers, or other electronic devices when necessary in order to have a reliable spokesperson always available but make certain that the job gets done. Media deadlines are inflexible and you rarely can afford to yield an entire sound byte or news story to the competition. (See chapter 10 on crisis communication).

IN SUMMARY

Communication plans, programs, campaigns, special events, and crisis management strategies differ little in structure and design. These communication efforts cover different time spans and, as a result, differ in intensity. Programs usually are structured in annual formats. Campaigns can range from months to several years. Special events usually cover shorter time spans than campaigns. Crisis responses can range from days to several months.

Objectives, strategies, and methodologies are the primary variables within campaigns. Campaigns almost always are designed to influence beliefs and behaviors. Most also can be defined in terms of sponsors' intentions and by the nature of the benefits they are intended to produce.

Campaigns usually are adversarial in nature. They are "we against them" efforts. The intensity and nature of campaigns, especially those of the political variety, tend to tempt participants to engage in less-than-ethical behaviors.

Campaigns progress through three distinct and equally important stages: pre-implementation, implementation, and post-implementation. Success or failure usually is determined during the pre-implementation stage, which consists of a series of logical steps. First, objectives must be defined. Then, resources must be cataloged and research undertaken. Campaign assumptions must be critically examined and potential for success evaluated before policies, strategies, and tactics can be prescribed. Materials then are prepared and organizing and scheduling are completed.

The implementation phase in some ways is the least demanding of the three if pre-implementation steps are well-handled. On-going monitoring is essential and adjustments often are necessary in response to changing circumstances but the bulk of the implementation phase deals with manipulating the machine constructed during pre-implementation.

Post-implementation is another matter. The post-implementation process, often referred to as a post mortem, is designed to assess accomplishments and to examine the cost and efficiency of strategies and tactics. Post-implementation steps are undertaken to assure that those involved learn by experience and, in the process, prepare themselves for the next campaign.

ADDITIONAL READING

Anshen, Melvin, ed. *Managing the Socially Responsible Corporation*. New York: Macmillan, 1974.

_____. *Corporate Strategies for Social Performance*. New York: Columbia University Press, 1980.

Atkin, Charles R. "Mass Media Information Campaign Effectiveness." In Ronald Rice and William Paisley, eds., *Public Communication Campaigns*, Beverly Hills, CA: Sage, 1981.

Bucholz, Rogene A., William D. Evans, and Robert A. Wagley. *Management Response to Public Issues: Concepts & Cases in Strategy Formulation*. Englewood Cliffs, NJ: Prentice-Hall, 1985.

"Effective Coalition-Building Can Be Invaluable To Your Organization," *pr reporter*, (October 30, 1989).

Haller, Robert T. *Creative Power! Grow Faster with New ProActive Tactics in Advertising and Public Relations*. London: Leister and Sons, 1987.

Heitpas, Quentin, "Planning," In *Experts in Action: Inside Public Relations*, Bill Cantor, ed. New York: Longman, 1984.

Helm, Lewis M., Ray E. Hiebert, Michael R. Naver, and Kenneth Rabin, *Informing the People: A Public Affairs Handbook*, New York: Longman, 1981.

Hennessy, Bernard. *Public Opinion*. Monterey, CA: Brooks/Cole Publishing, 1985.

Mason, Richard O., and Ian I. Mitroff. *Challenging Strategic Planning Assumptions: Theory, Cases and Techniques*. New York: Wiley, 1981.

Rice, Ronald E., and William J. Paisley. *Public Communication Campaigns*. Beverly Hills, CA: Sage, 1981.

Salmon, Charles T., ed. *Information Campaigns: Balancing Social Values and Social Change*. Newbury Park, CA.: Sage, 1989.

Simmons, Robert E. *Communication Campaign Management: A Systems Approach*. New York: Longman, 1990.

Van Leuven, James K. "Theoretical Models for Public Relations
    Campaigns." Paper presented to the Conference on Communication
    Theory on Public Relations, Illinois State University, Normal, IL,
    May 1987.
————. "A Planning Matrix for Message Design, Channel Selection and
    Scheduling," Paper presented to the meeting of the Association for
    Education in Journalism and Mass Communication, Norman, OK,
    1986.

9

Special Events

Special events bear striking similarities to programs and campaigns. From the communication perspective, they are more akin to these other types of efforts than they are different from them. Operationally, however, special events constitute a different breed. They are unique in the extent to which they are wholly managed by communicators, and in the level of detail required in their development and execution.

In broad terms, planning and executing special events are processes almost identical to those used in communication programming. The processes differ only in the time periods they cover and the levels of detail they require. The nature of special events becomes evident through examination of the differences and similarities they share with programs and campaigns.

Special event time spans typically range from hours to weeks while communication programs usually are designed on annual bases. Programs shape basic communication structures that support multiple activities oriented to specific stakeholder groups. Detailed planning in most organizations begins at the activity rather than the programming level, and special events usually are cast as activities—components of programs.

Special events in other ways are more akin to campaigns than to programs. Campaigns and special events both are cast in narrower time frames. Where programming is on-going, campaigns and special events, like crisis responses, are episodic in nature. Campaigns and special events require careful management of a myriad of detail, and most are tightly controlled from inception to completion.

Special events also differ from campaigns in several respects. Most campaigns are of the political or fund-raising varieties and therefore are repetitive or cyclical in nature. Special events may or may not be repetitive. Annual meetings, conferences, and trade shows usually are cyclical but grand openings, groundbreaking ceremonies, and open houses follow no predetermined patterns. Special events linked to special occasions are designed to capitalize on opportunities that occur relatively rarely in organizational lifetimes. Were "special events" defined to include shows, exhibits, and benefits of the sort regularly staged at galleries, shopping malls and elsewhere, the "free-standing" and repetitive categories might be approximately equal in size.

Development of special events follows a predetermined pattern. Some variation occurs from one event to another but the process involves four phases usually initiated in order despite considerable overlap among them. The steps are scheduling, planning, implementation, and communication. Before examining each of these processes, the term special events must be examined in some detail.

SPECIAL EVENTS IN CONTEXT

The term special events encompasses a set of activities so broad as to defy precise definition. The literature of special events suggests that the definition continues to expand with the ingenuity of promoters and communicators.

Some 30 years ago, in 1960, Hal Golden and Kitty Hanson defined "special event" to include almost any formal activity. They counted club meetings, luncheons, and sales meetings as well as conventions, store openings, film screenings, and trade shows in their survey of the field.

Since 1960, special events managers have found a host of new fields to conquer. Shopping center and mall openings have become commonplace. Mall promotions, designed to attract traffic to operating malls, are routine in many communities. Special events and promotions have become so large a component of communication practice, in fact, that a number of firms now specialize in special events production and in such esoteric subspecialties as meeting planning and special event security.

Special events succeed or fail primarily on the basis of their suitability to specific circumstances. Special events planner Mira J. Sheerin (1986) specifies five questions that require attention in the planning process:

1. Can we use our own constituency successfully? In other words, can organization members be induced to contribute time and effort. Will there be sufficient personnel to sell tickets? Will the board of directors support the effort?
2. Is a sponsorship or underwriting available? Is there a major donor who will support or co-sponsor the event, minimizing financial risk? Major donors or sponsors can make the difference between profit

and loss. Budgeting can not logically begin until donor and/or
sponsor arrangements have been completed.
3. Can community assets be used in staging the event? Can an
existing occasion be used as a platform for the effort or must the
organization develop an event from the ground up?
4. Who will want to attend and/or be willing to pay the price of the
ticket? Can the event be made profitable within these limitations?
5. Can the same type of event be conducted by other organizations?
(102)

Some events are more suitable to specific organizations than others.
Perhaps more important, is the event worth doing at all? That question
deserves a great deal of thought. Special events can be costly, and
should be undertaken only where they will produce results of at least
equal value. A series of questions posed by The Coca-Cola Company's
Carlton L. Curtis helps practitioners sort out special events—good, bad
and marginal:

- Why is the event being staged?
- What message is to be delivered?
- Is the event necessary?
- What are the target audiences?
- Can those audiences be reached by the event on a cost-effective
  basis?

Special event planning should begin only where these questions can
be satisfactorily answered, or in one other set of circumstances. The
economics of special events often become more attractive where they
can be repeated relatively easily on annual or more frequent bases.
Repetition tends to enhance effectiveness and profitability. Where
repetition is impossible, prospective events should be re-evaluated. If
repetition is feasible, according to Pembroke Hill School Development
Director Thomas J. Mulligan (1987, p. 36) several questions then
should be considered to determine whether the event is "just right" for
the organization involved.

Dollar Potential—How much money can the event reasonably be
expected to produce? Will that amount grow if the event is
repeated year after year? Is the potential great enough to merit
the time and effort required to put this event together?

Audience—Who do you expect to patronize the event? Only one of your
constituencies? All of your constituencies? The public at large?
Or a combination? Is the potential audience large enough to
support the event? Should the target audience be expanded or
the event scaled down to fit the audience?

Appropriateness—Is the event appropriate for your organization or institution? Will you patrons think it's a great idea or will they raise their eyebrows when they hear about it?

Timeliness—Is the event new and unusual or is it "old hat?" Are you ahead of or behind the times? Will attendance be viewed as being "in" or "out?"

Attractiveness to Volunteer Leaders—Is this an event that people will want to work on? Or will the first three people asked to take leadership roles respond with "Ugh!?"

Specialized assistance in event programming has developed out of the complexity of the process. A sample planning calendar for an uncomplicated key promotional event in a small shopping mall, as outlined by Alan R. Mount and John P. LaPlace (1987, p. 46), demonstrates this point. Their calendar is reproduced below. (From Mount, Alan R., and John P. LaPlace, "Effective Promotions at Small Shopping Centers," *Journal of Property Management*, November-December 1987. Reprinted by permission.)

Twelve months
A community group and/or commercial organization will approach the property manager with a promotion idea. (It may be the other way around.) Meetings will be held with the tenants and the merchants' association to judge the value of the event for the mall. In the next months, the following can take place.

• Approve activity and budget
• Select site
• Select date
• Create ideas for the event
• Approve final structure of the event
• Begin arranging for necessary equipment, visuals, staff
• Draft brochure (if appropriate)

Six months
• Prepare invitation lists, including media, key officials (if appropriate)
• Make arrangements with caterers and entertainment

Two months
• Check hotel accommodations
• Develop series of news releases to build public interest

Six weeks
• Begin preparing invitations
• Set approval of invitations

Five weeks
- Send all printed material to printer
- News conferences (if appropriate)
- Disseminate news releases

Four weeks
- Mail invitations
- Send public service announcements to local media

Three weeks
- Receive first responses from invitees
- Review written material and redraft as necessary
- Distribute fliers, stuffers and any other inexpensive forms of publicity

Two weeks
- Follow up with media personally
- Write more news releases
- Arrange photography for the event

One week
- Do telephone follow-up as needed
- Assemble press kits (if appropriate)
- Print news releases
- Hire personnel for events including hosts, hostesses, emcee
- Double check special equipment
- Keep caterer up to date on number of acceptances
- Prepare final lists of acceptances and participants

Day of event
- Check staffing of event (take the telephone numbers with you)
- Check out equipment
- Make sure participants are in the right locations

Mount and LaPlace deal with a small event at a single mall. Few special events fall into this category. Most are more complex, whether undertaken on free-standing bases or in series. As such, they require considerable time, effort, and resources.

Planning and Organizing

The extent of planning and organizing efforts necessary in developing special events was underscored by Coca-Cola's Carlton L. Curtis (1989) in describing his company's centennial celebration. Two years of detailed planning were required, and facilities were reserved as much as five years in advance.

The Coca-Cola centennial was planned and executed through an ad hoc organization established within the company for that purpose. The organization consisted of a management committee of three top officers and a nine-member coordinating committee that included officers and managers. The structure was designed to ensure that all activities were consistent with centennial objectives; that expenses were controlled; and that costs could be identified in advance. Management committee approval was required for activities and supporting budgets. Coordinating committee members handled day-to-day supervision and coordination.

The Coca-Cola approach involved senior management early in the planning process, ensuring that objectives were clearly defined and mutually understood, and that the event was designed within limitations imposed by time, money and resources. Like most familiar with special events, Curtis repeatedly emphasizes the criticality of time factors:

> There seemed to be a significant amount of time remaining to plan the centennial—it was a good 20 months before the actual event. But even with this much time, we found, as is often the case, that we still could have used more time. It is impossible to predict what delays may arise, so again, begin planning at the earliest possible moment. (1989, p. 246)

Similarly detailed planning and management are essential even in the case of smaller events. One of the more imaginative promotions of the 1980s, for example, occurred in Pasadena, CA, where Read Communications developed an innovative concept to breath new life into the vintage Pasadena Hotel. Nat Read's vehicle: Have the nation's "most romantic couple" marry aboard a Tournament of Roses parade float and honeymoon at the hotel. Read's efforts won a 1988 Silver Anvil award from the Public Relations Society of America.

The flamboyance that paid off for Read is not essential in special event programming, as has been demonstrated by national and international public relations agencies. One of them, Manning, Selvage & Lee, has used mall events extensively in behalf of clients such as Ortho Pharmaceutical Corporation, U.S. Shoes, Quaker Oats, the Bahamas Ministry of Tourism, and the California State Lottery. Other firms have been no less aggressive. They have been joined in the special events arena by a number of organizations that specialize in that field.

Specialization has been encouraged by several factors. The complexities and labor-intensive nature of special event programming encourage organizations to retain specialists. Many sponsors use this form of communication relatively rarely. Their communicators often lack adequate experience to assure success in special events programming. More important, day-to-day work loads may preclude handling the volume of added effort a special event can require.

Organizations nevertheless should exercise caution in employing special events consultants. Consultant Joe J. Goldblatt of Washington, D.C., offers these guidelines:

- Check references.
- Will on-site personnel be trained and supervised?
- Is the producer's organization strong enough to deal directly with entertainers rather than working through agents, saving money in the process?
- Will the producer negotiate talent fees to enhance cost effectiveness?
- Is the company insured and/or bonded? Does it have a good reputation?
- Will the company evaluate the event with you to ensure sound handling?
- Will the event be tailored to the needs of your community? (1985, p. 35)

BUDGETING

Where all factors appear favorable, decisions to proceed with special events nevertheless should be deferred pending development of comprehensive budgets. Budgets encompass three elements: estimated income, estimated expenses, and net income—the difference between the estimates.

Expenses always include food and beverages, printing, postage, entertainment, clerical and secretarial help, telephone, postage, messenger services, and other office expenses. Some will also involve theater rentals, transportation costs, music, audio-visual equipment, and the like. Awards, accommodations, and other expenses all must be calculated and included. Early estimates should be made as accurate as possible through careful shopping and conservative estimating.

Income in most cases is a function of ticket or other prices. Additional revenues often can be generated by printing souvenir programs, group ticket sales, and partial or total sponsorship or underwriting.

SCHEDULING

Two primary factors require attention in scheduling special events: conflicts and lead time. Potential for failure, or for less-than-resounding success, compounds where events are scheduled in conflict with others, or where schedules create difficulties for planners.

Potential conflicts create more difficult problems. Limitations or pressures created by schedules that permit too little preparatory time can be overcome. More personnel can be assigned, for example, to ensure that preparations are completed on a timely basis. Neither additional personnel nor more promotional dollars, in contrast, can overcome limitations imposed by conflicting events.

Conflicting Events

Scheduling problems created by conflicting events are a function of the interests of prospective audiences. Planners experience little difficulty, for example, where a benefit performance by an opera company and a major sports event are scheduled on the same evening. The audiences involved are not "mutually exclusive," but few rabid sports fans are apt to be potential opera patrons. Scheduling the opening of a major art gallery showing on the evening that a symphony orchestra performance has been scheduled, on the other hand, would create a conflict. The two events are apt to draw their audiences from among the same socioeconomic groups.

No perfect conflict avoidance system exists. Special event planners nevertheless must make every effort to avoid conflict and several techniques have been developed that help in that process. Potential for conflict is minimized where planners:

1. Consult calendars for potential holiday observances.
2. Examine the prior year's newspapers for repetitive annual events that might have been conducted on or about all dates under consideration.
3. Ask each of the following individuals to check their calendars for potential conflicts:
   a. Local newspaper city or metropolitan editors
   b. Local television news directors
   c. Managers of stadiums/coliseums/auditoriums
   d. Sales directors of large hotels
   e. Convention/visitor bureau directors
   f. Sports/entertainment promoters
   g. Governmental agencies that issue permits for parades and other events conducted on public property

No guarantees attach to the foregoing procedures but the process enables special event planners to accomplish two objectives. First, and most important, they avoid conflicts. Second, they may encounter conditions that could encourage participation in public events. Special events designed to attract the general public, for example, might gain in attendance where scheduled immediately before or after a holiday parade, concert, or similar event.

Restrictive Schedules

Restrictive scheduling can create as many problems in developing special events as potential conflicts in dates. Events developed under undue time pressures seldom achieve their potential, if only because planners' ability to attract celebrities, politicians, and other notables is limited.

"Earlier is better" should be the special event planner's guiding principle, even where the event is something as uncomplicated as a retirement dinner. Finding appropriate locations for such events grows progressively more difficult as dates grow nearer and can be all but impossible during holiday periods. Banquet facilities for holiday parties usually are committed a year in advance. Convention hotels, auditoriums and sports arenas may be booked three to five years in advance.

PLANNING

Timing of special events is perceived by some as the second phase of the scheduling process and by others as the first step in the planning process. The boundary between scheduling and planning is hazy in that the former flows naturally into the latter. Timing is a major factor in planning because events often must be tailored to available time. The planning process therefore begins with timing. Other factors requiring attention include staffing, budgeting, and prospectus development. The prospectus, a detailed, step-by-step summary of the proposed event, becomes the special event plan when approval processes have been completed.

Staffing

Developing and executing special event plans become labor-intensive processes due to the level of detail involved. Organization and control of the multiple tasks requires special attention regardless of the scope and magnitude of the events.

Scope and magnitude govern the complexity of special event staffing. Lesser events, such as retirement dinners, can be successfully organized by one individual. More complex events require large organizations. Committees often are appointed to oversee planning for complex special events, but an administrator should be made responsible for execution. The administrator or coordinating chairman may have one or more assistants as well as a steering committee. Steering committees usually consist of the chairpersons of major operating subcommittees but others may be involved as well.

Special event subcommittees often are formed to deal with community contacts, program development, advertising and promotion, budgets, and any other major function. Numbers of subcommittees created are governed by the magnitude and complexity of events.

Budgeting

The budgeting process arguably is most important in special event programming. Special events usually involve multiple revenue sources and diverse expense items. Potential for red ink is considerable unless budgets are carefully prepared and expenditures are tightly controlled.

Budgeting for complex events is most logically attacked through committee structures. Budget requests are then solicited from committees and/or subcommittees and assembled in composite form for consideration by the project steering committee. Requests are detailed and divided into essentials and non-essentials for steering committee consideration. Committee expenditures and obligations are limited to approved amounts. To assure control, chairpersons are held responsible for departures from approved budgets.

Steering committees establish necessary procedural guidelines in approving budgets. Guidelines cover purchasing procedures, requirements for receipts, check issuance procedures, and necessary record-keeping requirements.

Prospectus Development

The approved budget becomes the first component of what alternatively has been called a strategic plan or prospectus for the special event. This document or verbal blueprint also includes a calendar and schedules, a program listing preliminary and sub-events as well as the major event; media timetables, and agendas for each event and sub-event.

The calendar, as the word implies, is a chronological summary of events. Chronologies can be as simple as meeting agendas and as complex as breakdowns of the weeks of activities associated with the opening of a World's Fair.

While calendars list events for a day or week, schedules provide hour-by-hour breakdowns of the same activities. Schedules usually describe as well as itemize events and, in many cases, identify coordinators and some participants. While seldom incorporated into strategic plans or prospectuses, schedules often are later used as beginning points in developing agendas for individual events.

Strategic plans or prospectuses also usually include preliminary plans to publicize the event. Media plans, as they are called, are based on schedules, agendas, and media opportunities that will be created by listed activities. Releases and illustrations to be distributed during the course of the event are listed together with distribution dates and target media.

IMPLEMENTATION

Strategic plans often include critical path flow charts illustrating the tasks involved in developing a special event and the time frames in which each will be accomplished. When steering committees have finally approved all plans, these documents can be reproduced in ultra-large size to provide continuing guidance to managers and their staffs.

Whether maintained as sheets in planning binders or enlarged to wall size, critical path or other calendar-based systems are necessary to track the myriad of elements that must be brought together to assure success. Hundreds of individuals may be involved in implementing the plan. Each must always be aware of "what comes next," and visual displays enable managers to avoid lengthy and repetitive explanations.

Responsibility for executing the component tasks of the strategic plan are assigned to subcommittees or task forces. Most special event managers appoint contacts, program, and arrangements committees; others may be created as well.

Contacts Committee

The nature of special events governs the relative importance of committee efforts. Contacts committees are vital wherever and whenever events are designed to attract public participation. Contacts committee members are responsible for maintaining liaison with all of the many public and quasi-public organizations that are, or perceive themselves to be, vitally interested in the event.

Governmental agencies are especially important where permits must be obtained for parades, for special parking arrangements, or for other activities that may be disruptive to the community. Disruptions also may attract the attention of special interest groups. Merchants may not be well-disposed, for example, toward an organization or event that might keep patrons from their doors. Neighborhood residents may object to the noise attendant to a block party, and fishermen are likely to complain about the impact of boat racing on their fishing grounds.

Contacts committee members are responsible for dealing with all these groups, preferably before rather than after objections lead them to create potentially disruptive public issues. Members of the Contacts committee therefore attempt to anticipate sources of potential complaints and act to neutralize prospective difficulties.

Contacts committees also may be assigned responsibility for discouraging the scheduling of potentially conflicting events. This objective often can be achieved by maintaining contact with hotel sales managers, theater and coliseum managers, and others who often are first to become aware of event planners' activities. Conflict avoidance can be a diplomatically delicate process in that commercial interest often are involved. The process nevertheless can be productive in that other groups share the organization's interest in avoiding potentially troublesome conflicts.

Program Committee

Depending on time factors, program committee tasks can be more formidable than those of the contacts committee. Assembling the vital components of a successful program in a short period of time can challenge the most effective organizer.

Speakers seldom are available on short notice. Politicians, entertainers, and athletes make schedule arrangements months or years in advance. Where specific individuals are considered essential to the success of events, planning processes must be made contingent on their availability. Selection of dates, in other words, can be governed by the schedules of key participants.

Program committees' primary concerns usually revolve around participants, masters of ceremonies, entertainers, and others identified on the event program. Scope of program activities therefore governs the complexity of the special event. The dedication of a bank's new headquarters building, for example, may involve a series of separately programmed events for different groups and conducted over a period of weeks or months.

Arrangements Committee

The most demanding of program committee situations is no less complex than the set of tasks that must be completed by the arrangements committee. Where the program committee may be responsible for identifying, contacting, and recruiting those who will appear on the program, the arrangements committee must deal with their needs before, during, and after the event.

Associated problems are greater in number and complexity than appear to be the case. Each speaker or entertainer has special requirements—reasonable or unreasonable—that must be satisfied to obtain his or her participation. Each will be following a different travel schedule and may or may not be traveling alone. Demands on arrangements committee members compound where the latter conditions prevail.

In general, arrangements committees assume responsibility for speakers and entertainers from the time they leave their homes or prior engagements until the time they have returned home or reached their next engagements. Each must be assumed to be wholly incapable of performing the slightest task for himself or herself. They must be met at airport gates, for example, rather than in baggage areas. They must be transported by limousine rather than taxi, and their hotel rooms must be selected, furnished, and otherwise equipped to exacting standards. Their agents usually make such requirements known well in advance and in excruciating detail.

Arrangements and communication committees together must assume responsibility for an inordinate amount of detail. In addition to recruiting, transporting, and housing event participants, committee members will handle printing, signs and displays, parking, accommodations, entertainment, souvenirs, food and catering, prizes, gratuities, temporary help, and all of the necessities of media relations.

COMMUNICATION

Complete and timely information from steering and arrangements committees is critical to special event communicators. Special events presumably are designed to induce predetermined responses from specific audience or stakeholder groups. The best of events will fail to achieve that objective unless pertinent information reaches the groups involved.

Information about special events usually is transmitted through two primary communication systems: advertising and public relations. The two must function effectively together and separately if the event is to achieve the best possible results. Communication committees for larger special events often are subdivided into advertising and public relations groups for greater ease in operation.

Advertising

Members of the advertising committee are responsible for developing and producing commercial messages for dissemination through the mass media. Design and placement of signs and banners, purchase and scheduling of broadcast and print media advertising, and related activities also are part of the advertising function.

The advertising committee also may be assigned responsibility for developing booklets, brochures, programs, announcements, and other printed materials necessary in special event production. These tasks in some cases are assigned to the public relations committee where that committee's work load is less demanding.

Public Relations

Complexity in public relations tasks is governed by the dimensions of the event involved. Where special events attract large numbers of out-of-town media representatives and require maintaining extensive media facilities, the public relations committee's work may be limited to the relatively narrow publicity sector.

Preparation of media kits and their content, development of news releases, scheduling of interviews, and similar activities can be time-consuming where events attract national as well as local media. Demand is even greater where international, business, professional, or trade media are present as well.

Public relations personnel in any circumstances are responsible for supervising photography, establishing media schedules, arranging accommodations for media, and seeing that their transportation and communication needs are met. The latter alone can require buses or aircraft and hosts of telephone or microwave communication links.

ASSESSING RESULTS

As in any other communication effort, planners should determine well in advance how results are to be measured. For the Coca Cola centennial, the company used clipping and video monitoring services supplemented by international field offices to calculate numbers of publicity placements and potential audience exposure. This approach probably was the most sophisticated available given the nature of the event and the sponsoring company. Corporate anniversary celebrations usually are not expected to produce significant change in product sales.

Different, and more demanding, measurement criteria often are applied in other circumstances. Results of a mall promotion, for example, may be measured in incremental gain in sales for the period. A voter rally's outcome is measured in attendance. Only rarely, as in the Coca-Cola case, is media exposure a satisfactory gauge of results.

IN SUMMARY

Special events are miniatures of communication programs. They are developed through an identical set of procedural steps. They require almost identical levels of effort. They differ only in that they are conducted over shorter periods of time. Where communication programs are on-going in nature and usually are cast in annual cycles, special events range in duration from hours to weeks although planning can require a year or more.

The term special event covers a broad range of activities. Luncheons and meetings can be managed as special events and, in special circumstances, require such attention. Contemporary special events range from parades and mall events to festivals and promotional activities of all kinds.

A number of critical concerns must be addressed in special event planning regardless of the type of event involved. Factors that require attention include the extent to which organizational resources can be applied, availability of underwriting and community assets, size of potential audiences and the relevance of the event to the organization. Economic potential, timeliness, and attractiveness to volunteers also require attention.

Special event development involves several complex processes and overlapping: budgeting, scheduling, planning, implementation, and communication. Budgeting involves the development and management of fiscal control procedures. Scheduling, as the name implies, deals with selecting dates and making arrangements for participants. Planning and implementation encompass the "putting it together" stages of the process while communication requires "getting the word" to stakeholder groups of all kinds.

ADDITIONAL READING

Goldblatt, Joe J. "How to Buy Special Event Professionals," *Association Management* 37, no. 12 (December 1985).

Golden, Hal, and Kitty Hanson. *How to Plan, Produce and Publicize Special Events*. New York: Oceana Publications, 1960.

Harper, Doug, "Grand Openings," *Incentive* 162, no. 10 (December 1988).

Curtis, Carlton L. "Special Events: How They're Planned and Organized," In *Experts in Action: Inside Public Relations*, 2nd ed., Chester Burger, ed. New York: Longman, 1989.

"'I Do' Did It: How Vintage Pasadena Hotel Floated Facts of Life to Audience of 350 Mil." *Bulldog Reporter* (June 21, 1989).

Lant, Jeffrey, "Secrets to a Successful Special Event," *Nonprofit World* 5, no. 2 (March/April 1987).

"Malls Used by PR Firms to Stage Special Events," *O'Dwyer's PR Services Report* (September 1989) 26-27.

McIvor, Patrick J. "Special Events: Making Them Work for You," *Medical Marketing & Media* 22, no. 7 (June 1987) 44-50.

Mount, Alan R., and John P. LaPlace, "Effective Promotions at Small Shopping Centers," *Journal of Property Management* (November-December, 1987).

Mulligan, Thomas J. "There's More to Special Events Than Raising Money," *Fund Raising Management* 18, no. 2 (April 1987).

"Planning the Special Event: Negotiating the Do's & Don'ts," *Fund Raising Management* 15, no. 11 (January 1985).

Sheerin, Mira J. "Budgeting Special Events: Key to a Successful Benefit," *Fund Raising Management* 16, no. 10, (December 1985).

———. "Some Guidelines for Selecting the Right Type of Special Event," *Fund Raising Management* 17 no. 2 (April 1986).

10

Issues and Crises

Terminology associated with communication in abnormal circumstances has become more than a little confusing. *Crisis*, *disaster*, and *emergency* all have been linked to *communication* to create terms more impressive than enlightening. Organizations' communication needs intensify with crises, emergencies, and disasters, but these are different types of events.

Crisis is among the most misused words in the language of communication. A *crisis* is a decisive turning point in a condition or state of affairs. The word often is associated with turning points in acute diseases. Most important from a communication standpoint, crises are not disasters.

A *disaster* is an unfortunate sudden and unexpected event. Disasters occur through carelessness, negligence, or bad judgement, or are produced by natural forces such as hurricanes or floods. Organizations must communicate with stakeholders about the impact of disasters, but disasters are not crises. Disasters can create crises, but crises and disasters are not identical.

Disasters are better classified as emergencies. An *emergency* is an unforseen occurrence; a sudden and urgent occasion for action. Crises and disasters create communication emergencies of different kinds. *Crisis communication* and *disaster communication*, as a result, are equally separate and different functions.

CRISIS AND DISASTER COMMUNICATION

Disaster communication involves a set of planned procedures that begin immediately and automatically when a disaster occurs. Communication plans usually are incorporated into organizational disaster response plans but may be separately maintained by communication departments. Well-conceived plans meet the informational needs of all stakeholders. Disaster communication plans are activated in the face of natural and man-made disasters. They are implemented with equal speed in the face of hurricanes, oil spills, and nuclear accidents.

Disaster communication and crisis communication differ because crises develop more slowly than disasters and in relatively predictable fashion. Crises occur where issues are neglected or otherwise mishandled. Issues originate in organizational environments or through the behavior of their stakeholders. A strike is a crisis in employee relations resulting from organizational inability to achieve accommodation with workers. Crises develop equally readily in consumer relations, stockholder relations, and similar areas.

Crises of another sort occur "downstream" from natural disasters. Second-, third- and fourth-order effects of disasters can create crises. Consider, for example, the results of disruptions after a hurricane. Interrupted deliveries to a plant producing parts for manufacturers thousands of miles away can cripple production there and create economic crises at points far removed from the disaster.

Crises produced by disasters, like those that originate in stakeholder groups, should not create surprises. Disasters may be unforseen and unpredictable, but resulting crises almost always can be anticipated. The term *crisis communication* thus is inappropriate where applied to responses to the unforseen or the unpredictable.

Developmental Processes

Crises such as strikes or supply shortages are produced by interactions between organizations and environments. Crises usually develop slowly, permitting communicators the luxury of planning and measured response. From a time standpoint, the demands of crisis communication are similar to those of campaign planning.

Disasters, in contrast, are sudden, unpredictable, and usually unpreventable. Most are natural rather than human in origin, as with earthquakes, tidal waves, droughts, and floods. Some disasters, such as chemical spills and airplane crashes, are created through human accident.

Organizations must respond to disasters as well as crises, but the communication aspects of crises and disasters are different. Disasters require instantaneous response and permit almost no time for planning. Forward-looking organizations anticipate disasters by preparing necessarily ambiguous disaster plans designed to cover every eventuality. The ambiguities extend to communication responses, which may or may not be successfully implemented when disaster occurs.

Planning Processes

Planning for crises and disasters, and for attendant communication, varies because of differences between the types of events. Disasters at best can be anticipated only by monitoring the experiences of others. Few packaged goods organizations, for example, anticipated the product tampering that Johnson & Johnson experienced with Tylenol. Most changed packaging methods and took other after-the-fact precautions in the wake of the Tylenol case. A few may have modified standing disaster plans, but little else could be done.

Crises are another matter. Crises are more predictable events that usually occur because organizations or managers permit them to develop. With few exceptions, crises are products of neglected issues. Yesterday's problems are today's issues and tomorrow's crises.

These circumstances lead to imbalance in allocating communication resources. Crises are almost certain to arise from neglected problems and issues, while disasters are virtually unpredictable. Communicators routinely commit more resources to avoiding crises than to preparing for disasters. Resources may be quickly reallocated when disaster occurs, but day-to-day communication practices focus more on the crises and their precursors than on possible disasters. Organizations have become so sensitive to potential crises, in fact, that many dedicate substantial resources to communication subdisciplines called issues management and risk management.

Neither issues management nor risk management are generally accepted concepts among communicators. Public relations counselors especially have taken exception to the premise that issues management is a separate and distinct discipline. Analyses of the writings of early issues managers reveals little to differentiate their efforts from public relations practice. Issues managers claim to deal with events and trends leading to governmental intervention, as in environmental and energy matters. Risk managers begin a step earlier.

RISK MANAGEMENT

Viewed objectively, risk management is a tactic applied to prevent issues from deteriorating into crises. Risk management is a complex process that includes building organizational credibility, identifying problems, assessing and weighing risk, establishing standardized response mechanisms, and aggressively managing the program.

Risk management processes enable managers to act on Peter Drucker's concept of organizations: "The single most important thing to remember about any enterprise," Drucker says, "is that results exist only on the outside. The result of a business is a satisfied customer. The result of a hospital is a healed patient. The result of a school is a student who has learned something and puts it to work ten years later. Inside an enterprise there are only costs"(1989, p. 230).

Risk management involves three primary components. First, risks are identified and weighed. Second, problems are identified and categorized as they develop. Finally, and most importantly, an honest approach is essential in problem identification and to maintain organizational credibility.

Risks and Weights

While applied to prevent issues from becoming crises, risk management also is useful in assessing the potential vulnerability of organizations. Magnitude of risk, prospective visibility, and potential liability vary from issue to issue and industry to industry. Problems such as layoffs and plant closing usually are self-inflicted, but others originate externally. Origins of most problems can be sorted into nine categories:

1. Change in public perception of organizations or the quality of their products or services.
2. Change in market or competitive conditions.
3. Change in management resulting from board room battles or executive death or disability.
4. Product failures and attendant liabilities, especially where governmental investigations result.
5. Labor problems in the form of conflicts or shortages.
6. Economic problems.
7. Difficulties attendant to regulation or deregulation.
8. Adverse international events.
9. Attack by outsiders in one form or another.

The latter category includes hostile takeover attempts, lawsuits, complaints by environmentalists or special interest groups, and similar occurrences.

Categorizing potential problems is helpful in damage control but several other factors must be considered in weighing associated risks. The problem potential of industrial accidents, for example, varies with preparedness, the conditions under which mishaps occur, the places they occur, the nature of individuals involved, whether the incidents are isolated or serial events, and so forth.

Problem Identification

Early identification of potential problems requires personal and professional information networks. At least ten information sources usually are used:

1. Reviews of historical organizational records including news clippings, news releases, internal correspondence, board and executive committee minutes, and so forth.
2. Periodic interviews with managerial and supervisory personnel concerning their experiences with the organization and in the industry.
3. Regular interviews with legal, quality control, training, safety, governmental affairs, security, medical, legislative, marketing and other organizational specialists as well as those who serve as consultants to the organization.
4. Networking with colleagues, formal and informal, at business and professional association meetings.
5. Attending industry and professional meetings.
6. Monitoring journals, newsletters and books as well as mass media content related to the organization and its stakeholders.
7. Getting on mailing lists of other organizations in the industry and associated industries to identify (a) problems they are experiencing and (b) the ways those problems are being solved.
8. Subscribing to one or more insider newsletters.
9. Cataloging media reports to track developing trends.
10. Regularly applying survey research to monitor change in attitude and opinion among stakeholder groups.

Resulting information enables communicators to view organizational environments honestly; to avoid the blindness that permits some to delude themselves about the seriousness of environmental developments. Monitoring should produce objective views of organizations, their stakeholders, news media, and the industry or industries in which organizations operate.

Where the latter objective is achieved, existing and potential issues can be sorted into four management categories. Each type of issue—latent, emerging, critical, and follow up—requires different handling. The impact of latent issues can be anticipated. The organization should be able to resolve potential difficulty through accommodation. Emerging issues demand immediate attention and preventive action to preclude their reaching crisis proportions. Issues in the critical category literally are crises and deserve handling as such. Follow-up issues are the still-troublesome remnants of crisis settlements that require continuing attention lest they revert to crisis status or trigger additional problems.

TYPOLOGIES AND ORIGINS

Students of crises and crisis resolution have applied several analytical tools in examining these phenomena and the ways in which they can be anticipated and managed. Most of the tools involve typologies that permit crises to be categorized by type or origin.

Boston University Professor Otto Lerbinger (1986) has established a typology based on causal factors. Curtis G. Linke (1989, p. 166) of United Technologies' Pratt & Whitney Division has developed another in which he categorizes crises by developmental stages.

Crisis Typologies

Crises, Professor Lerbinger says, can be sorted into four categories:

- Technological, caused by human error or by unforeseen side effects arising out of processes or equipment used in the production of goods and services.
- Confrontational, arising out of the actions of governmental or social action groups seeking to block or change the activities or policies of the organization.
- Malevolent, caused by groups or individuals intent on destroying the organization and/or its operations.
- Managerial, arising out of ineptitude, negligence, callousness or misconduct on the part of senior managers.(6)

Alternatively, crises can be categorized as products of (a) misdeeds or (b) misunderstandings. The former consist of problems that occur because one or several individuals or groups of individuals did something wrong. Problems of this sort tend to escalate rapidly in the absence of intervention, which should consist of prompt, open, and truthful response. Crises of misunderstanding are equally troublesome but more readily corrected. They occur where stakeholders misunderstand organizational activities or policies. They are resolved through candid responses to stakeholder complaints. Involving stakeholders in problem resolution also can be helpful.

Finally, crises can be sorted into Linke's (1989) four categories: exploding, immediate, building, and continuing. Those in the exploding category, Linke says, include fires, accidents, and other self-defined, noticeable events that create immediate impacts. Immediate crises, in contrast, catch organizations by surprise but leave time to prepare, as in the case of environmental problems and governmental hearings. Building problems are those that can be anticipated, such as labor negotiations or layoffs, while continuing problems originate in chronic sources of difficulty such as drugs in the work place (167).

Crisis Origins

Crises may be products of external forces, internal ineptitude, or both. Communicators must guard against all eventualities. They must be especially alert, however, to managerial insensitivity. Senior managers are used to dealing in hard numbers rather than abstract concepts. They tend to be insensitive to human values that can't be expressed numerically. While decisive when dealing with clear choices, managers often experience difficulty where options are not well-defined. Among pitfalls that often entrap them:

1. Inability to understand the importance of popular perception. Managers often fail to comprehend that logical and rational decisions that look wrong will be perceived as wrong.
2. Acceptance of bad counsel. Lawyers, investment bankers and others perceived as "experts" often argue against honesty and openness. Strategies they advocate to avoid litigation or other contingent problems lead to concealment rather than candor, with predictable results.
3. Tendencies to deny simple, open explanations of organizational behavior, which in turn raise ethical and moral questions. Individual and organizational credibility suffer as a result.

These conditions often arise through weaknesses in managerial and supervisory education and training. Managers frequently find themselves at a loss to justify qualitative decisions in terms of public rather than organizational good. Most need considerable re-education before attempting to deal with advocates and media representatives more attuned to human than economic values.

Maintaining Credibility

The communicator's greatest asset in any effort—program, campaign, special event or crisis response—is organizational credibility. With credibility, all things are possible. Without credibility, little can be accomplished. Credibility is a commodity gained over time and at great expense in effort and consistency. Credibility is easily lost and, once lost, is doubly difficult to regain. Those who doubt soon learn the error of their ways, and the lessons are painful.

The foregoing is not a lecture in morality but a statement of fact. Society is intolerant of deceit and deception, real or perceived. Breaches of faith—in advertising and all other forms of communication—are long remembered, seldom forgiven, and never forgotten. These circumstances impose stringent requirements on those who seek to prevent crises. Keys to success include:

1. Correctness of purpose. Organizational operations must match reasonable and rational stakeholder expectations.
2. Acceptance of legitimacy in the arguments of others. Efforts to discredit are apt to be self-destructive. Public tendencies to support underdogs and to look askance at large organizations can be doubly troublesome.
3. Effectiveness in communication; in explaining the organization and its mission. The process can be difficult where organizations or their functions are technical, complex or otherwise hard to understand.
4. Fairness. Organizational policies, procedures, and behaviors always must meet the test of fairness. Public trust is greatest where organizational objectives are coincident with stakeholders' human and economic needs.

Organizations seldom fail where these principals are adopted and universally followed. Organizations seldom succeed where they are ignored. Adherence protects the organization's franchise to exist. Organizations continue to exist only where their behaviors are understood and generally approved, as demonstrated during prohibition and in the campaign against smoking.

FROM ISSUES TO CRISES

Risk management requires little of communicators in their traditional communication roles. Considerable may be expected, however, where communicators participate in strategic planning and subsequent affirmative communication activities. Communicators' roles expand at the strategic level to encompass issues management and risk management. These conditions require an understanding of the nature of issues, the manner in which they become crises, and the ways in which organizations contain issues and prevent crises.

Those who have written about issues management disagree as often as they agree on the finer points of the process. They are almost unanimous, however, in declaring that most issues are more complex than they appear. The complexities are most readily grasped by examining the phases or stages through which issues evolve.

Issue Development

Issues have been examined from several developmental perspectives. They have been viewed as current, emerging, and strategic, and as passing through social, political, legislative, and regulatory phases. Issues also can be categorized as nonexistent, dormant, potential, imminent, current, and critical. Finally, they can viewed as operational, corporate, and societal. No one of these perspectives adequately explains the evolution of issues. They are collectively helpful, however, in dealing with issues management.

Sources. Those who have examined issue origins sort them into four categories: operational, corporate, societal, and personal. The operational and corporate categories are relatively straightforward. The societal and personal are more complex. Operational issues involve matters such as hazardous waste disposal, acid rain, water shortages, traffic congestion, and other factors that relate to or may influence organizational operations. Corporate issues encompass legal and ethical matters, public disclosure requirements, and governance.

Societal issues subdivide into two categories: political-/governmental and personal rights or entitlements. The political-/governmental include reform movements dealing with initiative processes, election campaigns, and the organization of Congress. National economic planning and openness of government also fall into the societal category. The personal rights and entitlements category encompasses some of the more volatile contemporary issues. Among them are health care, personal privacy, sexual preference, comparable worth, and job ownership.

Types. Since issues are group-specific, they are most readily examined from organizational perspectives as falling into one of six types: nonexistent, dormant, potential, imminent, current, and critical. Nonexistent issues are those designated by parties to other issues as "not an issue" in their discussions. The other types are more complex.

Potential issues are those that may engage two or more parties, as can be the case, for example, where government considers alternative locations for a waste disposal plant. The issue will be joined between the agency and residents of any neighborhood selected.

Dormant issues arise intermittently where, for example, the completed waste disposal system might create odor problems during warmer weather or under other recurrent conditions.

Imminent issues are those expected to arise out of other events. Electrical brown-outs inevitably make energy production an issue.

Freezes in Brazil ultimately bring higher coffee prices and consumer protests.

Current issues are those with which organizations are presently involved while critical issues are potentially most damaging, as in the case of an oil or chemical spill.

Life cycles. Issues also have been categorized by developmental phase or life cycle. Areas of concern destined to become issues may first be observed in a "social expectation" stage in which public expectations of organizations change and changes capture media attention.

Issues that organizations fail to address during the social expectation stage progress to the political. The beginnings of the political stage are marked by the coalescing of ad hoc advocacy groups. Formal organizations then take shape to advance their own solutions to perceived problems.

Unless resolved at the political stage, issues move to the legislative. Legislative arenas can be municipal, county, state or federal. Governments are prone to act wherever elected officials perceive action to be in their interest, or inaction to be to their detriment.

The regulatory phase begins as legislative action is completed. Some call this the litigative-regulatory phase for two reasons. Statutes are reduced to regulations before they can be implemented. Litigation designed to shape final outcomes often occurs in the wake of legislation and during regulatory processes.

Stages. Finally, from the organizational perspective, issues can be viewed from what might be called a "calendar standpoint." Three distinct calendar categories are involved for current, emerging, and strategic issues.

Current issues, under this system of categories, are those moving toward resolution through legislative or regulatory processes. Current issues are the domain of organizations' lobbyists and governmental relations staffs. Emerging issues are expected to reach current status in 18 to 36 months and are handled by senior managers or issues management teams. Strategic issues are potentially troublesome, more than three years in the future, and handled by long-range or strategic planners.

Complexity. Issues always are complex. Most produce varied results that influence different groups in different ways. Battle lines that form over issues usually involve efforts to protect selfish interests. Consider, for example, the manner in which global warming will impact several groups. This trend doubtless will progress through predictable stages:

1. Support for alternative energy sources to the detriment of economic interests linked to existing sources.

2. Legislation to support alternative energy sources.
3. Changes in transportation systems and emergence of new systems.

The automotive industry could suffer economically while alternative transportation systems prosper. At the same time, heating costs would decline while air-conditioning expenses increase. Fishing seasons would grow longer, to the benefit of the recreation industry, but beach erosion could increase rapidly and coastal toxic waste disposal sites could be flooded. Tourism industry components, depending on locations and seasonal orientations, would boom or self-destruct. These are the sort of complexities that compel organizations to manage issues.

Issues Management

No potentially damaging issue can be ignored regardless of the category or categories to which it is assigned. Most are more complex than they appear. Many who would outlaw agricultural chemicals, for example, ignore potential for smaller harvests and higher prices.

Issues are further complicated because they often are intentionally obscured by the parties. Corporate issues usually are cost-shifting issues, says former issues manager Raymond Ewing. They involve demands for equity among those without political or economic power and can be viewed as conflicts between efficiency (the goal of business) and equity (the goal of citizen groups and, presumably, government).

Organizational efforts to manage issues and prevent their becoming crises involve six steps: identification, evaluation, research and analysis, defining strategic options, implementing programs, and evaluating results.

Identification. Issue identification requires understanding the process that leads to public policy. The process begins with growing public concern over a real or perceived problem. The interests of the political system are engaged as concerns grow and legislation and/or regulation ultimately result. Communicators involved in issues management track social, economic, technological, and political changes that might influence their organizations. They identify areas in which issue advocates' objectives overlap organizational interests. Issues arise where these interests are in conflict.

Evaluation. The interests of most organizations necessarily conflict to some extent with those of every stakeholder group. Each group seeks to satisfy its needs at the expense of other groups. Management's tasks therefore require on-going efforts to equitably resolve intergroup conflict. The evaluation process permits assigning priorities to identified issues, enabling the organization to respond accordingly.

Research and analysis. Ranking issues in order of organizational importance often requires more information than is readily available. Complex political, social, and economic forces involved in environmental issues, for example, make appropriate responses difficult to identify. Research permits managers to trace issues to their origins, identify sources of influence, and gain insight into how emerging issues are apt to develop.

Strategy options. Most organizations establish issue priorities by examining risks to organizational welfare. Nature of risk, level of confidence in available information, and likelihood that issues will subside all are considered in defining strategy options.

Action programs. Where issues pose immediate threats to organizations' ability to achieve their objectives, early response is in order. Action programs require identifying the interests of the parties involved, deciding on responses, designing messages, selecting communication channels, and executing plans and strategies.

Strategy evaluation. Strategies and tactics applied in action programs require constant monitoring. Results must be measured to ensure that objectives are achieved as planned and to enable program administrators to fine tune their efforts. Management techniques used in issue action programs are similar to those used in communication campaigns. On-going monitoring and fine tuning can make the difference between success and failure.

DEALING WITH STAKEHOLDERS

Issues management is doubly complex in that stakeholders involved rarely are kooks, cranks, or crackpots. Contemporary pressure groups tend to consist of well-educated, socially conscious and deeply committed activists prepared to use confrontational techniques to achieve their objectives. Organizations that respond with tactics once used in dealing with hippies and yippies flirt with disaster.

Intelligence and skill are vital in shaping responses to activists. Rather than being manipulated by dissidents and responding to pressure, organizations must join in framing and shaping public agendas to ensure that their interests are considered.

Management Pitfalls

Organizations' first steps in coping with stakeholders should be management-oriented and preventive. Senior managers must be protected from the isolation that can distort their perspectives and lead to flawed decision-making processes. Four major pitfalls require special attention.

First, managers must avoid running organizations as if the public does not exist. No organizational activity long remains secret. Aggressive reporters distrustful of organizations and spurred by public interest in business and government frustrate efforts toward secrecy. Bad news is best handled by early release.

Second, managers must avoid isolation. Bad news too often gets "filtered out" as it moves up the organization. Loyal, intelligent dissent among subordinates should be encouraged. Minority opinions appended to memos can be especially helpful in protecting against isolation.

Third, managers should beware of inexperienced spokespersons. Potential ineptitude is less dangerous than a tendency among the inexperienced to oversell, or to talk themselves into awkward corners.

Finally, senior managers must be wary of legal counsel. Ill-advised legal advice can invite disaster. Star Kist Foods, apparently on advice of counsel, elected not to respond to a Canadian Broadcasting Corporation charge that it had shipped a million cans of "rancid and decomposing tuna." Company profits dropped 90 percent.

Response to Activism

Successful response to activism is based on logic and rationality rather than emotionalism. The nature of activists must be known and their motivations understood before appropriate responses can be designed. Most importantly, their ethical legitimacy and seriousness must be accepted. Efforts to discredit activists rather than seriously consider and equitably respond to their claims can be disastrous.

Organizational legitimacy is conferred by the public and can be quickly withdrawn. Organizations are held accountable for their actions and must be sensitive to change in public and societal expectations and demands. General Motors Corporation's experiences with Ralph Nader are exemplary of disasters that can befall those tempted to deal with legitimate public interests in cavalier fashion.

Good works no longer are an adequate response to activists and the urgency associated with many of their concerns. Organizations that would succeed in contemporary society must help frame public agendas, a process that requires openness.

Leadership in openness must come from the top of the organization. Conflicts over disparate interests should be expected and welcomed by senior manager as opportunities to establish or enhance intergroup relationships.

Activist Groups

While attempting to deal openly and equitably with stakeholders, organizations must recognize that some operate beyond the limits of rational dialog. Dissidents usually fall into three basic categories: reformers, activists, and protestors. Group characteristics require variation in organizational response.

Reformers usually are bent on improving the system through protests ranging from demonstrations conducted within statutory limits to consumer boycotts. Activists use all but the most violent forms of protest. Extremists are committed to violence for its own sake. Extremists are the mercenaries of social protest. They usually have no personal ideological attachments and are recruited by others in support of specific causes.

Organizations can deal rationally with reformers and activists, but extremists are another matter. Dialogue is the best tactical approach to the first two groups but efforts to deal with extremists usually are best directed toward exposing them as social deviants. Many individuals fail to adequately discriminate between types of dissidents, however, and organizations must proceed with caution.

Information about dissident groups is published by the Foundation for Public Affairs in Washington in *Public Interest Profiles*, a book containing data on 100 organizations. Staff size, membership, budget, scope of activity, basic purpose, operating methods, political orientation, publications, and funding sources all are listed together with summaries of organizational agendas and analyses of their effectiveness.

Coping With Activists

Organizational responses to activists and events are best carried out on two levels. Immediate reactions are essential to organizational appearances while more substantive responses are prepared. The immediate usually are more or less standardized damage control responses that have proven at least temporarily effective in coping with crises while marshaling resources. Damage control in accident cases, for example, should include assistance to victims and their families while the organization (a) re-examines procedures that may have contributed to the mishap and (b) makes and announces any changes that may be appropriate to guard against repetitions.

Where scandal occurs, spokespersons should differentiate between individual and organizational actions to achieve as much separation as practical. The same principle applies where interorganizational problems surface. Spokespersons should distance the organization from the accused without being judgmental. Disagreements should be recognized rather than papered over: "Our opponents have a right to their views, but . . . ."

Most importantly, where organizations fail to meet their obligations and problems result, responses must encompass two elements: acknowledgement of failure accompanied by expressions of regret, and detailed plans to prevent repetition.

Responding to Emergencies

Emergency response plans are necessary to deal with developing crises. Contemporary society, and contemporary organizations, are too complex to meet emerging problems on ad hoc bases. Emergency response plans therefore usually involve most of the following elements:

- A decision-making team separate from senior managers who may be involved in and/or embarrassed by the problem.
- One or more feedback networks to track stakeholder responses to organizational actions and statements.
- Designated respondents to handle inquiries from stakeholder groups and assure that the organization "speaks with one voice."
- Active rather than reactive communication systems to deliver the organizational messages to stakeholder groups.
- Investigative teams, where necessary or appropriate to ensure that problem causes are identified and facts are known.

The scope of these activities requires extensive resources, but resource allocations are readily justified where the long-term welfare of the organization is at stake.

RESPONDING TO CRISES

Early responses to crises can limit the extent to which organizations are damaged. Prompt, open responses minimize damage potential. The reverse is equally true. Efforts to evade, avoid, and conceal compound organizational difficulties.

Crisis response involves multiple processes, some more complex than others. Organizations must first respond to the needs of crisis victims, contain problems involved, and assess the extent of damage. Governmental agencies, manufacturers, vendors, and others then must be notified while internal crisis management procedures are implemented. Finally, the organization must communicate effectively with all involved, dealing with legal, corporate responsibility and media problems in the process. In handling these steps, however, three principles always must be applied:

- Don't compound the problem. Avoid speculation, lies, misleading statements, stalling, and stonewalling. Don't pretend things are going well when they're not. Never get in the way of reporters. Never assign blame. Treat reporters fairly and equitably. Adopt an open communication policy and make certain it's enforced. Remember, both the organization's reputation—and the communicator's— are at stake.
- Get the problem and the story behind you as quickly as possible. Gather and release all available information as rapidly as practicable. Announce any delays and the reasons for them. Make certain announcements are complete the first time. Where information must be omitted, point out omissions and the reasons they exist.
- Prepare for tomorrow. You'll deal with the same media again and again. Your stature and reputation will depend on how well you handle the crisis. Your career will outlive the crisis, provided you adhere to ethical standards.

Crisis Recognition

Recognizing and defining crises involve a series of steps that lead to information, control, and management. Stages in the recognition process include:

1. Surprise, a sense of helplessness, irritation, frustration and, often, a premonition that the worst may be yet to come.
2. Early response, including handling spot information problems and controlling access to premises and people.
3. Containment, during which the organization digests the impact of the problem and its ramifications.
4. Control, during which information can be used to organizational advantage provided that no strategic errors such as "stonewalling" intervene.

Definition and Planning

The recognition stage of the response process extends in part into definition and planning. Definition involves two steps: defining the reality of the situation and preparing for action. Realistic objectives must be agreed upon by all members of the management team.

Successful definition requires answers to a set of difficult questions:

- Can the crisis escalate? What is the maximum potential and how soon might it be reached? In other words, how big can the problem become and how fast might it reach that size?
- How much media attention is likely? Does the nature of the organization and the problem warrant undue media coverage? What of proximity to population areas?
- To what extent will the problem interfere with normal operations or production levels, and with what economic impact?
- Is the organization a victim, a culprit, or both? Is the organization to blame in whole or part for the crisis?

At least three responses usually occur during the definition process: fear, need for information, and focusing. Fear develops as the seriousness of crises become known and as executives anticipate personal and organizational repercussions. Information is essential in response planning. Events that have occurred must be known before communication can begin. In focusing, the organization concentrates resources to meet needs created by the crisis.

Strategic planning involves identifying primary needs, marshaling resources, coordinating messages, and keeping communication channels open while senior managers make critical decisions. Primary steps include deciding how to publicly react; how to contain the crisis; and how to prepare for adverse reactions. A communication strategy must be developed to enable the organization to (a) forecast anticipated developments and anticipate media speculation, (b) identify topics for discussion and communication channels to be used in reaching all stakeholders; and (c) establish follow-up procedures to ensure that plans are executed.

Communication Strategies

Most crisis communication strategies involve a series of steps:
1. Define the problem
2. Establish objectives
3. Catalog resources
4. Gather information
5. List assumptions
6. Assess program potential

7. Formulate policy
8. Define audiences
9. Establish strategies and tactics
10. Organize and assign tasks
11. Establish schedules and monitoring systems
12. Assess results

Problem Definition

"Know your enemy" is a long-established campaign dictum applicable to crisis communication. Communicators succeed or fail in crisis situations through their ability to define and analyze the problem or problems at hand. Problems usually are more complex than they appear and require careful analysis. Among primary questions to be considered:

- What is the problem and why does it exist?
- What is the rationale for the proposed communication effort? What is to be accomplished and how?
- What stakeholder groups are parties to the problem and/or will need to be informed?
- What measurable, behavioral response does the organization seek from each group?
- What communication resources are available and what will be the scope of the response?
- What measurable goals can be achieved through communication?

Establishing Objectives

Only when these questions have been answered is it possible for communication objectives to be established. Objectives cover a broader range of activities during crises because communicators assume broader roles in emergency situations. Communication is paramount but communicators often handle coalition-building and networking assignments as well.

Coalition-building involves identifying, contacting, and recruiting allies who share organizational interests and may be willing to support the organization in any of several ways. This approach is identical to that used by labor, environmental, and other groups that form temporary alliances to pursue issues of mutual interest.

Networking involves similar steps but the primary objective is to gain information that may be of value during the crisis. Other organizations that have experienced similar problems, or have had dealings with parties to the crisis, are primary networking targets. Their experiences may help in anticipating opponents' strategies, tactics, and demands, or in dealing with other problems at hand.

Cataloging Resources

Alliances established through coalition-building and information obtained in networking can be major assets during protracted crises. Allies are most helpful where they are not overtly involved, making them more influential in legislative and regulatory areas. Many also can provide behind-the-scenes assistance in the form of information. Union organizing campaigns, for example, tend to follow established patterns. Knowledge of those patterns arms planners to frustrate their opponents as readily as military intelligence assists generals.

Other resources also must be identified as planning begins. Planners must know what to expect in organizational resources, especially monetary and human. Crisis responses seldom are provided for in organizational budgets and must be met with resources reallocated from other functions. Planners require sufficient information to manage the process. Precise numbers are unnecessary but reasonable estimates are vital. Planners who fail to obtain firm commitments as to resources find planning frustrating if not impossible. Plans to climb Mt. Everest would be difficult to complete, for example, without knowing whether climbers will wear boots, tennis shoes, or bedroom slippers.

Gathering Information

Research is among the more demanding components of the crisis resolution process. Two processes are involved: gathering and validating data. Validation is essential in dealing with information from allies and other less-than-quotable sources. Media representatives hold communicators accountable for errors, so facts must be validated before they can be used.

Information gathering encompasses all the techniques described in Chapter 5, and one other: acquiring complete data concerning incidents, events, or organizations involved in the crisis. The planner's first priority in crises is complete information. What happened? How did it happen? Who was involved? Why did it happen? Where did it happen? When did it happen? Complete, accurate answers must be quickly obtained.

Information necessary to answer media questions must be supplemented by other data. Information from company files and computer
databases can illuminate the history of the problem or trend.

Listing Assumptions

As information is gathered, assumptions are made—consciously or
unconsciously. Each must be listed and validated to avoid unpleasant
surprises. The process is time-consuming but essential. Assumptions
about stakeholder groups, opponents and allies are equally important.
Neither individuals nor groups can be assumed certain to behave in
ways that organizations prefer. Planners hope for the best but
anticipate the worst in a process appropriately called worst case
planning.
Listing assumptions about stakeholders, opponents, allies, and
conditions in their environments assists communicators in evaluating
assumptions. Plans then can be adjusted to cope with worst case
results, minimizing potential for mid-campaign problems and risk of
failure.

Assessing Potential

Analyzing assumptions is a logical preliminary to a "cold light of
dawn" assessment of the crisis communication plan. Several questions
must be addressed in as searching a fashion as assumptions earlier
were examined.
What can be accomplished through communication? What can not?
What are the pros and cons in terms of each objective? What are the
potential costs, and will achieving the objectives justify the investments?
These questions are neither negative or capricious. They help
communicators strip away misconceptions that might create obstacles
to achieving organizational objectives. Only when the questions have
been answered, and discernible weaknesses addressed, should planners
proceed to more substantive issues.

Formulating Policy

Among the critical questions that must be addressed early in the
planning process is the matter of authority. Who will direct the crisis
communication effort? What authority will be reserved to senior

managers? What will be the responsibilities of staff members and others temporarily assigned to the effort?

As these questions are answered, managers also may elect to address another issue: Should the organization "go it alone" or seek assistance? Numbers and complexities of stakeholder groups often govern in this area. On-going communication efforts rarely can be shelved "for the duration."

Defining Audiences

Although a more straightforward process, audience definition is among the most critical components of communication planning. Messages must be received, assimilated, and acted upon if objectives are to be achieved. Equal attention therefore must be paid to the nature of stakeholder groups, media to which they are attuned, and types of messages those media convey most effectively.

Group demographic and sociographic characteristics are most important. Age, sex, educational level, occupation, and income level are among the significant factors involved. The more communicators know about stakeholders, the more precise they can be in fashioning messages and selecting media.

Precision requires that communicators look beyond the obvious in identifying and characterizing stakeholders. More than one union may be involved, for example, in a plant with labor problems. Unions are not homogeneous organizations. Local memberships and leaderships often are at odds with international leaderships and, occasionally, with one another. The interests of the groups differ, as do their demographic and sociographic characteristics. All these factors must be weighed in preparing messages and selecting media.

Strategies and Tactics

The assessment process assures that communication objectives are rationally prescribed. Only after objectives have been specified can communicators proceed to develop strategies and tactics. The development process is undertaken from two separate, distinct, and equally important perspectives. Communicators and senior managers must look first at organizational behaviors and only afterward toward communication strategies and tactics.

The first question the development process addresses deals with perception and reality: Does the problem at hand originate in stakeholder misperception, organizational misbehavior, or a combination of the two? Where organizational behavior is at the crux of the difficulty, behavioral change is prerequisite to communication. Successful communication requires fair and equitable exchanges or transactions followed by honesty and candor in communication. Environments and behaviors can not be permitted to conflict with interpersonal and mediated messages.

When prerequisites have been fulfilled, communicators can proceed to developing strategies and tactics. Primary strategic considerations include basic communication approaches, semantics, and timing. Tactics deal with message development, media selection, and timing of events and activities. Each must be developed within available resources, human and economic.

Tasks and Schedules

Program planners find scheduling and task assignment more easily managed during development of strategies and tactics than as a separate function. The processes complement one another where managed concurrently. Concurrent handling helps prevent overcommitment of human resources. Strategies and tactics must be revised or additional resources acquired where personnel are lacking. Whichever solution is selected is more easily accomplished where needs are identified during planning rather than afterward.

Two alternatives exist where strategies and tactics require more personnel. Consultants can be employed to supplement staff or strategies and tactics can be modified to remain within available resources. The critical nature of the adjustment process cannot be overstated. Crises always demand more of organizations than had been anticipated. The communication sector is not exempt from this "rule," which planners can anticipate only in part by holding resources in reserve in the same way contingency funds are used in budgeting.

Contingency resources are best allocated through schedules established on hour-by-hour bases for each event and activity, and for all personnel. Worst case planning always is preferable. Communicators should assume that what can go wrong will go wrong, and install "fallback systems" accordingly. The mechanics of scheduling can be handled on paper, with chalk boards, or by computer. Most contemporary planners prefer computers but many traditionalists continue to effectively use "schedule boards" that can cover the walls of "war rooms" in complex situations.

Monitoring and Assessment

While last considered during planning, monitoring and assessment are among the more important of communication functions. Monitoring enables planners to fine tune communication efforts; to modify messages and change media in response to change—or lack of change—in stakeholder perception, attitude, and opinion. The productivity of fine tuning has been demonstrated in political and fund-raising campaigns but remains a less-than-universally applied system.

Fine tuning requires sophisticated monitoring systems. Communicators must be able to track attitude and opinion among stakeholder groups through surveys, and data must be quickly processed to enhance speed of application. The process is manageable where measures of behavioral response and survey instruments are created as communication plans are developed.

Early development of measurement systems also assists in post-crisis assessment processes. Data collected then can be analyzed to pinpoint relative strengths and weaknesses and modify standing crisis and disaster plans. Post-crisis assessment should be a learning process for all involved, designed to enhance the capabilities of organizations and communicators and make them better prepared to cope with subsequent problems.

IN SUMMARY

Crisis, *disaster*, and *emergency* are not interchangeable terms. A crisis is a turning point in a developing state of affairs. A disaster is an unfortunate sudden and unexpected event of any origin. An emergency is an unforeseen occurrence requiring urgent action.

Disaster and crisis communication differ because most crises usually develop out of neglected issues or sets of circumstances that rationally could have been expected to give birth to crises. Planning for crises and disasters varies accordingly. Crisis planning begins with processes that have become identified with issues management. Issues that may lead to crises are identified and tracked through scanning and monitoring processes. Organizational responses therefore can be prepared with some degree of precision. Disaster planning is necessarily generic. Plans are drawn that presumably will enable the organization to respond efficiently and effectively to any disaster. Ambiguity inherent in all purpose plans makes them more problem prone than is the case in crisis planning.

Crisis planning logically begins with risk management, a process through which organizations maintain early warning, risk assessment, and response/management systems to cope with emerging crises. The process also enables planners to assess the vulnerability of their organizations.

Organizational ability to manage risks or issues, cope with crises, and respond effectively to disaster is governed in part by credibility. Credibility among stakeholders is difficult to obtain, easy to lose, and more difficult to recover.

Communicator participation in risk management is advisable but less than essential. Participation is valuable where communicators also are involved in strategic planning and issues management. The issues management process is complex because of the complexities that prevail in organizational environments. Those environments influence stakeholders as well as organizations, complicating communication processes.

Where crises develop, a 12-step management process usually is used:

1. Define the problem
2. Establish objectives
3. Catalog resources
4. Gather information
5. List assumptions
6. Assess program potential
7. Formulate policy
8. Define audiences
9. Establish strategies and tactics
10. Organize and assign tasks
11. Establish schedules and monitoring systems
12. Assess results

ADDITIONAL READING

Buchholz, Rogene A., William D. Evans, and Robert A. Wagley, *Management Response to Public Issues: Concepts & Cases in Strategy Formulation*. Englewood Cliffs, NJ: Prentice-Hall, 1985.

Chase, W. Howard. *Issue Management: Origins of the Future*. Stamford, CT: Issue Action Publications, 1984.

Coates, Joseph F. *Issues Management: How You Can Plan, Organize & Manage for the Future*. Mt. Airy, MD.: Lomond Publications, 1986.

Drucker, Peter F. *The New Realities: In Government and Politics / In Economics and Business / In Society and World View.* New York: Harper & Row, 1989.

Ewing, Raymond P. *Managing the Media: Proactive Strategy for Better Business-Press Relations.* New York: Quorum, 1987.

Heath, Robert L., and Richard A. Nelson. *Issues Management: Corporate Public Policymaking in an Information Society.* Beverly Hills, CA: Sage, 1986.

Howard, Carole, and Wilma Mathews. *On Deadline: Managing Media Relations.* New York: Longman, 1985.

Lerbinger, Otto. *Managing Corporate Crises: Strategies for Executives.* Boston: Barrington Press, 1986.

Linke, Curtis G. "Crisis—Dealing with the Unexpected." In Chester Burger, ed., *Experts in Action: Inside Public Relations.* 2nd ed. New York: Longman, 1989.

Merriam, John E., and Joel Makower. *Trend Watching: How the Media Create Trends and How to be the First to Uncover Them.* New York: AMACOM, 1988.

Nagelschmidt, Joseph S., ed. *The Public Affairs Handbook.* New York: AMACOM, 1982.

Pinsdorf, Marion K. *Communicating When Your Company is Under Siege: Surviving Public Crisis.* New York: Longman, 1987.

Walters, Lynne M., Lee Wilkins and Tim Walters. *Bad Tidings: Communication and Catastrophe.* Hillsdale, N.J.: Lawrence Erlbaum Associates, 1989.

11

Preparing the Budget

Success in communication is measured in two ways. The first and arguably most important measure consists of behavioral response among stakeholder groups. The second measure is the extent to which managers complete communication projects within established financial limits.

Financial limitations are prescribed by budgets. Budgets are mirror images of plans, programs, campaigns, and special events expressed in numbers rather than words. Budgets are designed to ensure that the economic aspects of communication projects are managed as efficiently as the organizational and creative. As such, they are applied in several ways.

Information contained in budgets usually is first compiled informally in the form of cost estimates. Cost estimates serve as preliminary indicators of project practicality. Information involved then is prepared in more precise form and incorporated into a plan or program to induce employers or clients to fund the projects involved. Later, budgets are used in tracking and controlling project-related expenditures to ensure that they remain within specified limits.

At worst, the budgeting process is a necessary evil—necessary in that senior managers require financial estimates before approving projects that involve significant resources. At best, budgets serve as another measure of success that communicators can use to their advantage.

Whether viewed as necessary evils or as opportunities, budgets are mandatory components of every communication project save one: crisis response. The extent and cost of responses to crises or disasters is governed by circumstances that rarely can be anticipated with any degree of accuracy. Time pressures preclude formal budget processes while organizations cope with such problems. Some organizations maintain contingency items in their budgets to cover eventualities, but these rarely are sufficient to fund communication efforts during sustained emergencies or disasters.

Some planners suggest that an organization's history of emergencies can be used to predict crisis communication funding needs with sufficient accuracy to permit development of all-inclusive budgets. Budgets ideally should be all-inclusive but communication needs associated with crises such as Exxon's 1989 Gulf of Alaska oil spill and the Three Mile Island nuclear reactor crisis rarely can be managed within any rational budgetary reserves. Budget contingency funds should be adequate, however, to permit communicators to capitalize on "targets of opportunity." These are unexpected circumstances the enable organizations to reap communication windfall in the form of media exposure or otherwise.

Other than in terms of crises or disasters, budgets usually are mandatory. Budgets may relatively concise or highly detailed. Those that accompany communication plans tend to be brief, often consisting of little more than approximate or "not-to-exceed" figures for each component program, campaign, or special event. Budgets for campaigns or special events can be very detailed, however, with every hour of secretarial time and every long distance telephone call estimated in advance.

Regardless of level of detail, budgets are nothing more than plans or programs expressed in dollars. Budgets are tools of communication management and ultimately must be mastered by every communicator. They appear less threatening, however, when viewed at closer range.

ALLOCATION VERSUS COMPETITION

Budgeting processes vary from one organization to another. At the organizational level, the budgets are designed to best allocate available resources to achieve outcomes specified in strategic and operating plans. Communication budgets can be viewed as a part of this process, through which organizational objectives are met, or as a competition for organizational resources. Each of the two perspectives usually applies to some extent. Competition often prevails in organizations where departmental and managerial stature is measured in size of budget and numbers of personnel. Conditions may be only marginally less competitive where budgets are proposed by external consultants. Competition can be intense where projects assigned externally are funded with what otherwise might be a portion of the communication department's budget.

Although competition persists, the allocation function of budgeting is equally important. Cost-sensitive organizations constantly review all operations in terms of costs and benefits, and the communication function is not exempt. Budgets therefore can also be viewed as opportunities to demonstrate the value of communication.

The Budget's Role

These conditions are best understood where budgets are examined both as requests for resources and as guidelines to control expenditures. The first approach involves getting enough money to do the job. The second focuses on making certain the money is used to produce the best possible results.

The extent to which each application occurs is a function of organizational management. Budgets usually exist as requests for resources only to the extent that managers are involved in planning processes. Plans imposed from above usually are accompanied by resources deemed sufficient to do the job.

Unilaterally established budgets nevertheless may require planning at the department level. Need for planning is governed by the level of budget detail prescribed from above. Funds may be allocated in a lump sum, by categories, or on a line item basis. Communication managers may be required to create departmental budgets within a lump sum allocation or within categories. Where senior management uses the line item approach, budgets arrive in the department in operational form.

Benefits can accrue to communicators, however, even where the process is wholly unilateral. Budgets create internal communication opportunities. The process, no matter how perfunctory, enables communicators to show senior managers or clients what they are doing and why their roles are important to organizational welfare. Communication organizations are like any others in that they ultimately are dependent on clients or constituents. The budget process can contribute to strengthening the relationships involved.

Potential for enhanced relationships is especially great in organizations where communicators may or may not enjoy total rapport with senior managers. Cooperatively managed, budgeting in these circumstances can lead to enhanced understanding between communicators and executives whose backgrounds usually are in management or accounting.

Budgeting can be formal or informal, complex or simple. In any case, communicators find the process most beneficial where financial and operational information is integrated to make documentation as informative as possible for senior managers. Program descriptions often are made a part of budget documents to ensure that senior managers are aware of the extent to which communication supports organizational objectives.

The Budgeting Process

Budgets usually are born in one of three ways. More often than not, organizations allocate specific sums to accomplish given tasks and communicators are asked to prepare detailed budgets based on the nature of tasks and allocated funds. Perhaps equally frequently, budgets are based on prior experience, with each annual or project budget serving as a model for the next. Only rarely, other than where new projects are "on the drawing board" do communicators deal in "zero-based budgeting."

The latter term refers to a process in which budget developers deliberately avoid using historical patterns in preparing new budget documents. This approach is intended to avoid tendencies to assume that prior expenditures necessarily should be repeated. Zero-based budgeting is designed to encourage careful evaluation of every proposed expenditure, specifically those included in earlier and similar projects. The zero-based process rarely is used in pure form because large parts of communication organizations' budgets usually consist of relatively inflexible commitments. Overhead is relatively fixed. Personnel costs usually are inflexible as well, at least in the short term. Current expenditures in these and similar areas are part of the starting point for next year's budget.

Recycled budgets. Many communication planners find that review and revision of prior year's budgets to be the most efficient approach to the annual cycle. This approach is most practical in two sets of circumstances. One occurs where funds and plans are handed down from above, and where implementation of specified plans consumes virtually all available resources. The second arises where programs consist of relatively constant sets of efforts, as in the case of a retail mall consumer communication program involving 12 monthly promotional events.

Recycling nevertheless should involve extensive reviews of planned activities and associated expenses in efforts to improve results. Some activities may be retained unchanged. Others are to be modified and

still others are replaced. Associated expense records then are reviewed
to formulate budgets for ensuing cycles.

Objective-based budgets. The most common alternative to the
recycled budget is a planning document based on an organizational
plan or on a strategic communication plan. This approach can be
similar to the zero-based concept where new programs or campaigns
are contemplated. More often, however, the objective-based approach
is used to link communication planning to organizational planning.

Formal management-by-objective (MBO) processes also are
occasionally used. Applied most often in larger organizations, the MBO
approach requires communication managers to develop communication
goals and objectives based on organizational goals and objectives.
Communication strategies and tactics then are devised in keeping with
goals and objectives. Budget documents are based on those strategies
and tactics.

BUDGET VARIABLES

Every budget deals with a relatively standard set of variables. They
include personnel, materials and supplies, capital investments, and
overhead. Most communication budgets deal only in expenses.
Revenues generated by communicator efforts are counted in sales,
reduced turnover and absenteeism, more stable securities prices, and
any number of other benefits to the organization. All revenues are
counted, however, in other departments or operating units.

These circumstances suggest that data necessary to communication
budgeting also can be used to enhance the stature of the discipline,
even in the absence of accountability. Too many organizational
communicators, left to their own devices, are prone to permit their
departments to become under-utilized resources. Considerable work
can be avoided in the process, but avoidance entails risk, especially
where the perceived value of communication within the organization
deteriorates. Departments perceived in this fashion are unnecessarily
vulnerable to economic bloodletting during the inevitable "economy
drive."

Those who prefer more risk-free environments consider each of the
variables specified above in establishing budgets. Most variables are
complex. Personnel, for example, should include full-time, part-time
and temporary workers. The personnel item also may include all fringe
benefits. Most variables also deserve examination from external as well
as internal perspective. Budgets, in other words, should include

internal expenses as well as costs involved in the purchase of products or services.

Budget development processes logically begin with activities rather than expenditures. The first question communicators must address is "what will work best?" Relative cost should be considered only after all potential activities have been analyzed and ranked in order of estimated productivity. Budgets then are established by proceeding "down the list" to the extent that funds are available. Estimates for approved or accepted projects then are re-examined and costs involved are sorted into appropriate categories to form the completed budget document.

Comprehensive Budgets

Communication budgets should be comprehensive. They should reflect all direct and indirect costs that can logically be assigned to any task or project. Communicators always should avoid allocating costs to general categories for two reasons. First, lumping costs into catch-all categories such as overhead, supplies, and miscellaneous create big targets for cost accountants, internal auditors, and others who may want to reduce ensuing years' budget allocations. More important, too liberal use of these categories reduces the accuracy of data compiled to pinpoint individual project costs.

The catch-all approach may be the easiest way to appear to conform to the sort of cost containment measures that most organizations impose. The fewer accounts to which costs are charged, the easier the process becomes. Resulting risks are unacceptable, however, because the catch-all approach provides virtually no information as to how resources have been used.

Diligent assignment of costs by project or budget category, in contrast, enables communicators to attach precise price tags to their efforts. Precise cost data permit accurate weighing of costs and benefits, which is especially valuable in attempting to determine the relative worth of sets of communication programs, campaigns, special events, strategies or tactics. Finally, precision in costing maintains relative balance between project costs and catch-all accounts, discouraging undue auditor attention.

In general, costs are best allocated by project and, within projects, to internal and external categories. External, in budgeting, refers to all costs ultimately shown on vendor invoices or statements. Internal refers to all organizational or departmental resources invested in each project. Within the two basic categories, budgets should reflect the costs of labor, material, supplies, capital equipment, and overhead.

External Costs

The nature of external costs, and the systems most organizations use to pay them, makes expenses of this variety more readily categorized than the internal varieties. External costs most often charged to communication departments or counseling firms consist of professional services and materials. Research costs, especially in the form of invoices from data base vendors, also are becoming significant. Supplies, other than where substantial media production work is handled internally, usually contribute little to total cost.

Most organizations maintain central purchasing departments to handle routine material and equipment acquisitions. Some require purchasing departments or operational components to obtain bids on every purchase above a specified amount. Resulting records, in either case, usually are available for communicator use.

Care must be taken to ensure that charges are assigned to pertinent projects or accounts, but tracking external costs otherwise presents few difficulties. The only potential problem source worthy of mention involves charges for professional services from counseling firms. Agencies and others, especially those who serve the organization on retainer or contract bases, may be less than diligent in providing detailed information with their invoices. Recipients should require sufficient detail to permit allocation of costs involved by project.

Internal Costs

Maintaining adequate internal records is another matter. Difficulties are especially great in organizations other than counseling firm. Communication counselors' revenues require tracking all charges billed to clients. Most install computer-based systems to handle the mechanics, and the systems are readily applied internally as well as externally.

Circumstances within most organizational communication departments usually are very different. Time sheets may be required, but personnel are only rarely required to allocate time in 15-minute increments to specific tasks or projects. The same conditions usually apply with regard to other factors that contribute to departmental costs. Efforts to track the cost of specific projects or the indirect costs associated with these projects are rare.

Project costs should be tracked, however, if only to enable communicators to relate success to dollars in analyzing project productivity. Non-specific costs, ranging from pro rata shares of equipment amortization to postage, ideally should be monitored as well.

Personnel costs. Labor costs associated with tasks or projects come in two basic forms: wages and benefits. Wage rates are known and organizational financial officers usually can supply a relatively precise multiplier to calculate benefit costs. Most organizations spend 30 to 40 cents on benefits for every salary dollar. While wage:benefit ratios tend to increase in higher salary brackets, simple multipliers suffice for budgeting purposes.

Benefit costs may accrue at varying rates, however, in keeping with the nature of the organization's system. Many organizations maintain what are called "tiered" benefit systems for several categories of personnel. Multipliers may have to be adjusted accordingly. Part-time personnel in some cases earn no benefits and those who work under contracts rarely receive benefits.

Multipliers also can be adjusted to include any number of worker-related expenses. In most organizations, these range from dues and subscriptions to attendance at conferences and other items not usually categorized as benefits. The most common approach to multiplier adjustment involves calculating the sum of worker-related expenses as a percentage of payroll and adding that factor to the multiplier. Spending for worker-related expenses usually varies with rank and compensation level but the differences seldom are significant other than across employee categories.

Cross-category differences are significant for two reasons. First, differences can influence project costs. Second, duties should be assigned in keeping with individual capabilities, which usually are reflected in wage rates. Cost control therefore dictates that duties should move "down the organization" to the lowest level at which they can be adequately performed.

Vendor charges. Printing, audiovisual production, and other tasks usually carried out by vendors usually are second only to salaries and benefits as a component of communication department budgets. The costs involved are more easily identified and traced, however, and therefore are readily assigned to specific projects.

Most organizations use relatively few vendors in any given area. Concentrating printing work with a few firms, for example, makes these firms more sensitive to buyer needs while making it easier for purchasers to track multiple projects. Accurate cost accounting requires, however, that every invoice be allocated against a specific budget item. Vendors therefore must be required to adequately identify every charge in preparing invoices.

For budgeting purposes, every outside provider of merchandise or services should be categorized as a vendor. Every purchase should be documented with a purchase order identifying the project account or budget category to which costs should be assigned. Payments should be authorized only in keeping with purchase orders.

Capital costs. Purchase order systems almost always are used for major purchases of durable items and are categorized as capital expenditures. Capital equipment, as it is called, is depreciated over a period of years. Depreciation rates vary with types of equipment. Counseling firms usually track associated costs and pass them along to clients. The practice is rare, however, within other organizations.

Equipment amortization may be monitored in the communication departments of large corporations, but this usually is part of an organization-wide process rather than a departmentally initiated function.

Supplies. Charges for supplies as well as equipment amortization can be another matter where new technologies are involved. Expenses associated with a sophisticated desktop publishing system can be considerable, for example, and associated costs logically can be charged against specific projects.

Supply charges also may be appropriate where projects consume large quantities of copies or require unusual use of telephone, delivery, or other services. Other supplies, from paper clips to envelopes, usually are allocated to a general overhead category.

Overhead. The overhead category usually includes office space, utilities, telephones, and maintenance in addition to supplies. Maintenance may or may not include equipment maintenance, which can involve considerable costs. Annual maintenance contracts on sophisticated computers, for example, often cost 10 percent of purchase prices.

As answering machines, facsimile machines, cellular telephones, laser printers, and similar equipment items proliferate, these costs will continue to escalate. As they grow as a percentage of overall budgets, pressure will increase to include them in direct charges against specific projects.

Contingencies. Every budget includes an item for contingencies or unanticipated expenses. In some cases, contingencies are covered in line items by increasing each of them a fixed percentage to compensate for anticipated cost increases or variations. In others, a contingency line is attached to the budget and about 10 percent of total available funds is allocated to that line.

Contingency funds are necessary for several reasons. First, costs rarely are stable and usually move upward at varying rates. Budgets usually are compiled more than a year in advance of expenditure dates, and must anticipate any increases in cost. Failure to do so results in over-expenditures by year's end, a circumstance that seldom finds favor in the executive suite.

Ability to respond to changing conditions is even more important in budgeting than adjusting to rising costs. Every budget period has its quota of unanticipated opportunities. Many involve relatively small expenditures in return for substantial media exposure. Voluntary assistance extended quickly to disaster victims, for example, often can produce such results, but resources must be available to permit immediate response.

Non-Routine Costs

All of the cost factors described above arise in almost every communication project of any size. Each is all but unavoidable. The list, however, is not complete. Campaigns and special events are major generators of unusual or non-routine costs, each of which must be anticipated with some degree of precision.

A special event such as an annual employee recognition dinner, for example, can produce a lengthy list of other items. In addition to the dining hall, the dinner may involve beverages, gratuities, awards, guest speakers, accommodations and/or travel for speakers, special audio-visual equipment, and a host of other items. Each item will have an associated cost; a cost often higher than logic would suggest. Audio-visual rentals, for example, often are quite expensive, especially where more sophisticated multi-media equipment is involved.

Larger special events, such as building dedications, are even more demanding, and campaigns compound in complexity. Campaigns may involve any number of large scale meetings and rallies at as many hotels in as many cities. Logistics alone can become overpowering and costs can quickly escalate if not carefully controlled.

Cost control for special events, campaigns, and other non-routine items can be accomplished only with difficulty. Nathaniel H. Sperber and Otto Lerbinger have compiled a number of generic check lists that provide considerable assistance but planners ultimately must rely on their own analytical abilities in establishing budgets.

A dance, for example, will require a band in addition to a hall. If it's a dinner dance, it may require two halls, or a hall with a dance floor. Unlike the dinner, the dance probably is going to require extra electrical outlets. Contemporary musical instruments, unlike many of their orchestral predecessors, require electricity. Additional electrical capacity may be necessary for lighting.

Lighting fixtures may have to be rented, and electricians may be needed to install them. In large cities, and especially in specialized exposition and trade show buildings, electricians and other technical craftsmen often are available only through building owners and under union contracts that prescribe exorbitant rates. Owners and tenants often are forbidden by such contracts even from such mundane tasks as putting a plug into a receptacle or putting a light bulb in a fixture.

Although seemingly insignificant in substance, trivial matters such as these can produce excessive charges against over-strained budgets, to the embarrassment of communication planners. Unless precise cost data are available from vendor organizations, planners are best advised to assume that costs involved in staging an event in hired facilities will be double, triple, or quadruple those that otherwise would be encountered. Every item, from decorations and name tags to soft drinks and pretzels, will bet at least triple those found in large drug or food stores.

EMERGING CONCEPTS

All of the anticipated costs of every communication task ultimately must be brought together into a document designed to meet two needs. Organizational budgets traditionally are used to ensure that expenditures remain within limits imposed by organizational plans. Where income projections are realized and spending is limited by budgets, senior management's economic objectives almost invariably are achieved.

Communication budgets are designed to achieve something more. The budget process should be managed to ensure that adequate funding is provided for projects that planners have determined will best meet organizational needs. Several techniques have been applied in efforts to produce that result.

Illinois Bell's System

One of the two techniques is communication-specific while the other is management-oriented. The management-oriented technique, as described by Illinois Bell Telephone vice president John A. Koten, is a component of the company's objective-oriented management system. The communication-specific approach advocated by Memphis State University's E. W. Brody (1987) generates communication budgets based on operating departments' commitments.

Illinois Bell's communication planning and budgeting systems are linked through a management-by-objective system to organizational planning. Communication department goals and objectives are based on organizational goals and objectives. Communication strategies formulated in support of organizational objectives become a comprehensive communication plan. Department managers use plans to rank order activities by priority and cost. Funding is determined, in Koten's words, ". . . by drawing a line at the level of available resources, thereby funding activities below the line and withholding support from those increments above the line" (1984, p. 328).

Decision-makers have more before them, however, than a mere list of activities and associated cost factors in rank order. The Illinois Bell system includes lists of benefits expected to be accomplished through each activity. Anticipated benefits that will be lost by drawing the line at any given point thus are evident to those wielding the pencils.

The Consultant Model

Brody's (1987) model differs from the Illinois Bell approach in positioning communication departments to function as intraorganizational consultants. Communication department revenues consists of monies allocated by other departments to fund specific communication activities. A human resources department, for example, might commission the communication department to publish an employee newsletter. Customer relations might request a series of promotional leaflets, and investor relations might ask communication to plan and execute a series of analyst meetings in major cities.

The cost of each project, including all overhead, would be transferred from the requesting department to the communication department. In systems of this sort, internal communication departments are permitted to grow to the extent that they can sell their services to organizational clients. More important, such systems encourage an entrepreneurial approach on the part of communicators. Communication department growth and prosperity is governed by the extent to which it can sell services on mutually productive bases to other organizational components.

Communicators using the consultant model deal with revenues as well as expenses in developing their budgets. They operate internally as a firm of communication consultants would operate externally, assuming responsibility for expenses and funding those expenses by selling their services. Communication operations change functionally only to the extent that those involved may offer a more diverse set of services than otherwise might be the case. The budgeting process becomes more complex in that communicators function within departmental revenues.

Where senior managements and/or communicators prefer, the consultant model also permits communication departments to function in competition with outside vendors. Extensive and continuing use of external audiovisual production facilities, for example, might encourage communication managers to examine the economic feasibility of developing internal capabilities. In the extreme, the communication department could become a profit center rather than an organizational expense.

MANAGING THE BUDGET

Budgets often are viewed as temporary preoccupations within organizations. Development and maintenance of budgets, however, are continuing tasks. Maintenance, or ensuring that the organization remains within prescribed economic parameters, usually requires more time and effort than is consumed in development.

Successful management requires month-to-month if not day-to-day monitoring of expenditures. Two purposes are served by the monitoring process. Spending is more readily controlled and detailed records are compiled, arming those involved with data necessary to forecast future expenses.

Record-keeping in larger organizations usually is handled by an accounting department that provides periodic summaries to communication managers. Usually generated on monthly bases, these summaries present expenditure data for the past month and for the year to date in dollars and as percentages of the budget items involved.

Accounting managers usually are supportive of communicators and others seeking to conform to spending plans. Accounting computer systems may or may not be as sympathetic however, which often encourages communicators to supplement centralized financial record-keeping with departmental microcomputers. A broad range of accounting software is available for virtually every microcomputer and few communication departments are without the necessary hardware.

Where charges are entered as expenditures are authorized, and where entries are completed on daily or weekly bases, managers have almost instant access to highly accurate data.

IN SUMMARY

Success in communication today is measured in economic as well as behavioral terms. Economic measurement and economic control together induce organizations to use relatively standardized budgeting processes.

Budgets are used for allocational and competitive purposes. They are used by organizations to allocate resources to operating units. In addition, budgets are often used competitively by operating managers in efforts to capture larger shares of available resources.

Budgeting processes vary in level of detail with organizations and with the positions of managers within organizations. Some departmental budgets are handed down from above in near-finished, line item form. In other cases, lump sums are allocated and managers are called upon to develop their own budgets.

In either case, budgets are nothing more than mirror images of operating plans, programs, campaigns, and special events expressed in dollar form. Crisis responses are excluded from the list in that they seldom can be planned in sufficient detail to permit inclusion in budgets other than in the most general terms. Budget development can begin with historical patterns, in zero-based fashion, or through a combination of techniques. Budget variables tend to be consistent, however, including internal and external costs. The internal consist primarily of personnel and overhead factors. The external involve vendor charges and capital costs. Supply, overhead, and contingency items round out the typical budget although campaigns and special events can involve a number of extraordinary items.

A number of different budgeting systems are used in organizations of different types but their objectives always are the same: management of organizational resources to ensure best results.

ADDITIONAL READING

Brody, E. W. *The Business of Public Relations*. New York: Praeger, 1987.

Koten, John A. "Budgeting," in Chester Burger, ed. *Inside Public Relations: Experts in Action.* New York: Longman, 1984.

Sperber, Nathaniel H., and Otto Lerbinger. *Manager's Public Relations Handbook*. Reading, MA: Addison-Wesley, 1982.

Bibliography

Ajzen, Icek, and Martin Fishbein, *Understanding Attitudes and Predicting Social Behavior*. Englewood Cliffs, NJ: Prentice-Hall, 1986.

Andriole, Stephen J., ed. *Corporate Crisis Management*, Princeton, NJ: Petrocelli, 1985.

Anshen, Melvin, ed. *Managing the Socially Responsible Corporation*. New York: Macmillan, 1974.

————. *Corporate Strategies for Social Performance*. New York: Columbia University Press, 1980.

Atkin, Charles R. "Mass Media Information Campaign Effectiveness," In *Public Communication Campaigns*, Ronald Rice and William Paisley, eds., Beverly Hills, CA: Sage, 1981.

Baker, Frank, ed. *Organization PR/Systems: General Systems Approaches to Complex Organizations*. Homewood, IL: Richard D. Irwin, 1973.

Bedeian, Arthur G. *Organizations: Theory and Analysis*. Hinsdale, IL: Dryden Press, 1980.

Berger, Bruce. "Closing the Client-Agency Credibility Gap," *Business Marketing* (November 1989).

Berko, Roy M., Andrew D. Wolvin and Ray Curtis. *This Business of Communicating*. 3rd ed. Dubuque, IA: Wm. C. Brown, 1986.

Blau, Peter M. *Exchange and Power in Social Life*. New York: Wiley, 1964.

————. *Exchange and Power in Social Life*, 2nd ed. New Brunswick, NJ: Transaction Publishers, 1989.

Bok, Sissela. *Lying: Moral Choice in Public and Private Life*. New York: Vintage Books, 1979.

————. *Secrets: On the Ethics of Concealment and Revelation*. New York: Pantheon Books, 1982.

Brody, E. W. *Public Relations Programming and Production*. New York: Praeger, 1988.

————. *The Business of Public Relations*. New York: Praeger, 1987.

Brody, E. W., and Gerald C. Stone. *Public Relations Research*. New York: Praeger, 1989.

Broom, Glen M., and David M. Dozier, *Using Research in Public Relations: Applications in Program Management.* Englewood Cliffs, NJ: Prentice-Hall, 1988.

Bucholz, Rogene. *Business Environment and Public Policy: Implications for Management.* Englewood Cliffs, NJ: Prentice-Hall, 1980.

Bucholz, Rogene A., William D. Evans, and Robert A. Wagley. *Management Response to Public Issues: Concepts & Cases in Strategy Formulation.* Englewood Cliffs, NJ: Prentice-Hall, 1985.

Burger, Chester. *The Chief Executive: Realities of Corporate Leadership.* Englewood Cliffs, NJ: Prentice-Hall, 1986.

Carpenter, Susan L., and W. J. D. Kennedy. *Managing Public Disputes.* San Francisco: Jossey-Bass, 1988.

Cattell, Mark E. "An Assessment of Public Relations and Issue Management in Relation to Strategic Planning in American Business Corporations," *Public Relations Review* 12, no. 3 (Fall 1986).

Center, Allen H., and Frank E. Walsh. *Public Relations Practices: Managerial Case Studies and Problems* 3rd ed. Englewood Cliffs, NJ: Prentice-Hall, 1985.

Chase, W. Howard. *Issues Management: Origins of the Future.* Stamford, CT: Issue Action Publications, 1984.

———. "The Corporate Imperative: Management of Profit and Policy," *Public Relations Quarterly* (March 1985): pp. 5-14.

Chung, Kae H. *Management: Critical Success Factors.* Boston, MA: Allyn and Bacon, 1987.

Cialdini, Robert. *Influence: How and Why People Agree to Things.* New York: Morrow, 1984.

Cantor, Bill. *Inside Public Relations: Experts in Action.* New York: Longman, 1989.

Coates, Joseph F. *Issues Management: How You Can Plan, Organize & Manage for the Future.* Mt. Airy, MD: Lomond Publications, 1986.

Crable, Richard E., and Steven L. Vibbert. *Public Relations as Communication Management.* Edina, MN: Bellwether Press, 1986.

Curtis, Carlton L. "Special Events: How They're Planned and Organized," In *Experts in Action: Inside Public Relations,* 2nd ed., Chester Burger, ed. New York: Longman, 1989.

Cutler, Blayne. "The Fifth Medium." *American Demographics* (June 1990).

Degan, Clara, ed. *Communicator's Guide to Marketing.* New York: Longman, 1987.

DeFleur, Melvin L., and Sandra J. Ball-Rokeach. *Theories of Mass Communication,* 5th ed. New York: Longman, 1982.

Dennis, Everette E. *Reshaping the Media: Mass Communication in an Information Age.* Newbury Park, CA: Sage, 1989.

Drucker, Peter F. *The New Realities: In Government and Politics / In Economics and Business / In Society and World View.* New York: Harper & Row, 1989.

Ebel, Richard G. "How to Integrate Specialty Advertising Into Your Campaign," *Public Relations Journal* (November 1988).

"Effective Coalition-Building Can Be Invaluable To Your Organization," *pr reporter* (October 30, 1989).

Ehling, William P., and Michael B. Hesse, "Use of 'Issue Management' in Public Relations," *Public Relations Review* 9, no. 2 (Summer 1983); pp. 18-35.

——. "PR Administration, Management Science and Purposive Systems," *Public Relations Review* 1, no. 2 (Fall 1975): pp. 15-54.

Eisenhart, Tom. "Where To Go When You Need To Know," *Business Marketing* 74 (November 1989).

Evans, Fred J. *Managing the Media: Proactive Strategy for Better Business-Press Relations*. New York: Quorum, 1987.

Ewing, Raymond P. *Managing the New Bottom Line: Issues Management for Senior Executives*. Homewood, IL: Dow Jones–Irwin, 1987.

——. "The Uses of Futurist Techniques in Issues Management, *Public Relations Quarterly* (Winter 1978): pp. 15-19.

Fink, Steven. *Crisis Management: Planning for the Inevitable*. New York: AMACOM, 1986.

Garbett, Thomas F. *How to Build a Corporation's Identity and Project Its Image*. Lexington, MA: Lexington Books, 1988.

Geier, Ted. *Make Your Events Special*. New York: Folkworks, 1986.

Goldblatt, Joe J., "How to Buy Special Events Professionals," *Association Management* 37, no. 12 (December 1985).

Golden, Hal, and Kitty Hanson. *How to Plan, Produce, and Publicize Special Events*. New York: Oceana Publications, 1960.

Gollner, Andrew. *Social Change and Corporate Strategy: The Expanding Role of Public Affairs*. Stamford, CT: IAP, 1984.

Gray, James G., Jr. *Managing the Corporate Image: The Key to Public Trust*. Westport, CT: Greenwood, 1986.

Greene, Charles N., Everett E. Adam, Jr., and Ronald O. Ebert. *Management for Effective Performance*. Englewood Cliffs, NJ: 1985.

Greenwood, William T. *Issues in Business and Society*. 3rd ed. Boston: Houghton Mifflin, 1977.

Grunig, James E. "A New Measure of Public Opinion on Corporate Social Responsibility," *Academy of Management Journal* 22 (December 1979): pp. 738-764.

Grunig, James E., and Todd Hunt. *Managing Public Relations*, New York: Holt, Rinehart and Winston, 1984.

Haber, George, "Special Events Without Surprises," *Business Marketing* (October 1986).

Haley, Russell I. *Developing Effective Communications Strategy: A Benefit Segmentation Approach*. New York: Wiley, 1985.

Hall, Richard H. *Organizations: Structure and Process*, 2nd ed. Englewood Cliffs, NJ: Prentice-Hall, 1977.

Haller, Robert T. *Creative Power! Grow Faster with New ProActive Tactics in Advertising and Public Relations*. London: Leister and Sons, 1987.

Harper, Doug. "Grand Openings," *Incentive* 162, no. 10 (December 1988).

Harris, Richard J. *A Cognitive Psychology of Mass Communication*. Hillsdale, NJ: Lawrence Erlbaum Associates, 1989.

Heath, Robert O., and Richard A. Nelson. *Issues Management: Corporate Public Policymaking in an Information Society*. Beverly Hills, CA: Sage, 1986.

Heitpas, Quentin. "Planning." In *Experts in Action: Inside Public Relations*, Bill Cantor, ed. New York: Longman, 1984.

Helm, Lewis M., Ray E. Hiebert, Michael R. Naver, and Kenneth Rabin. *Informing the People: A Public Affairs Handbook*. New York: Longman, 1981.

Hennessy, Bernard. *Public Opinion*. Monterey, CA: Brooks/Cole Publishing, 1985.

Hickman, Gerald. "Analyzing and Developing a Public Relations Strategy." In *Experts in Action: Inside Public Relations*. 2nd ed., Chester Burger, ed. New York: Longman, 1989.

Homans, George C. *Social Behavior: Its Elementary Forms*. New York: Harcourt, Brace & World, 1961.

Homans, George C., and David M. Schneider. *Marriage, Authority and Final Causes: A Study of Unilateral Cross-Cousin Marriages*. New York: Free Press, 1955.

Hovland, Carl I., I.L. Janis and H.H. Kelley. *Communication and Persuasion*. New Haven, CT: Yale University Press, 1953.

Howard, Carole, and Wilma Mathews. *On Deadline: Managing Media Relations*. New York: Longman, 1985.

"'I Do' Did It: How Vintage Pasadena Hotel Floated Facts of Life to Audience of 350 Mil." *Bulldog Reporter* (June 21, 1989).

"In New Decade of Personalized Relationships & Communication, Changes in Techniques, Strategies & Practitioner Attitudes are Predictable: How to Reach Thousands or Millions Personally?" *pr reporter* (January 1, 1990).

Irvine, Robert B. *When You Are the Headline: Managing a Major News Story*. Homewood, IL: Dow Jones-Irwin, 1987.

Jacoby, Neil H. *Corporate Power and Social Responsibility*. New York: Macmillan, 1973.

Janson, John J., Jr. "Special Event Security: No Magic Formula," *Security Management* (April 1985).

Kellerman, Donald S., Andrew Kohut, and Carol Bowman. *The Age of Indifference: A Study of Young Americans and How They View the News*. Washington, D.C.: Times Mirror Center for the People and the Press, 1990.

Kelly, John M. *How to Check Out Your Competition: A Complete Plan for Investigating Your Market*. New York: Wiley, 1987.

Koten, John A. "Budgeting." In *Inside Public Relations: Experts in Action*, Bill Cantor, ed. New York: Longman, 1984.

———. "Moving Toward Higher Standards for American Business," *Public Relations Review* 12, no. 3 (Fall 1986): pp. 3-11.

Lant, Jeffrey. "Secrets to a Successful Special Event," *Nonprofit World* 5, no. 2 (March-April 1987).

LeBoeuf, Michael L. *How to Win Customers and Keep Them for Life*. New York: Berkley, 1987.

Lerbinger, Otto. *Managing Corporate Crises: Strategies for Executives*. Boston: Barrington Press, 1986.

Lesly, Philip. *Overcoming Opposition: A Survival Manual for Executives*. Englewood Cliffs, NJ: Prentice-Hall, 1984.

Linke, Curtis G. "Crisis—Dealing with the Unexpected." In Chester Burger, ed., *Experts in Action: Inside Public Relations*. 2nd ed. New York: Longman, 1989.

Littlejohn, Stephen W. *Theories of Human Communication* 3rd ed. Belmont, CA.: Wadsworth, 1989.

Lorsch, Jay W. *Pawns or Potentates: The Reality of America's Corporate Boards*. Boston: Harvard Business School Press, 1989.

"Malls Used by PR Firms to Stage Special Events," *O'Dwyer's PR Services Report* (September 1989).

Mason, Richard O., and Ian I. Mitroff. *Challenging Strategic Planning Assumptions: Theory, Cases and Techniques*. New York: Wiley, 1981.

Mattman, Jurg W. "Checklist: Securing and Insuring Special Events" *Public Relations Journal* (March 1987).

Mattman, Jurg W., and Alexander E. Berlonghi. "The Mattman Model: The Risks of Special Events," *Risk Management* 34, no. 10 (October 1987).

McIvor, Patrick J. "Special Events: Make Them Work for You," *Medical Marketing and Media* 22, no. 7 (June 1987).

Merkel, Earl, "The Communicator as Manager: How To Plan Effective Communications Based On Organizational Goals," *CompuServe Information Service: PRSIG* (1989).

Merriam, John E., and Joel Makower. *Trend Watching: How the Media Create Trends and How to be the First to Uncover Them*. New York: AMACOM, 1988.

Meyers, Gerald. *When It Hits the Fan: Managing the Nine Crises of Business*. Boston: Houghton-Mifflin, 1986.

Mintzberg, Henry. *Power In and Around Organizations*. Chicago, IL: Rand-McNally, 1965.

Mount, Alan R., and John P. LaPlace. "Effective Promotions at Small Shopping Centers," *Journal of Property Management*, (November-December, 1987).

Mulligan, Thomas J. "There's More to Special Events Than Raising Money," *Fund Raising Management* 18, no. 2, (April 1987).

Nagelschmidt, Joseph S., ed. *The Public Affairs Handbook*. New York: AMACOM, 1982.

Nager, Norman R., and T. Harrell Allen. *Public Relations Management by Objectives*. New York: Longman, 1984.

Nager, Norman R., and Richard H. Truitt. *Strategic Public Relations: Models from the Counselors Academy*. New York: Longman, 1987.

Nanus, Burt, and Craig Lundberg, "In Quest of Strategic Planning," *Cornell H.R.A. Quarterly* (August, 1988).

Nelson, Richard Alan, and Robert L. Heath, "A Systems Model for Corporate Issues Management," *Public Relations Quarterly*, (Fall 1986); pp. 15-20.

Nudell, Mayer, and Norman Antokol. *The Handbook for Effective Emergency and Crisis Management*. Lexington, MA.: Lexington, 1988.

"Opening Day: A Cooperative Event," *Chain Store Age Executive* (December 1987).

Pagan, Rafael. "A New Era of Activism," *The Futurist* (May-June 1989).

"Parties for Fun and Profit," *Incentive Marketing* 160, no. 12 (December 1986).

Petty, Richard E., and John T. Cacioppo. *Communication and Persuasion: Central and Peripheral Routes to Attitude Change*. New York: Springer-Verlag, 1987.

Pincus, J. David, and Lalit Acharya. "Employee Communication Strategies for Organizational Crises," *pr reporter*, 27, no. 17, (October 23, 1989).

Pinsdorf, Marion K. *Communicating When Your Company is Under Siege: Surviving Public Crisis*. Lexington, MA: Lexington Books, 1987.

"Planning the Special Event: Negotiating Do's & Don'ts," *Fund Raising Management* 15, no. 11 (January 1985).

Post, James E. "Corporate Response Models and Public Affairs Management," *Public Relations Quarterly*, (Winter 1979); pp. 27-33.

Preston, Lee E., and James E. Post. *Private Management and Public Policy: The Principle of Public Responsibility*. Englewood Cliffs, NJ: Prentice-Hall, 1975.

Redding, W. Charles. *Corporate Manager's Guide to Better Communication*. Glenview, IL: Scott-Foresman, 1984.

Rein, Irving J., Philip Kotler and Martin R. Stoller. *High Visibility*. New York: Dodd, Mead, 1987.

Rice, Ronald E., and William J. Paisley. *Public Communication Campaigns*. Beverly Hills, CA: Sage, 1981.

Rice, Ronald E., and Charles K. Atkin. *Public Communication Campaigns* 2nd. ed. Newbury Park, CA: Sage, 1989.

Riggs, Lew, "Managing a Successful Public Affairs Response to an Initiative Attack," *Public Relations Quarterly*, (Winter 1985-86), pp. 28-30.

Robbins, Stephen P. *Organization Theory: Structure, Design and Applications*, Englewood Cliffs, NJ: Prentice-Hall, 1987.

Robinson, Edward J. *Public Relations and Survey Research*. New York: Appleton-Century-Crofts, 1969.

Rogers, Everett M. *Communication Technology: The New Media in Society*. New York: Free Press, 1986.

Rosenberg, Morris, and Ralph H. Turner. *Social Psychology: Sociological Perspectives*. New York: Basic Books, 1981.

Rubenstein, James. "A Grand Opening," *Bank Marketing* 21, no. 1, (January 1989).

Ruch, Richard S., and Ronald Goodman. *Image at the Top: Crisis and Renaissance in American Corporate Leadership*. New York: Macmillan, 1983.

Salmon, Charles T., ed. *Information Campaigns: Balancing Social Values and Social Change*. Newbury Park, CA.: Sage, 1989.

Salvaggio, Jerry L., and Jennings Bryant. *Media Use in the Information Age: Emerging Patterns of Adoption and Consumer Use*. Hillsdale, NJ: Lawrence Erlbaum Associates, 1989.

Salvaggio, Jerry L., ed. *The Information Society: Economic, Social & Structural Issues*. Hillsdale, NJ: Lawrence Erlbaum Associates, 1989.

Selame, Elinor, and Joe Selame. *The Company Image: Building Your Identity and Influence in the Marketplace*. New York: Wiley, 1988.

Settle, Robert B., and Pamela L. Alreck. *Why They Buy: American Consumers Inside and Out*. New York: Wiley, 1986.

Sheerin, Mira J. "Budgeting Special Events: Key to a Successful Benefit," *Fund Raising Management* 16, no. 10 (December 1985).

———. "Some Guidelines for Selecting the Right Type of Special Event," in *Fund Raising Management* 17, no. 2 (April 1986).

Simmons, Robert E. *Communication Campaign Management: A Systems Approach*. New York: Longman, 1990.

Sperber, Nathaniel H., and Otto Lerbinger. *Manager's Public Relations Handbook*. Reading, MA: Addison-Wesley, 1982.

Spitzer, Carlton E. *Raising the Bottom Line: Business Leadership in a Changing Society*, New York: Longman, 1982.

Steckmest, Francis W. *Corporate Performance: The Key to Public Trust*. New York: McGraw-Hill, 1982.

Strasser, Susan. *Satisfaction Guaranteed: The Making of the American Mass Market*. New York: Pantheon, 1989.

Stubbart, Charles I. "Improving the Quality of Crisis Thinking," *Columbia World of Business* (Spring 1987).

Thibaut, John W., and Harold H. Kelley, *The Social Psychology of Groups*, New Brunswick, NJ: Transaction Books, 1986.

Turk, Judy VanSlyke, "Forecasting Tomorrow's Public Relations" *Public Relations Review*, 12, no. 3 (Fall 1986); pp. 12-21.

Van Leuven, James K. "Theoretical Models for Public Relations Campaigns," Paper presented to the Conference on Communication Theory on Public Relations, Illinois State University, Normal, IL, May 1987.

———, "A Planning Matrix for Message Design, Channel Selection and Scheduling," Paper presented to the meeting of the Association for Education in Journalism and Mass Communication, Norman, OK, 1986.

Walters, Lynne M., Lee Wilkins, and Tim Walters. *Bad Tidings: Communication and Catastrophe*. Hillsdale, NJ: Lawrence Erlbaum Associates, 1988.

Winnett, Richard, *Information & Behavior: Systems of Influence*. Hillsdale, NJ: Lawrence Erlbaum Associates, 1986.

"Xerox Restores Its Position Thru Cultural Change, Long-Term Quest for Quality is based on Relationship Building," *pr reporter* (May 21, 1990).

Zillmann, Dolf, and Jennings Bryant, eds. *Selective Exposure to Communication*. Hillsdale, NJ: Lawrence Erlbaum Associates, 1985.

Index

ABOUT THE AUTHOR

E.W. BRODY teaches public relations in Memphis State University's Department of Journalism in Tennessee and maintains a public relations consulting practice in Memphis.

Managing Communication Processes is his tenth book. He edited the second edition of *New Technology and Public Relations* and previously wrote eight books for Praeger. They include *Public Relations Writing* (with Dan L. Lattimore, 1990), *Communication Tomorrow: New Audiences, New Technologies, New Media* (1990), *Public Relations Research* (with Gerald C. Stone, 1989), *Public Relations Programming and Production* (1988), *Communicating for Survival: Coping with Diminishing Human Resources* (1987) and *The Business of Public Relations* (1987).

Dr. Brody's articles on public relations have appeared in *Public Relations Journal, Public Relations Review, Journalism Quarterly, Legal Economics, Health Care Management Review, Journal of the Medical Group Management Association, Modern Healthcare, Hospital Public Relations,* and *Public Relations Quarterly.*

Dr. Brody holds degrees from Eastern Illinois University, California State University, and Memphis State University. He is accredited by the Public Relations Society of America.